HOW TO MAKE
CLASSIC AMERICAN FURNITURE

HOW TO MAKE
CLASSIC AMERICAN FURNITURE

James Clapper

CREATIVE HOMEOWNER PRESS®

Manufactured in United States of America

Current printing (last digit)
10   9   8   7   6   5   4   3   2   1

Produced by Roundtable Press, Inc.

Editorial: Judson Mead, Marguerite Ross, Joan Gregory, Betty Vera
Illustrations: Norman Nuding
Design: Jeffrey Fitschen
Jacket design: Jerry Demoney
Jacket photo: David Arky
Art production: Nadina Simon
Illustrated Techniques: Courtesy of Ralph Dorazio

LC:85-26976
ISBN: 0-932944-80-9 (paper)
      0-932944-81-7 (hardcover)

CREATIVE HOMEOWNER PRESS®
BOOK SERIES

A DIVISION OF FEDERAL
MARKETING CORPORATION
24 PARK WAY,
UPPER SADDLE RIVER, NJ 07458

KEY TO SYMBOLS

The projects in this book are
rated by the relative level of difficulty involved. These ratings are
indicated by symbols at the
beginning of each project.

Easy

Moderate

Difficult

INTRODUCTION

Building fine furniture can be a painstaking, time-consuming process—but it doesn't have to be! By making proper use of modern tools, techniques, and materials, you can construct handsome projects in less time and with less effort than you might suspect.

Author James Clapper found this out when operating his own furniture factory in Wisconsin. Over several years, he developed many furniture designs that could be built quickly and simply, using ordinary home workshop tools. As Clapper refined his designs and added new ones, they coalesced and grew to become a unique system of furniture construction. Clapper presents this system, along with more than thirty projects of his original furniture designs, for you to use in your own workshop.

As you work with Clapper's plans, you'll see that he makes ingenious use of hardware to strengthen the projects and simplify construction. For example, the drawers in most of his furniture designs are mounted on metal extension rollers and slides. This eliminates the need for building wooden web frames and drawer guides. Metal wears better than wood, so the drawers in Clapper-designed furniture are simpler to install and they last longer than drawers in more traditional projects.

The system also incorporates many different types of furniture. This book includes not only chests of drawers, but dressers, wardrobes, desks, tables, bookcases, benches, beds—projects of every description. And once you understand Clapper's system, you can easily adapt and combine these designs to build projects that meet your own special requirements. If you're so inclined, you could easily build an entire house full of furniture using just this book!

However, before you get started building your own furniture, we'd like to offer a few suggestions:

First, read the front sections of the book carefully, even if you're already an experienced woodworker. Not only do these chapters explain Clapper's construction system, they also contain many great woodworking tips. During his years as a furniture manufacturer, Clapper garnered some invaluable experience. He has collected, organized, and distilled this experience in the opening sections. No matter how many projects you may have built before (even if you've never built anything!), you're sure to find new ideas here that will make the reading worthwhile.

Next, check and recheck our dimensions on the projects before you cut good lumber. There are more than thirty projects in this book, and the design for each project incorporates dozens—sometimes hundreds—of dimensions. Each of these dimensions has been copied several times before this book reached its final form. We've checked over everything thoroughly, but authors and editors are only human. When you get ready to build something, sit down with a calculator and check the dimensions in the plans and the Materials Lists. Not only will this save you time in the long run; it will foster a better understanding of the project before you begin.

Finally, follow the safe woodworking procedures outlined in this book. Before you make each cut, think it through. Make prudent use of safety goggles, blade guards, spring boards, push sticks, push shoes, and other safety equipment in your shop. After all, your hands and eyes are the finest tools you own.

Baby Cradle (pages 136-138). A classic design such as this one can be passed down from one generation to the next. The decorative curves and the curve of the rockers require a skillful use of the band saw.

CONTENTS

TOOLS

A fully equipped home workshop can represent an investment of several thousand dollars, so the casual or occasional woodworker may settle for one or two major tools (a bench saw or radial arm saw, perhaps a drill press) or even resist buying any rather than tying up money in equipment that may be used only once or twice a year. But if you are bitten by the woodworking bug, you will eventually want, in addition to that saw and drill press, a full complement of workshop tools: band saw, saber saw, belt/disc sander, router, and jointer. With this lineup and your mastery of their use, you can do just about anything with wood.

Be a careful comparison shopper when you are in the market for a stationary power tool, for all are not created equal. A table saw is a table saw, but one saw may incorporate features and accessories that give it a greater range of capabilities than others. Peruse the manufacturer's literature before you buy, and ask a salesperson to display the various features of the tool. You can then see how it stacks up against others of its type. Often, when craftspeople are satisfied with a tool, they will outfit their entire workshops with tools of the same brand. That's not necessarily a bad idea, but you should compare just the same.

Almost as valuable as the tool itself is the instruction book that comes with it. It tells you exactly how to use that particular tool and all its accessories, and how to operate it safely. Study the book carefully and always follow its recommendations. Keep the book near the tool for ready reference when necessary. Pay particular attention to the sections that deal with alignment and adjustment. If your tools are properly aligned, your woodworking will seem much easier. Periodically, check that your tools are aligned and adjusted as precisely as possible.

TABLE SAW AND RADIAL ARM SAW

The table saw and the radial arm saw are the workhorses of the woodworking shop. Both will make all the basic cuts—crosscut, rip, miter, bevel—and, with the proper accessories, cut dadoes, make moldings, and sand workpieces. The radial arm saw can also be adapted to shaping, drilling, boring, and routing—all with speed and great accuracy. Various guides help the table saw perform with a high degree of precision.

On a table saw, the table remains horizontal and the blade can be tilted to make angle cuts from 90 to 45 degrees. The work is brought to the blade with the miter gage. Compound angles can be cut by tilting the blade and adjusting the miter gage. On a radial arm saw, the work remains stationary and the blade is brought to it along the arm, from above. The arm can be rotated for angle cuts. Anything that is done on the table saw can also be done on the radial arm saw.

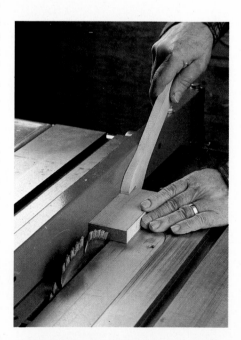

A table saw makes quick work of both large and small cuts. When you cut small pieces, use a push stick for safety.

The radial saw will cutoff, rip, miter, dado, slot, mold, notch, bevel, rabbet, tenon with dado blades, drill, sand, and plane.

A dado cutter is a useful accessory that can be used on either a table saw or a radial arm saw. There are two types: A wobble dado (with a single blade), and a dado set (with several blades). Either tool will cut a variety of joints—dadoes, rabbets, and grooves—quickly and easily. They can be configured to saw a kerf 1/8-inch wide up to ¾-inch or wider.

BAND SAW AND SABER SAW

The band saw and the saber saw are two power saws used primarily for cutting curves. The band saw has a continuous flexible steel blade that runs over two large pulleys. The capacity of the saw is determined by the distance between the blade and the frame. This can be 10, 12, or 14 inches for most home workshop saws. The band saw can be used for crosscutting and ripping, with accessories such as a miter gage and ripping fence, but it will not make these cuts as accurately as either a bench saw or radial arm saw. The band saw is best suited for cutting external curves and fine scrollwork.

The saber saw acts as a portable jig saw. The blade is fastened at one end to a shaft that moves up and down through the workpiece. The saw is extremely good for cutting curves and for making internal cuts. Varied blades for different types and thicknesses of wood are made for the saber saw, including very fine blades capable of accomplishing quite intricate cuts. Mounting your saw in a table accessory (available from most dealers) makes it easier to cut curves in small pieces.

DRILL AND DRILL PRESS

The electric drill and drill press are very important tools in any shop. The various attachments and accessories available for use with the drill give it a wide range of capabilities. For precision drilling, angled holes, or repetitive drilling of holes to a specified depth, the drill press is the best choice. There are drill stands available that, combined with your portable drill, can serve as a drill press. Used with care, they do a creditable job. The best bits to use in your drill are the spur-pointed wood bits. They are much more accurate than

Drill with 1/2-inch chuck.

high-speed drill bits used for metal and wood.

Your drill or drill press should have a feature that allows you to vary the speed. Different bits and different materials will require different drill speeds. Operating at the wrong speed could overheat and ruin a drill bit.

JOINTER

Although the jointer does a limited number of jobs, it does them extremely well, and fine cabinetry would be next to impossible without this tool. Most readily available commercial lumber, although dressed, is rough-cut and imperfect. The jointer is used to finish the lumber surface prior to cutting on a bench or radial arm saw.

The essential parts of a jointer are the base, front, and rear tables, cutter head (with three or four blades), safety guard, and fence. The front table is adjustable to control the depth of cut. The fence tilts and locks for bevel cutting. The safety guard should be left in place at all times.

For safety, use push blocks when surfacing a board on the jointer. Hold the board firmly against the fence and the table, and do not stand directly behind the work. Always wear safety goggles when operating this tool. When you need to join a board at an angle, tilt the fence in towards the table (making an angle of less than 90°). If the fence is tilted away from the table, the work may slip.

ROUTER

The router has an almost limitless capacity for cutting intricate contours in wood, and even an amateur

Cutting curves is a job most easily done on the band saw. The work can be steered through the thin blade at any angle.

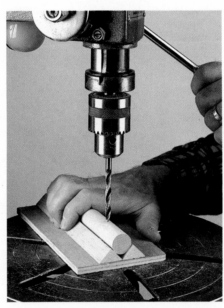

After the table saw, the drill press is probably the most generally useful power tool in any home workshop.

This jig saw with an edge guide attached makes rip cuts easily. It also bevels, cuts perfect circles, and makes pocket cuts with ease.

Jointers can taper, bevel, smooth, and flatten edges or faces of wood in one quick pass.

Router bits can do rabbeting, dovetailing, box coring, coving, ogee cutting, and trimming.

When inverted and mounted under a worktable, the router becomes a light-duty shaper.

with only moderate skill can use this tool to produce artistic edgings, multi-curved moldings, relief panels, delicate grooves for inlay work, perfect rabbets and dovetails for joints, and precise mortises.

Accessories for the router include straight, circle, and slot guides, as well as special template guides that can be pre-cut so that you can rout just about any shape. Special tables hold the router upside-down, with the bit up, so that it can be used as a stationary shaper. Such tables should be equipped with guards to protect the user. These guards must never be removed if the tool is to be safely operated.

Routers operate at extremely high speeds—up to 24,000 rpm in some cases—and this requires that you take some special safety precautions when using them. Of course, you should always wear protective goggles. You should also wear hearing protectors. The high speed generates a high frequency sound, and this sound can cause a permanent hearing loss if you're exposed to it for long periods.

When using the router as a hand-held power tool, make absolutely certain that the workpiece is clamped to the workbench so that it can't budge. Otherwise, the router may catch the workpiece and throw it across the room—or at you.

The router, which is basically a high-speed chisel, cuts a dado accurately and quickly.

GLUING

Unless you have your own hardwood forest and sawmill, you will find that boards of appropriate width for many of the projects in this book are not readily available. So you will have to create boards of sufficient width by gluing narrower pieces together. This is a skill you can master with a little practice.

MAKING A GLUING TABLE

This is a piece of equipment you can build for yourself which will make gluing operations relatively easy. The table can be whatever size and shape is best suited for the type of work you plan to do, although it should allow for at least 30 inches of space between the two pieces of the gluing jig, as shown in the plan. The width should be at least 36 inches to accommodate the dowel anchors on the jig.

Cut the top from ¾-inch fir plywood. Cut the legs from 2 × 4 stock—make the table whatever height is comfortable for you, but between 30 and 33 inches is recommended. Install sliding glides to the legs to make the table easy to move. Brace the legs with a piece of plywood, as shown in the plan, or with 2 × 4 braces. For strength, use wood screws throughout.

Cut curves at the corners of the table to make inevitable collisions with the table less painful; you can also round the top edge of the tabletop with a ½-inch quarter round router bit.

MAKING A GLUING JIG

Cut a 2 × 4 to a length of 57 inches. Mark two spots on each end of both of the narrow sides of the board, centered, 13½ inches in from each end, as shown in the jig plan. On these points drill ⅜-inch-diameter holes, 1 inch deep.

On the wide side, drill 1-inch-diameter holes every 3 inches, centered on the width of the side, as shown in the plan (see Detail A).

These holes must go all the way through, but to do this so that the board does not splinter, drill just through the board, and then turn the piece over and complete the holes from the other side. Round the edges of these holes (on both sides) with a router. Then cut the 2 × 4 from end to end (see Detail B).

Glue 3-inch-long ⅜-inch dowels into the two sets of holes on both pieces. When the glue has dried, round the exposed dowel ends with sandpaper.

Return to the table and drill ⅜-inch-diameter holes in the top to accommodate the dowels on the jig pieces (these holes will, of course, be 30 inches apart). Be sure that you lay out the holes so that the jig pieces will be parallel when fitted onto the table (see Detail C). The table is now equipped to hold bar or pipe clamps in the rounded notches on the jig.

GLUING A TOP

Assume that you are going to glue up a top for a chest. You need an 18-inch width, and so start with three boards a little more than 6 inches wide so that there will be enough extra to trim the top down to 18 inches. The long edges of the boards must be jointed so that they are perfectly smooth for a good glue joint. If you have a jointer, do this yourself; if you don't, have it done. Lay out the boards so that the end grain of each turns in the opposite direction from that of the next board (see Detail D). Mark the boards so that you can find this same arrangement when you lay them in the clamps; also draw light lines across the joints so that you can adjust the boards back into position in case they shift.

Place two pipe clamps in the gluing-table jig, as close as possible to the ends of the boards being glued up. Lay two pieces of narrow wood scraps across the pipe clamps to protect the edges from the clamps.

Put glue (Franklin®, Tite-Bond®,

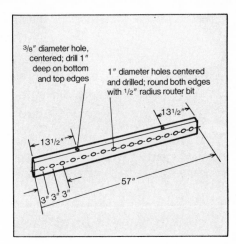

DETAIL A

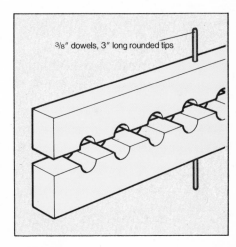

DETAIL B

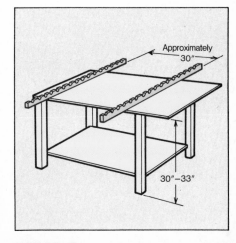

DETAIL C

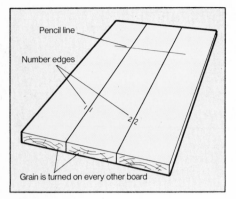

DETAIL D

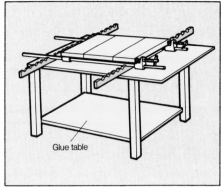

DETAIL E

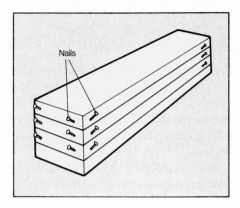

DETAIL F

Borden's White®, or Weldwood White®) on both edges of the boards where they join and work the glue well into the wood fibers. Lay the boards across the clamps and pull up the bottom piece of each clamp so that it just touches the edge of the wood (see Detail E). Place a third clamp over the tops of the boards, between the other two clamps. Tighten just the center clamp, making sure that the boards don't shift left or right (check your pencil marks) or that one board does not rise above or sink below the surfaces of the others.

Taking the same care, tighten the two clamps on either end of the boards. If your boards are at all warped, you can correct this by working outward from the center, first getting the boards flat, and then tightening clamps to hold them in place; bending the boards to flatten them further out toward the ends and tightening these in place; until you reach the ends of the boards, which you can C-clamp flat (use strips of scrap wood above and below to protect the ends of the wood from the C clamps).

Note the time the boards were clamped so you won't have to guess when the glue has set up. Let them sit a little longer than recommended to be sure the joints are sound. Remove any excess glue with a putty knife and wipe away with a clean, damp rag. If this glue is not removed, it will clog sandpaper during the sanding stage.

Also, before leaving the boards to set up, fill any knots or flawed areas with wood putty in a color close to the color of the finish. Use the time

while the glue is setting up to machine the other parts of the project to size.

GLUING A BLOCK

For pedestal legs and other thick pieces that you will turn on a lathe (you can usually get this done for you if you don't have a lathe), you will need to fabricate a block of wood. This is a somewhat simpler procedure than edge-gluing because you are gluing flat pieces together on their flat surfaces. But, as with edge-gluing, you must keep the pieces from slipping as you clamp.

Starting with two pieces, apply a thin layer of glue to both surfaces that will mate. To keep the pieces in place, spot-nail one piece to the other along the edge, as shown here; then glue and spot-nail the next piece to the block, and so on, until the block is complete (see Detail F). After the glue has set, remove the nails. Nail only in those areas that will be milled away when you turn the piece.

GLUING UP THICK STOCK

For the most part, the projects in this book use standard thicknesses of lumber—¼-inch and ¾-inch. This stock is readily available at any lumberyard. However, some projects specify 1¼-inch thick lumber for a few parts, mostly table and desk tops. You may have to glue up thick stock for these parts. The technique varies depending on the materials you are using.

PLYWOOD

If you're working with plywood, sand-

wich sheets of ½-inch and ¾-inch thick plywood. Bond them together with contact cement and cover the edges with wood tape or veneer to make the stock look like a single, solid piece of 1¼-inch thick wood. Tip: If you're making a table or desk top, you'll see only one side of the stock in the completed project. You can save money by substituting particle board or wafer board for the bottom pieces of plywood.

SOFTWOOD

If you're working with softwood, buy several 1½-inch thick boards and glue them edge to edge, as described elsewhere in this chapter. Let the glue set up for at least twenty-four hours. Carefully scrape off any excess glue from the boards, and then take the stock to a lumberyard and have it planed down to 1¼ inches thick. Most lumberyards also offer milling services and should be able to plane boards up to 24 inches wide for a small fee. Tip: If you don't want knots in your desk or table top, buy clear two-by lumber. Most of the larger lumberyards will have this.

HARDWOOD

If you're working with hardwood, follow the same procedure as for softwood. Purchase lumber slightly thicker than you need, glue it edge to edge, then take it back to the lumberyard and have it planed down.

Safety Note: If you're gluing up thick stock to turn on a lathe, let the glue set up for at least twenty-four hours before turning. Otherwise, the stock may fly apart while you're working.

SANDING

There are proper techniques for sanding, and they are not hard to learn. The most important thing to keep in mind is that not all sanding is a removal process. You will, of course, have to sand away rough edges and sometimes sand a piece to make it the right shape. But much of the sanding required in these projects is simply smoothing to a perfect finish. Remember that patience is the most important ingredient in a successful sanding job. Remember also that a good sanding job is more important than any other single aspect of these projects.

There are two stages of pre-assembly sanding called for in these projects—rough and finish sanding. When a piece has been assembled, there are two further stages of sanding—critical and inspection sanding—that get the wood ready to accept a finish that shows no flaws. In each project you will be told which parts (and parts of parts) require what level of sanding.

SELECTING SANDPAPER

Technically, there is no longer an item called sandpaper. Today, these gritty sheets are called abrasive papers, because they are made of abrasive materials other than sand. Five kinds of abrasive are used: flint, garnet, silicon carbide, aluminum oxide, and emery. The cheapest papers use flint. They neither cut as fast nor last as long as the better papers. If you expect to do much sanding, it will pay you to buy better papers coated with one of the other abrasives.

Abrasive papers come in half a dozen thicknesses. The thinner papers are good for working in tight places because these weights fold easily. However, they are not as good for use on sanding blocks or power sanders because the paper will tear. The heavier papers feel very stiff and may crack when folded, but they

stand up longer in the power and hand sanders. You should have some of each weight.

There are two kinds of papers, open grain and closed grain. The open-grain type has only a light coating of abrasive material so that the material being sanded doesn't cling to the abrasive granules and clog the paper. The closed-grain type has a dense coating of abrasive material and does its work most quickly. For general smoothing and finishing, the closed-grain type is better. Buy some light-weight papers for sanding in and around corners, but buy mostly heavier papers for their longer life.

The accompanying chart shows the relationship between the different grading systems for indicating the coarseness of grit for abrasive papers and tells the most common use for each type.

In addition to standard abrasive

papers, you can buy waterproof sandpaper. This is usually sold only in the finer grits and is made to be used with water or oil for the final rubdown in hand finishing.

ROUGH SANDING

Rough sanding eliminates glue left on the surface at glue joints, chatter marks made by a jointer or planer, tear-out around swirling grain and knot areas, and other miscellaneous flaws and gouges found in the surface of wood.

Use 80-grit aluminum oxide or garnet paper for rough sanding. Ideally you should have, or have access to, a large stationary belt sander—especially for sanding large pieces. You may want to have the tops of cabinets sanded for you if you do not have a belt sander large enough to accommodate their size. The top will show the quality of the sanding job

Sandpapers

Manufacturers grade their abrasive papers by one of three methods, and there are no national standards to serve as a guide. Some give their papers a name (fine, medium, etc.); some rate them by grit number (30, 180, 400, etc.), referring to the abrasive particle size; and others use a numbering system (3/0, 5/0, 8/0), the oldest of all grading methods. The chart below shows all three methods in relation to each other, so that no matter which rating is used, you can buy the paper you need.

Number	Grit	Name	When to use
10/0 9/0	600, 500, 400 360	Superfine	Last sanding of a new furniture or toy finish; final sanding of fine woods; hand-rubbed finish
8/0 7/0	320, 280 240	Extra fine	Same as above
6/0	200, 220	Very fine	Sanding between coats of paint or varnish
5/0 4/0 3/0 2/0	180, 150 120, 100	Fine	Sanding hardwood and softwood before and after you stain, seal, or apply a priming coat
1 0 1/0 1/2	80, 60 50	Medium	Removing deep scratches, shaping of parts, or rough sanding
1½ 2 2½	40, 36 30	Coarse	Wood removal, shaping, rough sanding

more than any other part of a cabinet. You can mount a portable belt sander on a work table for smaller jobs. An unmounted portable belt sander can also be used, though you will have to work harder to achieve equivalent results.

It is imperative that you sand with the grain right from the beginning of the rough-sanding process. You must also be careful not to sand off so much that the dimension of the piece is changed significantly. Allow an extra 1/16 inch when cutting parts to allow for what you lose in the sanding process.

Rough sanding is always done on unassembled parts so that if something goes wrong the parts can be replaced with the least amount of trouble. Mistakes happen!

FINISH SANDING

Some parts need a second level of sanding; some don't. Directions for each project will specify whether or not to go to this stage. Using a belt sander with 120-grit aluminum oxide or garnet paper, sand until all flaws and unsightly blemishes have been eradicated and the scratch pattern of the rough sanding has been obliterated. This process should not take off too much wood.

CRITICAL SANDING

Critical sanding is for surfaces that will be seen and finished. This stage occurs after the cabinet has been assembled and is ready to be finished. As you assemble the piece and move it to your finishing area (assuming that you have a spacious shop), little scratches and dings will inevitably occur. Also, clamp marks, glue joints, fastener marks, hammer "half moons," and other slips will have taken their toll on the surfaces of the cabinet. The result is almost always one that no finishing-shop supervisor would appreciate. Stain magnifies these small flaws to monumental proportions and makes an otherwise very satisfactory job look second-rate.

This final, critical sanding job should be done with 120-grit aluminum oxide or garnet paper in an

High power, auto-tracking, and a large 4-inch belt size characterize this belt sander.

This 3-inch belt sander provides moderate smoothing power.

orbital finish sander or by hand. All flaws should be eliminated at this stage. Also, at this time all sharp edges and corners should be rounded off slightly by hand.

INSPECTION SANDING

When you are all finished with the critical sanding and the piece is free of flaws, it is time to step back and approach the project as if you were a professional finisher working on pieces prepared by a lazy sander. Treat the surfaces with great suspi-

cion and you will find flaws even after having completed the critical stage.

Use a stain-dampened cloth (damp, not saturated or even wet) to rub over suspect areas such as glue joints, miter joints, areas filled with wood putty or critically important surfaces such as the top. New flaws will appear in the wood under this treatment. The inspection sanding just before staining is your last chance to correct these problems.

When you find a flaw, rub the stain-dampened area with a clean cloth

This 1/4-sheet orbital pad sander is used one-handed before applying the finish.

This orbital 1/2-sheet pad sander can be used with one or two hands.

instructions for achieving the best results.

☐ Always sand with, not across, the grain of the wood.

☐ Use a straight back-and-forth movement of the sanding block. Don't use a circular or irregular motion.

☐ Apply even pressure to the top of the sanding block. Don't lean more heavily on the front or back of it. The pressure should be light, not forced.

☐ When sanding a flat surface, be especially careful as you approach the edge. There is a tendency to lean on the block at this time, which results in heavier pressure near the edge of the work. Keep the sanding surface level and the pressure even to avoid tapering the work surface downward.

☐ Tap the sawdust out of the sandpaper at regular intervals. The sawdust clogs the paper and prevents the paper from cutting properly. You can use a small brush (an old toothbrush will do).

to dry the small amount of stain. Then sand the area lightly by hand with 120-grit paper. Wipe again with the stain-dampened cloth to see whether or not the flaw is gone. If it isn't, repeat the procedure until it is. Remember, anything you leave at this point will stay forever.

USING A TACK CLOTH

When you finish sanding, wipe the sawdust from the surface of the work with a tack cloth. (You can buy tack cloth already made at your home center, or you can make one by moistening a cloth with a mixture of one part turpentine and three parts varnish.) The advantage of a tack cloth over a regular dust rag is that the sawdust clings to the tack cloth; it doesn't fly into the air, only to settle on the work again in a few minutes.

SANDING TECHNIQUES

Sanding is easy if you are aware of the basic techniques. Follow these

MACHINING

While the woodworking projects in this book are all different, the joints in the projects are often similar. Consequently, the machine setups used to make similar joints will be identical. To simplify our instructions, we've standardized some of the more common joinery and machining techniques. Whenever a plan calls for making a simple dado or rabbet, we'll refer you to this section for the exact specifications. Each joint and technique is illustrated so you can see exactly what to do. In addition, we've provided a Quick Reference List of machining standards on the last page of this chapter.

ENLARGING PATTERNS

Many of the projects in this book have parts that must be cut according to certain patterns, that are included with the plans. Because the size of any book is limited, these patterns are never shown full size. You'll have to enlarge and trace them onto the stock.

To enlarge a pattern, first remember that the measurements in the Materials Lists are finished sizes. Cut the stock for a patterned piece a little bit larger than listed so you have room to work. Most of the patterns have grids laid over them, so that you can enlarge them using the traditional squares methods. Simply draw a full-size grid on a large sheet of paper with the same number of squares horizontally and vertically as shown in the plan. Examine the plan and note where each pattern line intersects a grid line. Make a pencil dot at the corresponding point on your full-size grid. Then simply connect the dots.

Connecting the dots requires some artistic ability, and many woodworkers aren't comfortable doing it. There is an easier method that requires a little more equipment, but not much skill.

Take a picture of the pattern you wish to enlarge using 35mm slide film. Shoot the picture straight on, not off to one side. Project this slide directly onto the stock you want to cut. Once again, you must project the picture straight on. Move the projector closer or farther away from the board until the projected pattern is exactly full size. Then trace over the projected pattern with a pencil.

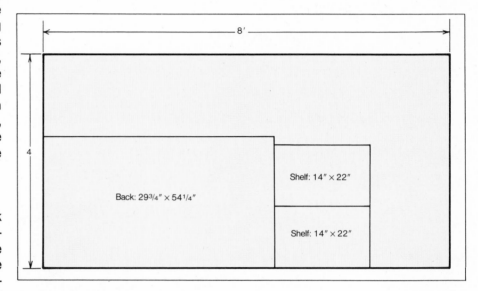

ECONOMICALLY CUTTING PLYWOOD SHEETS

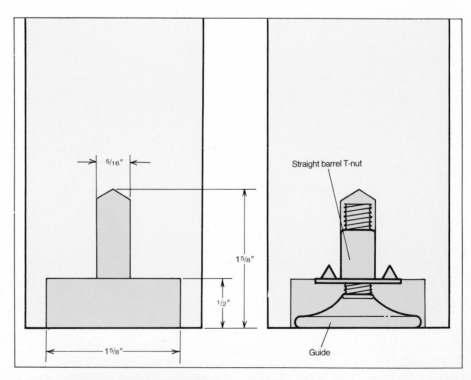

ADJUSTABLE TABLE GLIDES

GROOVES

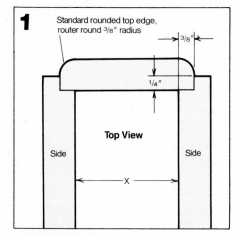

1

Standard rounded top edge, router round ³/₈″ radius

³/₈″

¹/₄″

Top View

Side   Side

X

STANDARD BACK RABBET

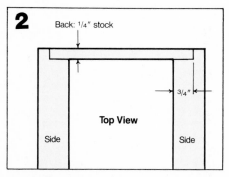

2

Back: ¹/₄″ stock

³/₄″

Top View

Side   Side

STANDARD FLUSH BACK RABBET

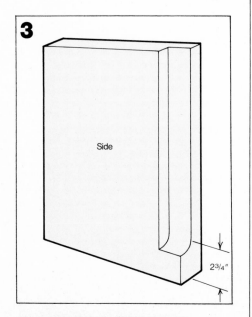

3

Side

2³/₄″

**STANDARD FLUSH BACK
STOPPED RABBET**

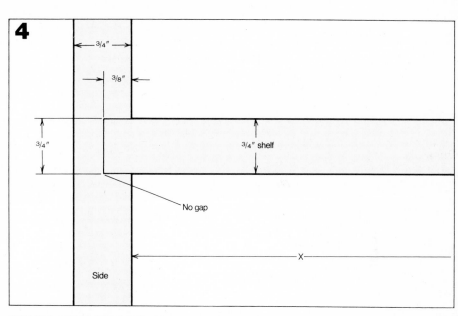

4

³/₄″

³/₈″

³/₄″

³/₄″ shelf

No gap

Side

X

STANDARD SHELF DADO

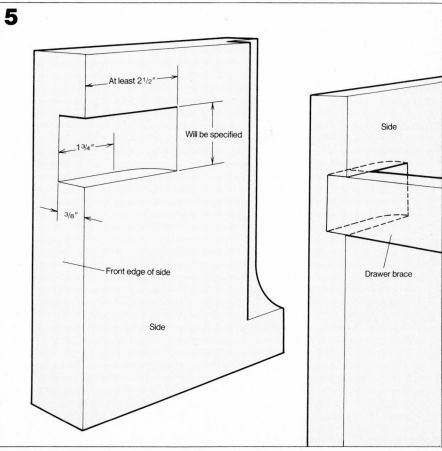

5

At least 2¹/₂″

1³/₄″

Will be specified

³/₈″

Front edge of side

Side

Side

Drawer brace

STANDARD DRAWER BRACE STOPPED DADO

6

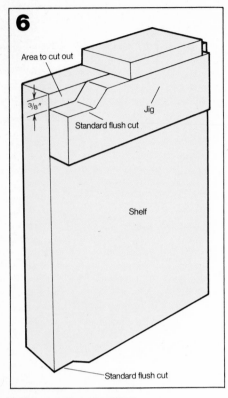

Area to cut out

3/8"

Jig

Standard flush cut

Shelf

Standard flush cut

SHELF FLUSH CUT

7

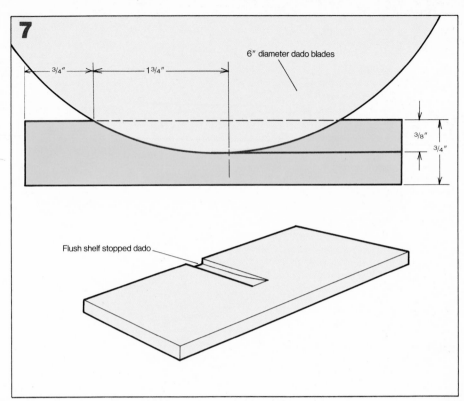

6" diameter dado blades

3/4"   1 3/4"

3/8"

3/4"

Flush shelf stopped dado

STANDARD FLUSH SHELF STOPPED DADO

8

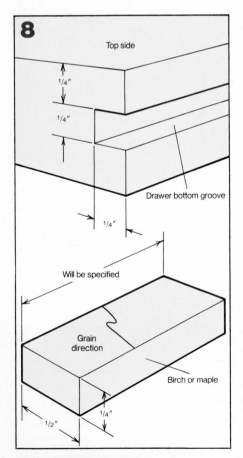

Top side

1/4"

1/4"

Drawer bottom groove

1/4"

Will be specified

Grain direction

Birch or maple

1/4"

1/2"

STANDARD SPLINE GROOVE IN ³/₄″ STOCK AND STANDARD SPLINE

9

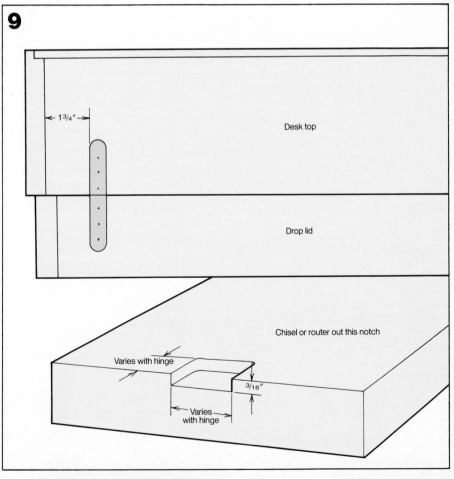

1 3/4"

Desk top

Drop lid

Chisel or router out this notch

Varies with hinge

3/16"

Varies with hinge

HINGE MORTISE FOR DESK LID

DOORS

10

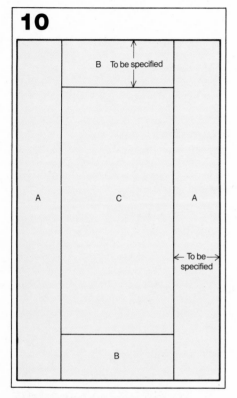

B   To be specified

A   C   A

To be specified

B

BASIC DESIGN STANDARD DOOR CONSTRUCTION FOR 3/4" STOCK

11

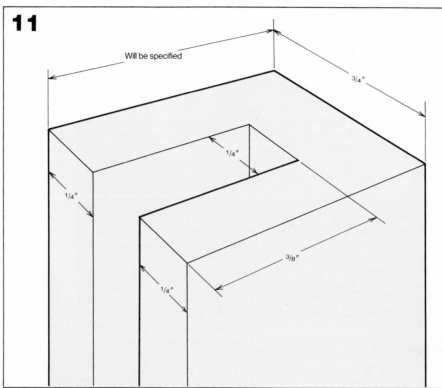

Will be specified

3/4"

1/4"

1/4"

1/4"

3/8"

STANDARD DOOR CONSTRUCTION, A STILE

12

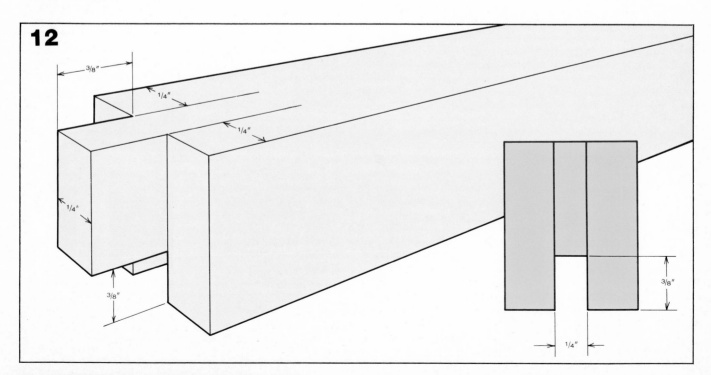

3/8"

1/4"

1/4"

1/4"

1/4"

3/8"

3/8"

1/4"

STANDARD DOOR CONSTRUCTION, A RAIL

13

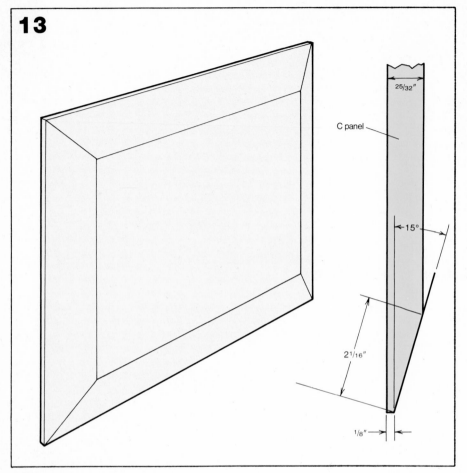

25/32"

C panel

15°

2¹/₁₆"

1/8"

RAISED PANEL DESIGN

14

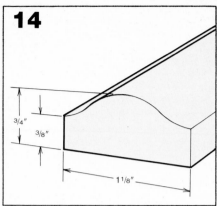

3/4"

3/8"

1¹/₈"

STANDARD DOOR RAIL MOLDING

15

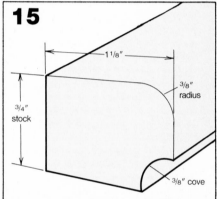

1¹/₈"

3/8" radius

3/4" stock

3/8" cove

STANDARD COVE MOLDING

16

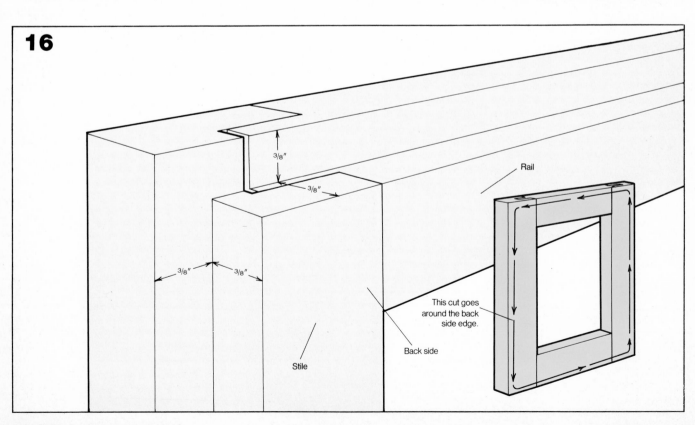

3/8"

3/8"

3/8"

3/8"

Rail

This cut goes around the back side edge.

Back side

Stile

CABINET LIP FOR DOORS

DRAWERS

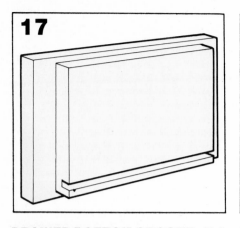

17

DRAWER BOTTOM GROOVE, 1/4″ DEEP

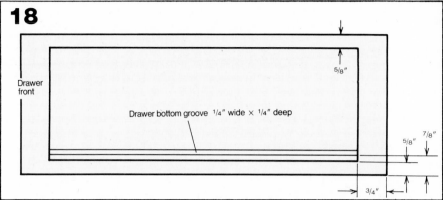

18

Drawer front

Drawer bottom groove 1/4″ wide × 1/4″ deep

5/8″

5/8″   7/8″

3/4″

DRAWER FRONT FOR USE WITH MONORAIL DRAWER SLIDES WITH OVERLAP DRAWER FRONTS

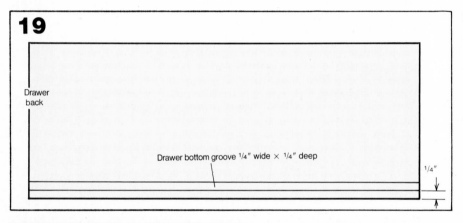

19

Drawer back

Drawer bottom groove 1/4″ wide × 1/4″ deep

1/4″

DRAWER BACK FOR USE WITH MONORAIL DRAWER SLIDES WITH OVERLAP DRAWER FRONTS

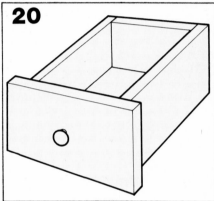

20

FINISHED DRAWER

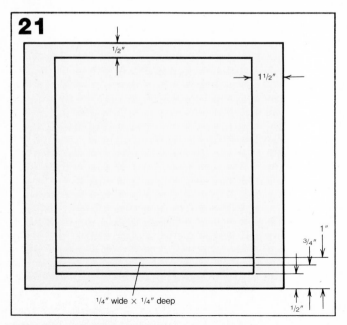

21

1/2″

1 1/2″

1″

3/4″

1/4″ wide × 1/4″ deep

1/2″

DRAWER FRONT FOR USE WITH SIDE-MOUNTED ROLLER SYSTEMS FOR DRAWERS WITH OVERLAP FRONTS

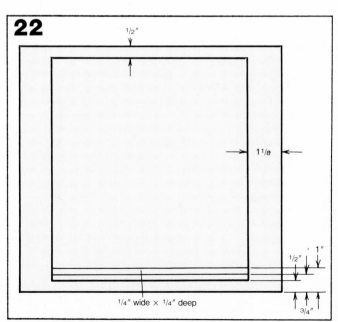

22

1/2″

1 1/8″

1″

1/2″

1/4″ wide × 1/4″ deep

3/4″

DRAWER FRONT FOR USE WITH SIDE-MOUNTED ROLLER SYSTEMS WITH DRAWER FRONT INSTALLED FLUSH WITH CABINET

23

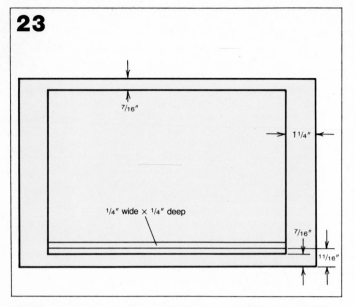

7/16"

1 1/4"

1/4" wide × 1/4" deep

7/16"

1 1/16"

OVERLAPPING HAND-FITTED DRAWER FRONT

24

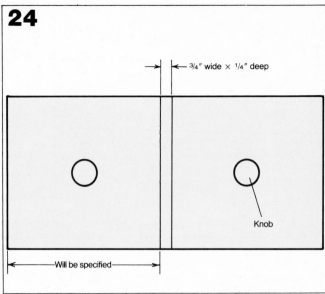

3/4" wide × 1/4" deep

Knob

Will be specified

APOTHECARY DRAWER FRONT DESIGN

25

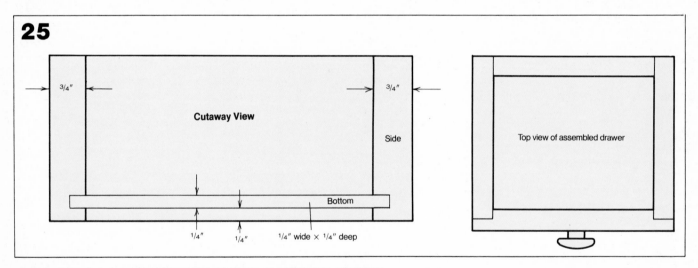

3/4"

Cutaway View

3/4"

Side

Bottom

1/4"   1/4"   1/4" wide × 1/4" deep

Top view of assembled drawer

HAND-FITTED DRAWER WITH FLUSH-MOUNTED FRONT

26

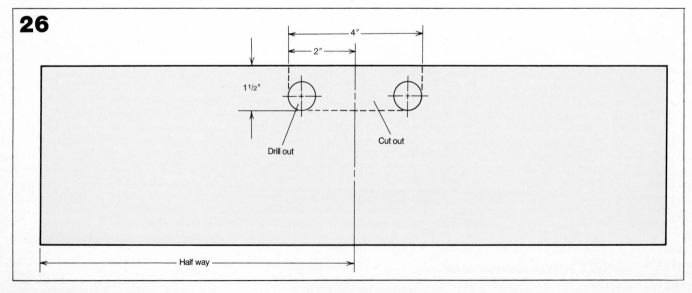

4"

2"

1 1/2"

Drill out

Cut out

Half way

DRAWERS: TRAY CUT-OUT

MOLDINGS

27

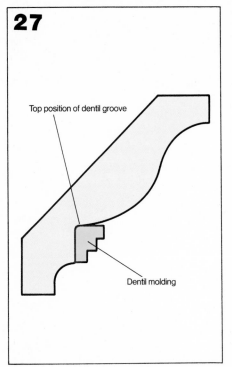

Top position of dentil groove

Dentil molding

CROWN MOLDING WITH DENTIL MOLDING

28

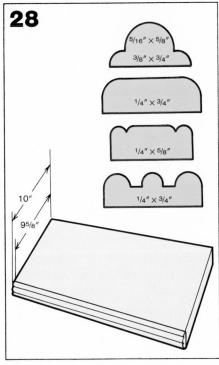

5/16" × 5/8"

3/8" × 3/4"

1/4" × 3/4"

1/4" × 5/8"

1/4" × 3/4"

10"

9 5/8"

SCREEN MOLDINGS FOR SHELF EDGING

29

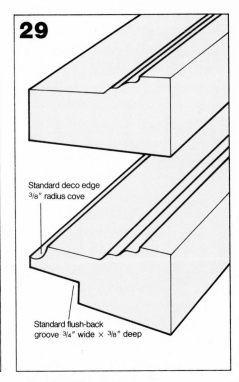

Standard deco edge 3/8" radius cove

Standard flush-back groove 3/4" wide × 3/8" deep

STANDARD 2" BRICK FRAME MOLDING

30

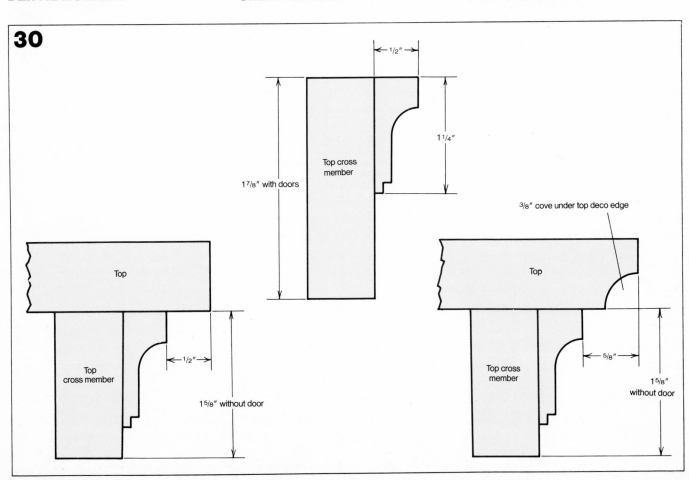

1/2"

1 1/4"

Top cross member

1 7/8" with doors

Top

Top cross member

1/2"

1 5/8" without door

3/8" cove under top deco edge

Top

Top cross member

5/8"

1 5/8" without door

TOP MOLDINGS

PATTERNS

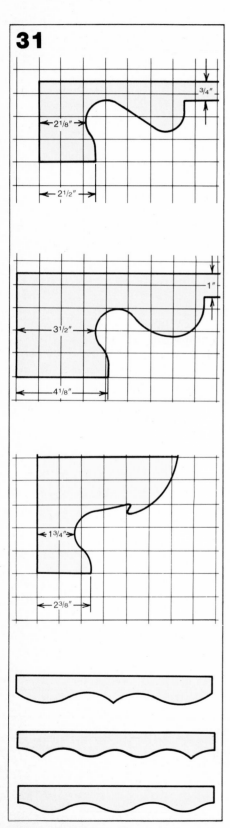

31

SCALLOP AND FOOT VARIATIONS

MACHINING STANDARDS QUICK REFERENCE LIST

Joint or Technique	Specifications	Tools Used
Cabinet lip	3/8" wide × 3/8" deep	Table saw or router
Dado, shelf	3/4" wide × 3/8" deep	Table saw or router
Dado, stopped, flush shelf	3/4" wide × 3/8" deep, stopped 3/4" from edge	Table saw with dado accessory
Dado, stopped, drawer brace	3/4" wide × 3/8" deep, stopped 3/4" from edge	Table saw or router
Divider, records	Parallel holes, 6 3/4" apart	Drill or drill press
Drawer fronts, apothecary	Overlapping lips are 1/4" wide, 1/4" between fronts	Table saw or router
Drawer fronts, overlapping	Fronts overlap case by 3/8". Other dimensions may vary depending on hardware	Table saw or router
Drawer, tray cut-out	4" long × 1 1/2" wide	Drill and saber saw
Feet, bracket	5 1/2 tall, width variable with design	Band saw or saber saw
Flush cut	3/8" wide × 1 3/4" long	Band saw or saber saw
Frame-and-panel doors	Rails and stiles have 1/4" wide × 3/8" deep groove on inside edge. Rails have 1/4" wide × 3/8" long tenons. Bevel at 15°, tapering to 1/8" thick at edge.	Table saw or router
Groove, drawer bottom	1/4" wide × 1/4" deep, 1/4" from edge	Table saw or router
Groove, spline	1/4" wide × 1/4" deep	Table saw or router
Molding, brick	1" thick, 2" wide, may have 3/8" deep × 3/4" wide rabbet in back	Molder or shaper
Molding, cove	1 1/8" wide × 3/4" thick with 3/8" cove in lower edge and upper edge rounded to 3/8" radius	Molder, shaper, or router
Molding, crown	Dimensions variable, may have dentil molding inset	Molder or shaper
Molding, door rail	1 1/8" wide, 3/4" thick, tapering to 3/8" at edges	Molder, shaper or router
Molding, screen	1/4"–3/8" thick, 5/8"–3/4" wide	Molder or shaper
Molding, top	1/2" thick × 1 1/4" wide	Molder or shaper
Mortise, hinge, desk lid	3/16" deep, length and width varies with hinge. Position 1 3/4" from edge	Chisel or router
Rabbet, back	3/8" wide × 3/8" deep	Table saw or router
Rabbet, flush back	3/8" wide × 1/4" deep	Table saw or router
Rabbet, stopped, flush back	3/8" wide × 1/4" deep, stopped 2 3/4" from edge	Table saw or router
Spline	1/4" thick × 1/2" wide	Table saw or band saw
Table glides, adjustable	Hole #1, 5/16" dia. × 1 5/8" Hole #2, 1 5/8" dia. × 1/2"	Drill or drill press

ASSEMBLY

There are many assembly procedures, such as installing shelves and assembling drawers, that are common to most of the projects in this book. They are given here in some detail and will be referred to in each project where assembly of cabinets, doors, or drawers is called for.

The key to successful cabinetwork is making precise cuts and keeping assemblies square as you put them together. Always use a carpenter's square or try square as you clamp parts; you may have to push or pull parts into square as you work.

No matter how attentive you are, you may find that the shell of a cabinet is not perfectly square when you position it on the top for attachment. At this last stage of assembly, you can still square up the cabinet, using the top to hold it true.

There are two reasons you must pay particular attention to the angle at which you drive nails and screws. Screws and nails can split the wood into which they are driven if two are driven in parallel and fairly close together. When attaching narrow pieces, such as drawer braces, where screws or nails must be relatively close, angle the fasteners so that their paths into the end grain of the brace are not parallel. Also, for extra strength, the specified length of some fasteners (especially those attaching the top to a cabinet) is close to the total depth of the two pieces being attached. Check the fastener length against the depth of the pieces and, where necessary, angle the fastener slightly to prevent its breaking through the top surface.

Doors and drawers are no trouble to assemble if the parts are cut exactly as called for. A door is held square by the panel (if it is square), but a drawer may require some adjusting for square before securing the bottom. Both assembly procedures are given here and are also shown in photographs on pages 41-45 in the front section of this book.

CABINET ASSEMBLY: CROSS MEMBERS AND DRAWER BRACES

Top and bottom cross members and drawer braces should be nailed as well as glued in place. Because of their position, holes for the nails should be pre-drilled and angled as shown below to prevent either the side or the cross member or brace from splitting. Use 4d finishing nails unless otherwise directed. When constructing hardwood cabinets, you can usually eliminate nailing, although you give up some strength if you do.

Clamp the pieces in place as indicated in the drawing to secure for nailing. Tighten the clamps with your fingertips; nail; square the unit; and finally, tighten the clamps fully.

Locate the top nail that goes into each cross member or brace farther in from the edge of the side than the lower nail, and drive each nail at a slight angle to the length of the cross member or brace for extra strength.

CABINET ASSEMBLY: BOTTOM AND SHELF INSTALLATION

Whenever possible, shelves and cabinet bottoms that fit into grooves in the sides should be glued and nailed with 4d finishing nails driven through the bottom surface of the shelf, as shown at the bottom, right. This adds strength to the cabinet.

Use a nailset to drive the nails home—you can't do it with a hammer alone because the angle is too shallow.

Once the shelves (or cabinet bottoms) are glued and nailed in place, pull the pieces even more tightly together with pipe or bar clamps while the glue sets. It is very important here to make sure the various components are in square with each other while the glue is setting.

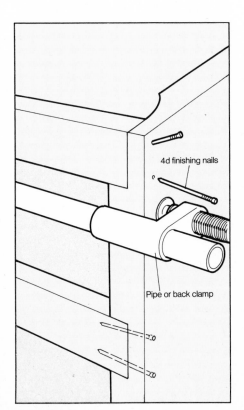

ASSEMBLY A

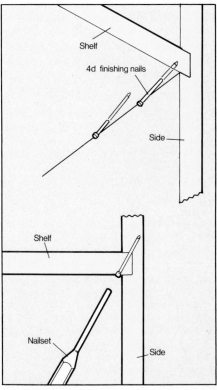

ASSEMBLY B

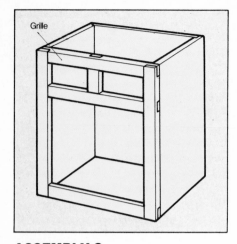

ASSEMBLY C

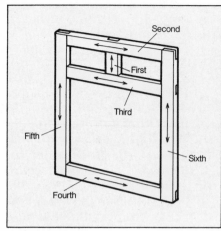

ASSEMBLY D

CABINET ASSEMBLY: GRILLE SUBASSEMBLY

In cabinets, the grille is a subassembly that defines the openings for doors or drawers. The cross pieces in the grille also serve the function of drawer braces; doors are attached directly to and close against the grille. In many of these projects, the grille is attached to the leading edges of the sides, as shown.

Like doors and drawers, the grille should be glued and clamped early in the assembly process so the glue has a chance to set up. To ensure the best possible fit of the parts, do not sand grille pieces until assembly. This saves a step because you will need to sand the glue joints on the grille after the glue has set up anyway. Because the parts are only glued together, the only tools you

need for this job are C clamps (with pads to protect the wood) for holding the individual joints together, and pipe or bar clamps to hold the entire grille square. As you glue and clamp the parts, check the door and drawer openings for square several times. After the glue has set up completely, sand the grille with a portable belt sander and a finish sander in the sequence shown at top, right.

CABINET ASSEMBLY: GRILLE INSTALLATION

The grille is now ready to be glued, nailed, and clamped onto the front edges of the cabinet's sides and the bottom (if there is one). Spread plenty of glue on the leading edges of the sides and the bottom. Use 4d finishing nails to hold the position of the sides, bottom, and grille while you

tighten pipe or bar clamps to pull the parts tightly together and square, as shown. If necessary, pre-drill for the nails.

On some cabinets a top cross-member support will provide the reinforcement its name suggests and also ensure the correct inside distance between the sides; the same is true for a top brace. A bottom back brace glued and screwed onto the inside surface of the plywood back at its bottom edge, as shown bottom left, serves the same dual purpose.

When the grille is secure, remove the clamps and rough- and finish-sand the grille edges flush with the sides. Be careful not to sand through the thin outer layer of a plywood side.

CABINET ASSEMBLY: FINAL SQUARING

During the assembly process up to this point, you will, of course, have made an effort to keep the cabinet square. But things don't always work out as planned, and your cabinet may be out of square when you finish assembling the body. If this happens, you can use the attachment of the top to pull the rest of the assembly square.

To square the cabinet while attaching the top, first set the top upside down on a flat surface, padded so the top won't be scratched. Set the assembled cabinet body upside down on the top and position it according to the plan for that project.

Spot-nail through the attachment point at the front of the cabinet (top cross-member, top brace, or top cross member support) with finishing nails. Spot nailing means nailing to secure something in place without driving the nails all the way in. When the front of the cabinet has been spot-nailed to the top, attach it permanently with No. 8 x 1¼- or 1½-inch (or longer, depending on the thickness of the two pieces joined) wood screws. With the screws driven home, drive home the spot nails in the front.

With the front edge of the cabinet secure, spot finishing nails into the side braces and top back brace, but do not drive these nails into the top at

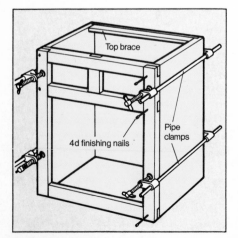

ASSEMBLY E

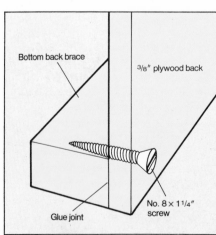

ASSEMBLY F

all. Use a carpenter's square to check the cabinet for square. Twist the cabinet until you get it square against the carpenter's square; then tap the spot nails into the top to hold the squared sides in place. Secure the sides and back of the cabinet with No. 8 × 1¼-inch or 4d wood screws, as with the front.

Twisting the cabinet to square it will make the overlap of the top on either side slightly uneven, but it is much more important to have a square cabinet.

As you attach the top, you will notice that screws driven through the top braces (set slightly below the tops of the sides) create a springlike tension on the braces. This allows the top to flex slightly, responding to weather changes without cracking.

CABINET ASSEMBLY: WRAPAROUND FOOT

Many furniture pieces have a foot that wraps around three adjacent sides or all four sides. If this is the case on the project you're building, it is necessary to C-clamp the front foot (which has two 45° miters) onto

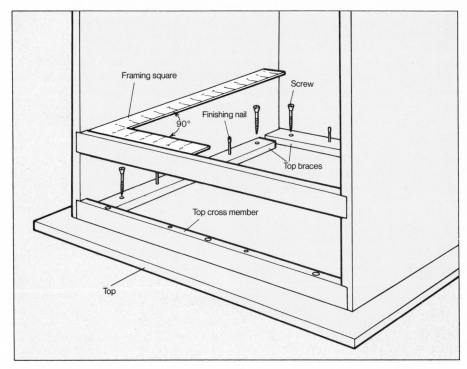

ASSEMBLY G

the bottom cross member. With the front foot clamped in place, you can position and attach the side feet, to which you will then glue and nail the front foot.

Put the side feet in position so that they mate smoothly with the ends of the front foot, and pre-drill holes (if necessary) for screws to be driven through from the inside of the cabinet. Spread glue on the mitered ends of the front and side feet—working the glue well into the grain—and attach the side feet in place with No. 8 × 1¼- or 1½-inch wood screws (depending on the thickness of the sides). When the side feet are secure, cross-nail each miter joint, as shown, with 4d finishing nails (through pre-drilled holes if necessary). Countersink the nails and fill with wood putty. Finally, clamp the assembly with pipe or bar clamps until the glue sets up.

DOOR ASSEMBLY: SANDING

Cut the A stiles and B rails and C panels for doors according to the dimensions given in the project and the specifications #10, #11, #12 on page 19. For success with these doors,

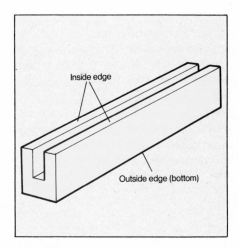

ASSEMBLY J

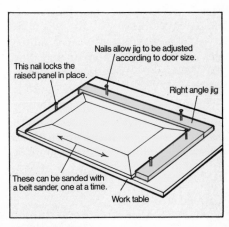

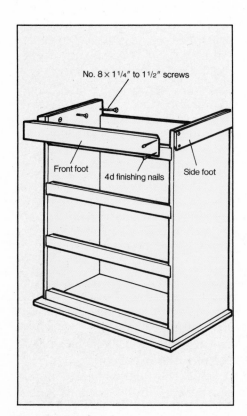

ASSEMBLY H

ASSEMBLY K

great care should be taken to make the machining quite precise; see the illustrated sequence on pages 41-42 for cutting instructions. If you are building one of these doors for the first time, it is a good idea to try one or two strictly for practice.

After the A stiles and B rails and the C panel are machined, they must be sanded. Refer to the Sanding section, pages 13-15, if necessary. Rough-sand the front and back surfaces and the outside and inside edges of the A stiles and B rails, but do not sand the grooves for the C panel at all. Do this sanding with care, and do not sand off much at all. The rails and stiles will be finish-sanded after the door has been assembled.

If you are using a piece of plywood for a flat C panel, you will not need to do more than touch it up with fine sandpaper. If you are using a raised panel, it must be finish-sanded before the door is assembled. This is most easily accomplished with the simple jig illustrated on page 27 and shown also on page 42. Position the panel in the jig, lock it in place with a spot nail, and use a portable belt sander along the angled surfaces. Rotate the panel to do the next angled surface, and continue until the panel is sanded all the way around. The flat (raised) surface of the door should be rough- and finished-sanded at this time.

DOOR ASSEMBLY

To assemble a door, you will need a very flat piece of ¾-inch plywood slightly wider than the door, newspaper to cover the plywood, two pipe clamps, a straight piece of scrap wood to serve as a spacer, and four C clamps with pads to protect the wood.

Start the assembly by spreading glue on the tongues of the B rails with a brush (wipe away any excess before continuing). Also squeeze a little glue into the groove in the A stiles, where the tongues of the B rails will sit.

Place two A stiles on the ends of a B rail, as shown at top. Slip the C

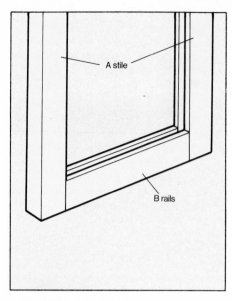

ASSEMBLY L

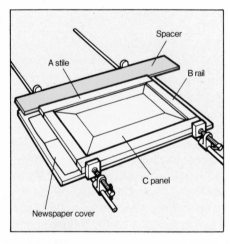

ASSEMBLY M

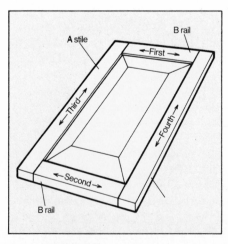

ASSEMBLY N

panel into place and fit the remaining B rail into place. Set this assembly onto the piece of plywood covered with newspapers, as shown at middle left. The panel sits on the two pipe clamps. The spacer sits on the panel between one edge of the door and the clamps so that the clamps can tighten against the door while the door remains entirely on the plywood. Fingertip-tighten the pipe clamps and check for square. If the door is not square, loosen the clamps and make the necessary adjustments.

When the door is square, place a C clamp with protective pads on each of the four joints at the corners of the door so that the door is clamped to the plywood panel beneath at these joints. This will flatten the door against the panel and force the door to be flat, square, and perfect. For good measure, place one more pipe clamp across the door on the side to oppose the buckling pressure of the other two. The entire glued-up door assembly should set up before any of the clamps are removed.

This method of door construction will produce a door as free from problems of warpage and twist as is possible. It takes a little longer than other methods but is worth the effort to make a door without flaws.

When the door has set up, remove the clamps and give it a final sanding. Use a portable belt sander with 80-grit paper to smooth the A stiles and B rails. Sand the B rails first, as shown at bottom, which will cause scratching at the ends of the A stiles. Then sand the A stiles to remove these scratches. Finally, sand the perimeter of the door with a belt sander. Use great caution not to sand off too much around these edges, and especially not to change the width of the door. If you sand off too much, it is possible that the doors will not meet when closed (if this is what the project calls for), but rather leave a gap that will spoil the appearance of your cabinetwork.

Lastly, use a straight-line or orbital finish sander with 120-grit sandpaper to ready the front surfaces of the rails for finishing.

DOORS: DECORATIVE MOLDING

If you are making flat panel doors, you may want to add a decorative molding to the C panel around the inside edges of the rails. This molding is mitered like a picture frame and attached to the assembled door with glue and brads, as shown.

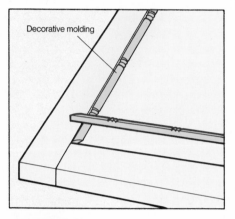

Decorative molding

ASSEMBLY P

DOORS: INSTALLATION

Doors should be installed on a cabinet before the cabinet is given its finish to ensure that they fit, that the hinges operate properly, that the drill holes for knobs or pulls are properly aligned, and that the magnetic catches or other devices are operating properly. Once everything is properly positioned and working, the doors should be removed while both they and the cabinet are finished.

To install a door, place it on the cabinet and locate the hinges where you think they should be. Generally speaking, the placement of a hinge will look best at a point on the door where the top of its hinge pin lines up with the inner edge of the B rail, as shown above. Also, the knob or door pull usually should be halfway down the A rail. The magnetic catch should be placed as close to the doorknob as possible. If this isn't possible, then place the catch at the top of the door and adjust the magnetic grab to the minimum amount required to keep the door closed.

When you remove the doors for finishing, label the hinges so that you can remount them in the same places. Don't remove the magnetic catch or strike plate, but simply use masking tape to protect them from the finish. Don't bother to install knobs or backplates (or drawer pulls, for that matter) until after finishing, since all of the hardware components must be removed to finish the door properly.

When both cabinet and doors are finished, reinstall the doors.

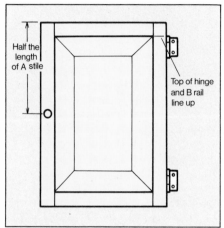

Half the length of A stile

Top of hinge and B rail line up

ASSEMBLY Q

DRAWER ASSEMBLY

Cut the drawer parts to the dimensions given for the project and according to the machining specifications given for that particular drawer on pages 21-22. The more precisely these parts are machined, the more squarely the drawer will fit together, so take the time to get it right. An illustrated sequence of these cuts will be found on pages 43-45. Rough- and finish-sand the front, sides, and back.

When the parts have all been cut and sanded, lay the drawer front face down on a padded workbench top, butted against an immovable object, as shown below.

Glue and nail the sides onto the front (pre-drill for the nails if necessary). Set the nails at this time. Slip the bottom into place and spread glue onto the ends of the drawer back. Lay the drawer on its side in order to nail through the drawer side into the back. Set these nails too.

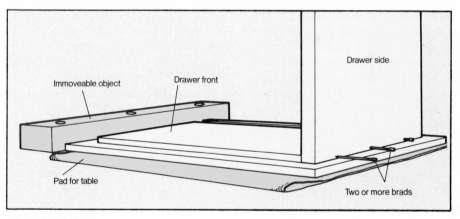

Immoveable object

Drawer front

Drawer side

Pad for table

Two or more brads

ASSEMBLY R

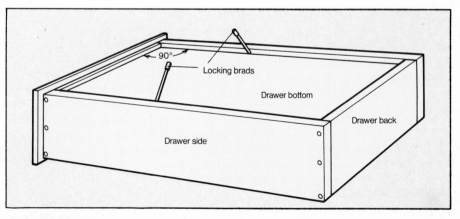

90°

Locking brads

Drawer bottom

Drawer back

Drawer side

ASSEMBLY S

Turn the drawer upside down and check for square. Once the drawer is square, drive a brad through the drawer bottom into each side, as shown at bottom of page 29, to lock the drawer into position while the glue in the joints sets.

Note: Square the drawer relative to the drawer front. If the drawer absolutely will not become square, then come as close as possible.

At this point the drawer should be rather firm and locked in square. Fill the nail holes neatly with wood filler so that additional sanding will not be necessary.

DRAWER INSTALLATION: MONORAIL ROLLER SYSTEM

Mark a vertical center line on the back of the drawer and attach the rear roller, centered on this line with the roller flange even with the bottom of the drawer back. Screws for this attachment come as a part of the roller system.

The monorail should be ⅛ inch shorter than the distance from the back edge of the drawer brace to the back of the cabinet. Cut the monorail to length with a hacksaw.

Install the bracket for the monorail in the back of the cabinet with wood screws, insert the monorail in the bracket, and attach the front of the monorail to the front of the cabinet. The monorail must be level, and it must be precisely centered in the drawer opening at both the front and the back of the cabinet. Measure carefully before you attach the parts of this system to the cabinet.

Attach the side rollers to either side of the drawer opening, as shown. Position these rollers so that they will contact the drawer sides, and keep the sides from rubbing on the front of the cabinet.

To install the drawer, tilt it forward slightly, as shown here, and insert the rear roller in the monorail. When you feel the roller drop into place, bring the drawer back to level and slide it smoothly into the cabinet.

DRAWER INSTALLATION: CHANNEL ROLLER SYSTEM

There are two ways to install a chan-

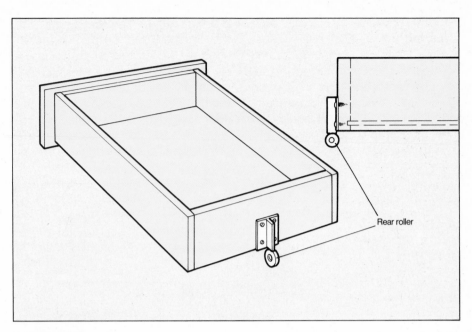

ASSEMBLY T-1

Rear roller

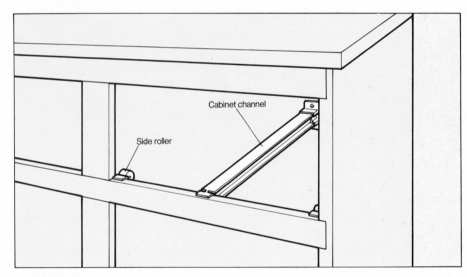

Cabinet channel

Side roller

ASSEMBLY T-2

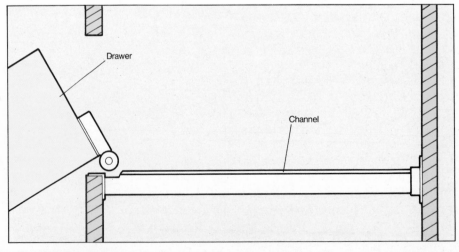

Drawer

Channel

ASSEMBLY T-3

nel-type drawer-roller system—either to the cabinet back or to the cabinet sides. Both methods are given here. Use the one called for in the project you are building. This type of roller system comes in a variety of lengths at 2-inch intervals and should be cut to exact size with a hacksaw. (Measure cabinet depth from the front of the drawer brace to the back, less 1/4 inch and drawer side length, less 1/4 inch.)

To attach the channels to the cabinet sides, first attach channels C-L and C-R (cabinet left and right) to the cabinet so that the front end of each channel is flush with the leading edge of the drawer brace, as shown at top left.

Attach the drawer channels (D-R and D-L) to the drawer, as shown. The roller plate at the back of the drawer should be flush with the bottom of the drawer. You are ready to insert the drawer into the side channels.

To attach the channels to the back of the cabinet, you will need a plastic bracket for each roller. Attach these brackets to the back of the cabinet with wood screws. Then insert the rear end of the side channels into the brackets, and attach the other ends to the front of the cabinet. The channels must be level, and they must be precisely parallel. Measure carefully before installing these parts.

Attach the drawer channels to the drawer as described previously, and insert the drawer into the side channels. When properly installed, the lower roller on the drawer will ride the side channels, and the upper roller on the side channels will ride in the drawer channels, as shown here.

DRAWER INSTALLATION: EXTENSION ROLLER SYSTEM

Mount the cabinet channels on top of the drawer brace, flush with the leading edge of the brace. Be sure that you drive the screws all the way in so that the screw heads will not impede movement of the drawer.

Butt the leading end of the drawer channels against the inside face of the drawer front, and install with a few screws driven through the slots in the channel. (Do not attach with all

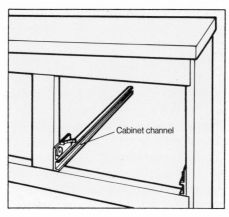

ASSEMBLY U-1

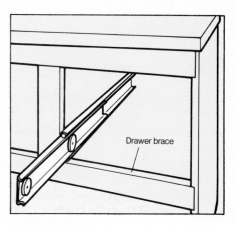

Drawer brace

ASSEMBLY V-1

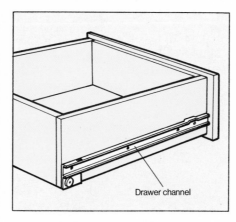

Drawer channel

ASSEMBLY U-2

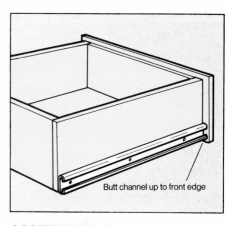

Butt channel up to front edge

ASSEMBLY V-2

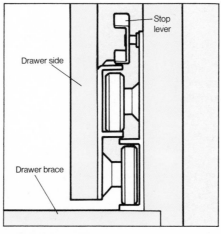

Stop lever

Drawer side

Drawer brace

ASSEMBLY U-3

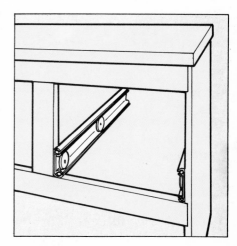

ASSEMBLY V-3

the screws or drive the screws all the way in at this point; you may need to adjust the position of the channels.) These screws should be located 1 1/16 inches above the drawer bottom.

To install the drawer, push the cabinet channels all the way into the cabinet; then slide the drawer into place. Adjust the drawer channels as necessary and install the screws.

Cabinet channel

HIDING SCREW HOLES

From time to time, you will have to insert a screw in a project where it will be seen unless you hide the screw head. To hide a screw head, countersink and counterbore the screw. A countersink is a beveled edge on a pilot hole that creates a seat for a flathead wood screw. A counterbore is a countersink that has been bored 1/8 to 1/4 inch beneath the surface of the wood, creating a hole or shaft. The screw head will sit in the bottom of the shaft, and the shaft can be filled to hide the screw.

Most hardware stores carry screw drills that will drill a pilot hole, countersink, and counterbore all in one operation. All of the screws specified for the projects in this book are either No. 8 or No. 10 screws, so you'll need to purchase two drills—one for each size.

Most No. 8 and No. 10 screw drills leave a 3/8-inch counterbore. You can fill this counterbore with wood putty if you want, but it's best to fill it with a plug of the same type of wood that you're working with. Most woodworking suppliers sell 3/8-inch screw plugs of common woods, such as birch, maple, oak, or walnut. You can also make your own plugs with a 3/8-inch plug cutter. This simple tool fits in your drill press just like an ordinary drill bit, and is usually available from the same suppliers that sell screw plugs.

SECURING DOWELS IN HOLES

When gluing a spindle or dowel into a hole, it is best to place an appropriate amount of glue in the hole by pouring it down around the sides of the hole. Then, using a matchstick or other suitable instrument, spread more glue entirely around the surface of the hole's passageway. Do not place glue on the shank of the dowel, since, as the dowel enters the hole, the extra glue will rub off and spread over the surface to be stained later.

The dowel and hole should be the same size. This causes a pressure fit, which requires clamping to force the dowel into the hole. Pinning or nailing the dowel should not be necessary, but it may be done. A hardwood wedge may be used when a dowel or spindle passes through the piece it enters. Back and front posts on chairs and deacon's benches are examples of spindles engaged in this manner. See the sketch below for instructions.

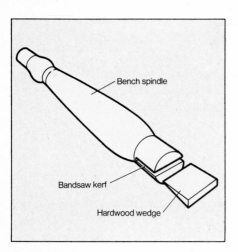

Bench spindle

Bandsaw kerf

Hardwood wedge

ASSEMBLY W

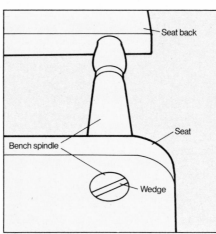

Seat back

Bench spindle

Seat

Wedge

ASSEMBLY X

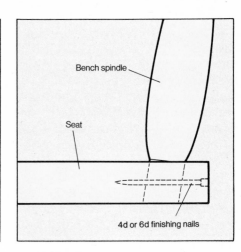

Bench spindle

Seat

4d or 6d finishing nails

ASSEMBLY Y

GALLERY

Simple Bookcase Desk (pages 117-118). Shelves for books and an ample work surface make this desk ideal for a child's room or a home office or library.

Simple Bookcase (pages 52-53). The machining and assembly operations required to build this bookcase are as simple as its design. When you need more book and display space for small collectibles, this project will come in handy.

Hall Cabinet (pages 57-59). Useful both as a decorative storage piece and as a server for the dining room, this cabinet is only 13 inches wide. The flip-top version converts the cabinet to a convenient sideboard.

Pedestal End Table (pages 92-94). The pedestal that supports the top of this sturdy table is turned from a block of glued-up stock. Your local lumberyard may be able to turn the piece for you.

Candlestand (pages 95-97). This is really an all-purpose table. You can use it as a lamp table, nightstand, end table, plant stand, or smoking stand. Also, the size of the top can be altered to suit.

Secretary Desk (pages 119-123). The top section of this classic desk features two small drawers and cubbyhole compartments. This is a challenging project, so be sure to take great care machining and assembling all the parts. You'll want someone to help you with the final assembly.

Seven-Drawer Desk with Organizer Top (pages 124-130). This is a challenging project that requires subassemblies before final construction, but it's well worth the effort. Be sure to get assistance with the final assembly, since the desk is too heavy for one person to handle.

Four-Door Buffet (pages 64-67). This is a spacious cabinet for the dining room or living room. Like the machining of all the cabinet projects in this book, precision is essential for keeping the assembly square.

Square-Edge Buffet (pages 60-63). Although this project is called a buffet, it can be used as a media cabinet to accommodate stereo and video equipment, or as a storage cabinet for almost any room in the house.

Large Dresser (pages 75-78). This spacious dresser with six deep drawers is designed for storing sweaters and other bulky items.

Portable Bar (pages 154-156). Two shelves for bottle and glass storage, not visible in this picture, provide adequate space for storage and serving when entertaining. It's compact and can be stored close to a wall and out of the way when not in use.

Wall Unit (pages 79-83). This is an all-purpose storage unit that is relatively easy to construct. There's plenty of shelf storage and display space along with drawers and a desk surface, making it suitable for use in a bedroom or study.

Sliding-Door Headboard (pages 150-153). Dimensions given for this headboard fit a queen-size bed, but they can be adjusted easily for a standard or king-size bed.

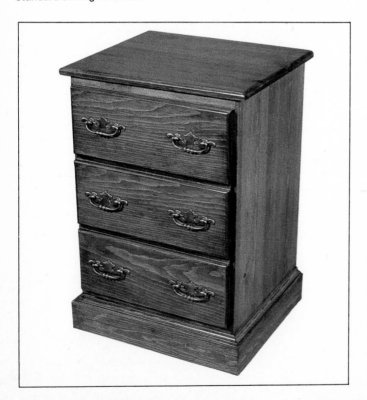

Record Cabinet (pages 72-74). The picture at the right reveals that the drawers here are actually decorative facings on the door. This is a relatively easy and satisfying project to build.

Nightstand (pages 90-91). The drawer and door combination provides useful storage space for books, tissues, and other nighttime necessities and it's just the right height for a reading lamp.

Baby-Changing Cabinet with Tray (pages 131-135). This is a relatively easy project to build since no subassemblies are required. And once baby has grown, it can be used for many other purposes.

Rounded-Post Headboard (pages 147-149). You can vary the center pattern to suit your room's decor by choosing from alternate patterns offered, or you can duplicate this simple, but attractive design. Little woodworking experience is required.

Drop-Leaf Trestle Table (pages 101-103). This is the perfect table for a country kitchen or dining room. Its classic design relies upon the beauty of the wood top, so be especially choosy when selecting wood for the top and leaves.

Heavy Trestle Bench (pages 104-106). As a companion to the drop-leaf trestle table, you may want to consider building two benches. It is a simple, sturdy design that is easy to build.

ILLUSTRATED TECHNIQUES

The following eight pages give illustrated directions for performing some of the important subassembly routines called for in many of the case-furniture projects in this book. Use these pages in conjunction with the information given for the project you are building and with the specifications given in the sections on Machining Standards and Assembly.

DOORS

The techniques for cutting the door parts are shown here on a table saw equipped with homemade jigs, plans for which are given on page 45. These cuts require the use of a dado cutter and a regular blade.

STEP 1
CUTTING THE RAILS AND STILES

Mark and cut the rails to length according to the dimensions given in the project you are building and the specifications given on pages 19–20 in the Machining Standards section.

Use a dado cutter to groove the rails and stiles to the depths indicated on page 19. Set the fence on your table saw so that the grooves are centered in the rails.

Mark the cuts for the tongues on the B rails (at both ends). The technique shown here for making those cuts involves two steps performed with a regular blade (shown top right and bottom): make the horizontal cuts with the blade set for ¼ inch. Raise the blade to ⅜ inches, stand the rail on end, and complete the cuts.

STEP 2
CUTTING A RAISED PANEL

Cut a blank for the raised panel to the dimensions given in the project you are building. Set the blade on your saw at a 15° angle and use the vertical jig shown on page 45 to support the panel as you run it through the blade. Cut all four of the sides in this manner.

Set the rip fence at the proper distance from the blade, so the groove is centered in the boards; run the door rails and stiles through.

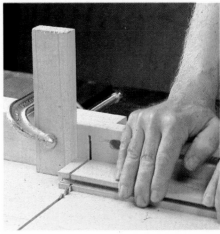

If you use a regular blade to cut the tongue ends of the B rails, set the depth of these horizontal cuts as specified on page 19.

A vertical pass through the blade completes the tongue on a B rail. Set the blade height at the length of the tongue.

Crank the blade up as high as it will go and set it at a 15° angle to cut the four sides of a raised door panel.

Don't try to sand the raised panel without securing it, or it will skate away. This jig is simple and easy to knock together.

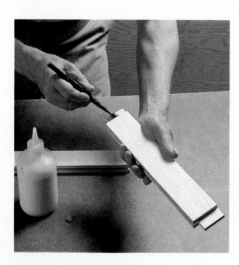

Use a brush for applying glue in order to control the amount of glue on the work. If you are careful, you save sanding later.

STEP 3
SANDING THE RAISED PANEL

Use the simple jig shown here to hold the raised panel in place for sanding the trimmed edges. Sand one edge; then rotate the panel to sand another.

STEP 4
STARTING ASSEMBLY

Brush glue onto one tongue on each of the B rails and into both ends of the groove on one of the A stiles where the pieces will mate. Take care to apply the glue so that as little glue as possible will squeeze out of the joint when the parts are assembled. Do not apply glue to the panel or the grooves where the panel rests. The panel must be allowed to "float" in the grooves, so that it can expand and contract with changes in temperature and humidity.

STEP 5
ASSEMBLING THE DOOR

Set the two B rails into the ends of one of the A stiles lying flat on your work table. Slip the raised panel (or flat plywood panel, if you are building a flat panel door) into the grooves in the B rails and slide it into the groove in the A stiles. Apply glue to the other two tongues on the B rails and the groove in the remaining A stile. Once you've done this, fit the A stile into place.

STEP 6
CLAMPING THE DOOR

Set the door on a very flat piece of plywood slightly wider than the door. Set this plywood on two pipe clamps with a piece of scrap wood between the clamps and the edge of the door, as shown, so that the clamps will apply pressure to the door and not to the plywood foundation panel. Tighten the clamps evenly to prevent distortion in the door. When the clamps are snug, use C clamps to secure each of the glue joints at the corners of the door to the plywood panel, as shown. Remember to pad all clamps to prevent pressure marks on the door. Such attention to detail is well worth the final results.

The rails are glued, but not secured, when you insert the door panel. The panel should sit evenly in the grooves on all four rails.

Clamp the door on a flat surface to ensure that the door will be flat. The pipe clamps should press against the A stiles.

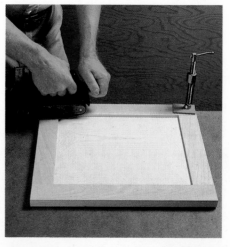

Sand down the joints after the glue has dried thoroughly. The door should be secured to the work surface for sanding.

STEP 7
FINAL SANDING

When the glue has dried, unclamp the door and sand the joints with 120-grit sandpaper to smooth away any glue that has squeezed out and any discrepancies in fit between the rails. Use a jig to hold the door while sanding, or clamp it down, as shown here.

DRAWERS

The secret to making drawers successfully is cutting the parts with precision: slight errors in cutting will be magnified as you assemble the drawer. A drawer that is significantly out of square will not move smoothly on its rollers or slides.

There are several kinds of drawers given for these projects. The dimensions depend on the roller system used to mount the drawer, as well as on whether or not the drawer front will overlap or fit into its opening flush with the front of the cabinet. The drawer shown here has an overlap front and is designed for use with a channel roller system.

STEP 1
CUTTING THE PARTS

The ¼- × ¼-inch grooves in the front, sides, and back of the drawer to accommodate the drawer bottom are made with a dado cutter, as shown. The location of the groove is the same on the sides and bottom; therefore these can be machined one after the other without changing the position of the rip fence on the saw. The corresponding groove on the front piece is farther from the bottom edge of the piece because the front is wider than the other three parts. The location of these grooves is shown on pages 21-22 in the Machining Standards section.

STEP 2
COMPLETING THE DRAWER FRONT

Use a regular cutting blade on the table saw to make the cuts for the drawer overlap. This is done in two steps: first make the horizontal cuts, as shown at top right; then make the vertical cuts, as shown at middle

Cut the grooves in the back, sides, and front with a dado cutter. Set the rip fence for the sides and back; then adjust for the front.

The additional cuts for the overlap drawer fronts are made here with two passes through a regular cutting blade.

Adjust the blade height as required to complete the second cuts. All grooves except the drawer bottom are ⅜ inch deep.

Cutting the ends of the drawer front requires clamping the piece to a jig because it is too long to ride securely against the fence.

Pre-drill for nails if the wood is hard to nail into. Drive the nails most of the way in; then use a nailset so you don't mar the surface.

Cut the back from ¼-inch plywood to the dimensions specified for the project you are building. It slips easily into place.

right and left. Notice that when you are cutting the ends of a long drawer front, it should be clamped to your jig to ensure a straight cut.

STEP 3
STARTING ASSEMBLY
You will need some immovable stop

Stand the drawer on end to nail in the back, which sits between the sides. The back's groove fits over the drawer bottom.

Check for square and don't be alarmed if you are slightly off—even though the joints have been nailed, there will be some give.

to hold the drawer parts fast while you nail them together. The one shown here is simply a piece of scrap wood tacked to the work surface.

Put the drawer front face down on the work surface, flush up against the stop, and nail one side in place. If you are using a wood that is at all hard or brittle, pre-drill holes for the nails. Set the nails with a nailset.

Attach both sides in this manner. When the sides are secure, slip the drawer bottom into place in the grooves in the sides, and seat it in the groove in the drawer front.

STEP 4
COMPLETING ASSEMBLY
Stand the drawer up on its front and set the back piece in place; the groove in the drawer back fits onto the drawer bottom, and the back sits between the sides. Turn the drawer on its side and nail the back in place through one side, as shown. Turn the drawer onto its other side and complete nailing.

STEP 5
SQUARING THE DRAWER
When the drawer has been assembled, turn it upside down and use a carpenter's square, as shown, to determine whether it is square. If it is out of square, grip opposite corners of the drawer and push and pull in toward the middle of the drawer. This should cause the drawer to distort slightly, bringing it into square. If you can't get the drawer absolutely square, it should still work in the cabinet if the deviation is minor.

A nail or brad driven through each side of the bottom into the front and back of the drawer will lock the drawer into its proper squared shape. If the drawer is out of square, you may need to hold it square while you drive these locking nails into place—another set of hands is the best way to do this.

TRAY CUT FOR A DRAWER FRONT
Where the plan calls for a tray cut on

a drawer front (see page 22 in the Machining Standards section), this can be done on a band saw alone, cutting along an outline marked on the drawer; or, as shown here, a drill press can be used to establish the curved corners of the cut, and then a band saw, to finish the cut. Using the

You can twist the drawer slightly to square it up. A second pair of hands is a big help through this stage of the work.

When you have pulled the drawer square, lock it into place with brads driven through the bottom into the drawer front and back.

drill press ensures smooth, regular curves for the corners of the cut.

To drill and then cut, mark the location of the ends of the tray cut, as indicated on page 22, and drill through both locations. Mark the straight sides of the cut, and complete on the band saw.

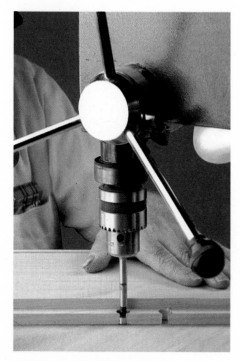

Drill starter holes for the tray cut.

Complete the cut with a band or saber saw.

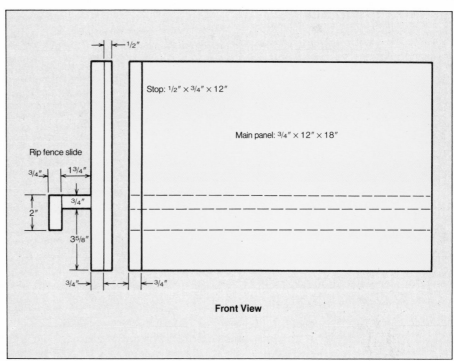

TENONING JIG FOR TABLE SAW

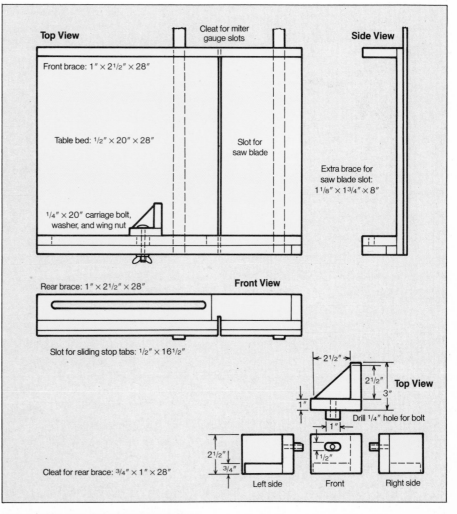

CUT-OFF JIG FOR TABLE SAW

CUTTING AND ASSEMBLING A GRILLE

A squared-up, perfectly flat grille is essential to successfully building a cabinet that calls for a grille. If the grille is not square, or if it is warped, the piece will not go together properly. If the grille you are building has these problems, discard it and make a new one. The cost in extra materials will be negligible compared with the aggravation of trying to build a cabinet around a faulty grille.

Grille parts can be cut on a table saw or radial arm saw with a dado cutter, as shown here for the middle lap cut. The end laps can be cut with the dado cutter or with two passes through a regular blade, as shown here. Make these cuts with precision, and the grille will go together right the first time.

Assemble the grille with glue; be sure to work glue well into the wood at each joint. Assemble the grille on a perfectly flat surface so the unit will be flat. Clamp a joint and then square the work; clamp another joint, and continue squaring as you go. Where you can't fit a clamp (as in the middle of the grille shown here) tack it tightly with brads to hold the joint while the glue sets.

Two passes through a regular blade make neat laps at the ends of grille components.

You have to use a dado cutter to make the cuts for middle lap joints in the grille.

Use the carpenter's square to make sure that the work is square while you clamp it onto a flat surface.

FLUSH SHELVES

A shelf cut and installed in the following manner will mask the dado groove in which it sits and add a professional touch to your work. The specifications for these cuts are given on page 18.

Set up a dado cutter the same width as the thickness of the shelf on a table saw or radial arm saw. Make the cuts in the sides where the shelf (or shelves) will sit, stopping the cuts an inch or two short of the edges of the board, as shown.

Make a template of wood or stiff cardboard that fits into the groove, follows the contour of the stopped cut, and fits flush against the leading edge of the side.

Lay this template over the end of the shelf, as shown in specification 7, page 18, and mark out the corner of the shelf to be cut. Do this at each end of the shelf. This cut (as shown here, completed) can be made with a band saw or saber saw. Cut each end of the shelf, and the resulting installation will look like the one shown here.

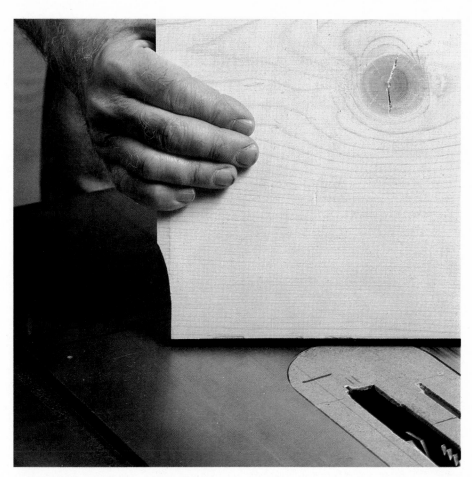

Use a band saw or saber saw to make the cuts at the leading corners of the shelf.

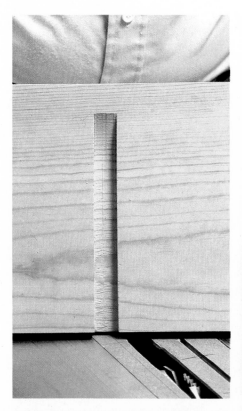

A dado that stops short of the edge of a side will hide this part of the construction.

The fit between shelf and side should be tight and show no gap at the side's edge.

CUTTING A DRAWER-BRACE GROOVE

A drawer-brace groove accommodates the drawer brace, and because it will not show from the front, the cut need not be squared off. Cutting a groove, as shown here, is a much quicker method than chiseling a notch that fits the brace exactly.

To make the cut, mark out the width of the cut according to the width of the brace (see specification 5, page 17). Fit a dado cutter on your table saw (or radial arm saw) and set the depth of the cut to ⅜ inch.

Because the cut needs to be wider than the dado cutter, you must make a few passes to complete it. Make the first pass through the blade at the edge of the cut. Run the board through the blade again, overlapping the cut, and repeat as necessary until you can make the last pass at the other edge of the cut.

WORKSHOP BASICS

If you want to build furniture from scratch, you need a workshop area designed for this purpose. It should be large enough to move around in without bumping into your tools and work surfaces, your materials, and the project itself—400 to 500 square feet is a comfortable size, about the same size as a one-car garage. Remember that you can store lumber for your projects in the ceiling-joist area, if your shop has an unfinished ceiling. Your shop should have good ventilation, as well as excellent lighting which is glare-and shadow-free on all your tools and work surfaces. When you have planned for your power tools, lighting, and ventilation, add up the amperage these will use and have the space wired with sufficient circuits and grounded outlets that have covers to keep out sawdust. Finally, if you plan to build large pieces, remember to make sure that the entrance to the shop is large enough to get the pieces out.

Rather than cutting a notch for a drawer brace with a chisel, you can make a few passes with a dado cutter, going far enough into the board to leave a flat surface for the end of the brace.

The curved end of this cut will not show when the cabinet is assembled. Be sure, when you mark for the cut, that you are using the actual width of the brace as a gauge for tight fit.

The brace should fit snugly in the groove. When you assemble the cabinet, this brace will be attached with glue and two nails driven through the sides into the ends of the brace.

FINISHING

Take your time with this procedure to bring out the best in the project.

MATERIALS:
Satin urethane finish or spar varnish
A high-quality 2″ or 2 1/2″ brush
Steel wool (0000)
Mineral spirits
Pumice (powdered)
Oil stain
Silicone carbide sandpaper, 150- and 180-grit
Aluminum oxide sandpaper, 120- and 80-grit
Waterproof silicone carbide sandpaper, 400- or 500-grit
Paraffin oil
Tack rags

PREPARING THE PIECE

Use 120-grit aluminum oxide sandpaper to inspect-sand the unfinished piece. See that the scratch pattern left by the sandpaper goes with the grain. If there are any tough-to-smooth-out spots, switch to 80-grit aluminum oxide sandpaper, and then resand with 120-grit.

APPLYING THE STAIN

First stain a scrap of wood, or use a section of the piece itself that will not show, to test the amount of stain needed. After testing, apply it to the piece of furniture with a rag, using a brush to get into corners. Continue putting on stain until you reach the desired color. To get a piece darker, add more stain, letting it stand until it starts to dry and then rubbing it into the wood. If the piece gets too dark, douse a rag with mineral spirits and wipe off the stain before it dries. Then let the piece dry thoroughly.

PLANNING THE JOB

Different areas of a piece call for different treatment because they vary in the number of urethane coats they require and in the sanding. The three categories of surface discussed here are labeled A, B, and C. A surfaces are those parts that get the heaviest wear, especially tabletops—these require five coats of urethane or var-nish. B surfaces get a fair amount of wear, especially drawer and door fronts, feet, and chest tops—these require four coats of finish. C surfaces are little seen and get no wear to speak of—these require only three coats.

APPLYING THE FIRST COAT

Apply a very heavy coat of urethane or varnish. Of course, you can't have any drips, so check the piece after fifteen minutes and scoop off any drips that have formed, or press them flat with your index finger. Let this coat dry between three and six hours.

APPLYING MORE FINISH

When the first coat has dried, leave it as it is, without sanding. Apply a second coat and let it dry about two hours.

APPLYING EVEN MORE FINISH

Leave the second coat as it is (again, do not sand) and apply a third heavy coat of urethane only to the A parts of the piece. Leave the B and C parts alone at this time. Let the third coat dry—again, about two hours.

SANDING

Use 150-grit silicone carbide sandpaper to sand the entire piece. Sand with the grain until the shine of the finish has all but disappeared. Go back over all the surfaces with a tack cloth to remove the dust. Be sure to remove all the dust.

APPLYING ADDITIONAL FINISH

Apply another heavy coat of urethane or varnish to the entire piece. This is the third coat for the B and C parts and the fourth for the A parts. This is likely to be the final coat for the C parts, so work carefully and make sure you leave no drips. Let this coat dry about two hours.

SANDING

Using 180-grit silicone carbide sandpaper, sand A and B surfaces. (If any of the C surfaces seem to need another coat, treat them as if they were B surfaces. Otherwise, leave them alone.) Sand away all the small bumps and bubbles first; then "scuff-sand" the entire surface—this means to scratch it lightly so as to remove some of the shiny look. Remove all dust with a tack cloth.

APPLYING THE FINAL COAT

Apply the final coat of finish to the A and B areas. This is the end of the finishing process; next the finish will be hand-rubbed to achieve a glossy surface. Allow the final coat to dry overnight or eight hours.

SANDING

Dip 400- or 500-grit waterproof silicone carbide sandpaper in water, and smooth down bumps and bubbles on the A and B surfaces. Sprinkle the water on the surface and keep dipping the sandpaper as you work. Be sure to rub with the grain. At this point rub down only the surface imperfections, not the areas that are already smooth and shiny. Then dry the surfaces.

RUBBING

Rub out the A and B surfaces with 0000 steel wool. At first this process will seem to scratch the nice, shiny finish, but stay with it. All of a sudden the surface will become as smooth as silk. Don't skip any area with the steel wool.

FINAL TOUCHES

This step is necessary for the A areas and optional for the others. Apply paraffin oil to the surface with your fingers. Sprinkle the surface with powdered pumice. Rub with a soft cloth in the direction of the grain. Rub until you wear yourself out (the more rubbing the better) and then wipe the surface clean. If you find any scratches or imperfections, return to them with the paraffin oil and pumice. Finally, wax the finished piece with your favorite furniture wax.

SAFETY

When you're working in your shop, and especially when using power tools, there are certain precautions that you should *always* take, as well as certain things you should *never* do. Follow these instructions:

• *Always* be sure that you've got a safe electrical setup; be sure that no circuit is overloaded, and there is no danger of short-circuiting, especially in wet locations.

• *Always* read the labels on containers of paint, solvent, and other chemical products; observe ventilation, and all other warnings.

• *Always* read the tool manufacturer's instructions for using the tool, especially the warnings.

• *Always* use holders or pushers to work pieces shorter than 3 inches on a jointer. Avoid working short pieces if you can.

• *Always* remove the key from any drill chuck (portable or press) before starting up.

• *Always* pay deliberate attention to how a tool works so that you can avoid being injured. For example, always observe the proper infeed direction and correct use of the anti-kickback pawls and chute when ripping stock on a radial saw.

• *Always* make sure that any adjustment is locked before proceeding. For example, always check the rip fence on a table saw or the bevel adjustment on a portable saw before starting to work.

• *Always* prevent the workpiece from spinning on a drill (press or portable). It will tend to spin clockwise, the same as the drill rotation. Clamp and block the piece whenever necessary.

• *Always* wear a mask when sanding or handling chemicals.

• *Always* wear eye protection, especially when striking metal on metal; a chip can fly off—for example, when hammering a chisel.

• *Always* know the limitations of your tools. Don't try to force them to do what they weren't designed to do.

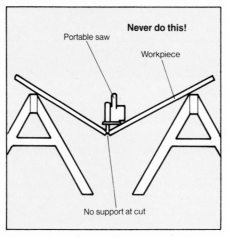

Kerf will close in unsupported area, jamming the blade, and causing kickback.

Eye protection must be used at all times when operating power tools.

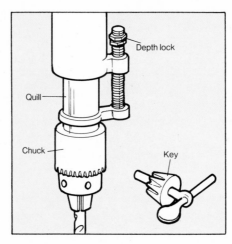

Always remove the chuck key before starting up a drill or drill press.

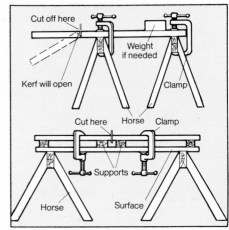

Use these safe methods when cutting off workpieces with portable saws.

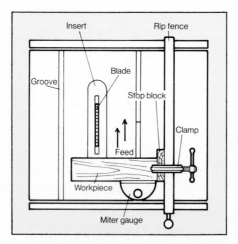

Use a stop block to prevent kickback when crosscutting short pieces.

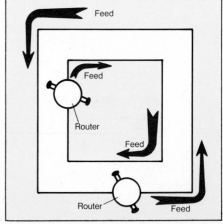

Always rout edges with work at left, feeding into the router bit from the right.

For example, don't force a thick piece of very dense wood such as maple through a consumer-grade table saw in one pass—use several shallow passes instead. Whenever possible, use carbide blades; they're cheaper in the long run—and safer.

• *Always* be aware that there is never time for your body's reflexes to save you from injury from a power tool in a dangerous situation; everything happens too fast. *Be alert!*

• *Always* keep your hands away from the business ends of blades, cutters, and bits. Use push sticks, jigs, and hold-downs instead of touching the workpiece.

• *Always* try to hold a portable saw with both hands so that you will know where your hands are.

• *Always* use a drill with an auxiliary handle to control the torque when large size bits are involved.

• *Never* work with power tools when you're tired or under the influence of alcohol or drugs.

• *Never* work with very small pieces of stock. Whenever possible, cut small pieces off larger pieces.

• *Never* change a blade or a bit unless the power cord is unplugged. Don't depend on the switch alone being off; you might accidentally hit it.

• *Never* work in insufficient light.

• *Never* work with loose clothing, hanging hair, open cuffs, or jewelry.

• *Never* work with dull tools. Have them sharpened, or learn how to do it yourself.

• *Never* use a power tool on a workpiece that is not firmly supported or clamped.

• *Never* saw a workpiece that spans a large distance between horses without close support on either side of the kerf; the piece can bend, closing the kerf and jamming the blade, causing saw kickback.

• *Never* support a workpiece with your leg or other part of your body if you intend to cut it with a portable or jig saw.

• *Never* carry sharp or pointed tools, such as utility knives, awls, or chisels in your pocket. If you want to carry tools, use a special-purpose tool belt with leather pockets and holders.

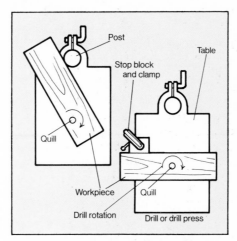

Always block small workpieces to prevent spinning while they are being drilled.

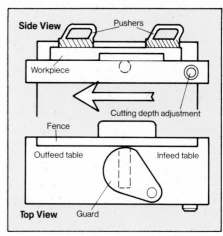

On jointers and planers, always leave guard in place, and use friction sole pushers.

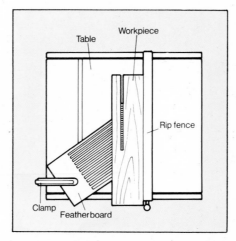

Use a featherboard to hold the workpiece against the rip fence.

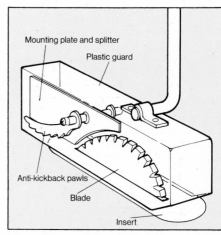

Always use the blade guard on a table saw when blade comes up through work.

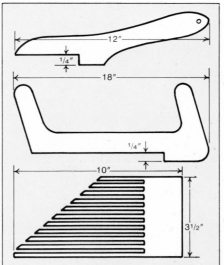

Make your own push sticks and featherboards, and use them for safety's sake.

Always keep the work area around power tools clear of all potential hazards.

SIMPLE BOOKCASE

MATERIALS LIST

A Top (1), 3/4" × 11" × 36"
B Shelves (3), 3/4" × 10" × 333/4"
C Sides (2), 3/4" × 101/4" × 351/4"
D Front foot (1), 3/4" × 31/2" × 341/2"
E Top back brace (1), 3/4" × 11/8" × 33"
F Top scallop (1), 3/4" × 2" × 33"
G Back (1), 1/4" × 321/2" × 333/4"

HARDWARE

No. 8 × 3/4" flathead wood screws
No. 8 × 11/4" flathead wood screws
No. 8 × 11/2" flathead wood screws
4d finishing nails
3/4" brads

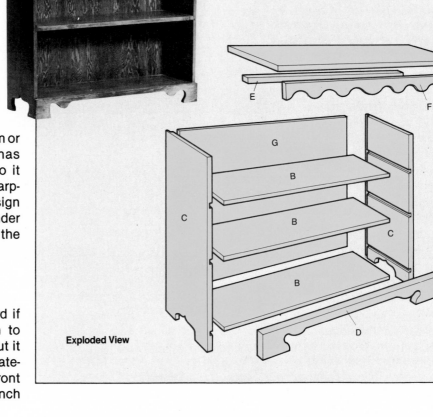

Exploded View

Suitable for almost any living room or child's room, this bookcase has shelves of 3/4-inch thick stock so it can carry heavy loads without warping. By simply changing the design of the foot and the scallop just under the top, you can easily change the style to suit your tastes.

STEP 1
MACHINING THE TOP

The top should be a single board if possible, especially if you plan to make the bookcase from pine. Cut it to the dimensions given in the Materials List and round the side and front edges (top and bottom) with a 3/8-inch quarter round router bit.

STEP 2
MACHINING THE BACK

The back can be any type of 1/4-inch plywood desired. If the bookcase is of pine, knotty pine plywood is ideal. If the bookcase is to be painted, then a less expensive plywood, such as fir, should be used. Birch and pine are very compatible woods in the way they accept a stain, and so it is also appropriate to use birch plywood for the back of a pine bookcase. Whatever plywood you choose, cut it to the dimensions given.

STEP 3
MACHINING THE SIDES

Cut the two sides to the dimensions given in the Materials List. You can cut a pattern in the sides for feet or leave them plain (a flush cut). See specification #31, page 24, for a selection of designs.

Cut standard shelf grooves and standard back grooves in the sides, as shown in Detail A, so that they are a mirror pair. See specifications #1 and #4, page 17, for details.

STEP 4
CUTTING THE TOP SCALLOP

Cut the top scallop piece to size and then copy and transfer one of the scallop patterns given in specification #31, page 24, onto it. Cut out the pattern with a saber or band saw.

STEP 5
MACHINING THE FRONT FOOT

The dimension given for the front foot is 1/16 inch longer than the bookcase to allow for sanding it flush after installation. If you wish, round the leading edge with a 3/8-inch quarter round router bit. Finally, cut a foot pattern, if desired. See specification #31, page 24, for a selection of designs, or create one of your own.

STEP 6
SANDING THE PIECES

Rough- and finish-sand the upper surface, the two ends, and the front edge of the top. There is no need to sand the back edge or underside of the top. Rough- and finish-sand the front face of the top scallop; the lower scalloped edge need only be rough-sanded. There is no need at all to sand the back side of the top scallop. Also, the shelves need not be sanded on the bottom surfaces, but rough- and finish-sand the top surfaces. Don't sand the front edges yet.

Rough- and finish-sand both surfaces of the sides. There is no need to sand the front edges. Sand the top edge of the front foot before it is put onto the cabinet; the front surface need only be rough-sanded before assembly. Usually, there is no reason at all for sanding the plywood back. It comes from the manufacturer sanded. The top back brace should be rough-sanded on the front surface and on the downward edge.

The bookcase will require additional sanding after certain stages of assembly: after the shelves are in place (flush with the back grooves at the back of the sides), the front edges should be sanded level with the sides; and when the front foot has been installed, use a belt sander to sand its ends flush with the sides.

STEP 7
ASSEMBLING SIDES AND SHELVES
Spread glue on the grooves and on the ends of the shelves. Work the glue into the end fibers and fit the shelves into the grooves. Check for square and clamp above each shelf. Use six bar clamps, three on the front and three on the back, to hold the shelves firmly until the glue has set. Use 4d finishing nails to nail from the underside of each shelf into the sides. Set the nails with a nailset. Check for square; use clamps to pull into square if necessary.

STEP 8
ADDING THE SCALLOP AND BACK BRACE
While the clamps are in place, apply glue to the ends of the top scallop and the back brace. Fit the back brace into place (set flush with the back groove), and nail through the sides into the ends of the top scallop and back brace with 4d finishing nails. Set the nails with a nailset.

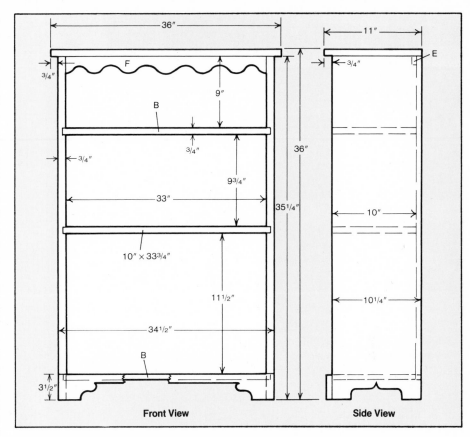

Front View **Side View**

Clamp the scallop and brace to assure that the glue will set well.

STEP 9
ADDING THE FRONT FOOT
Place glue on the leading edge of the sides and the bottom shelf before placing the front foot in position. Nail through the front foot into the leading edges of the sides and shelf with 4d finishing nails. Clamp until set.

STEP 10
ADDING THE TOP
Place the top upside down on a padded surface and invert the bookcase onto the top. The back edge of the top should be flush with the back edges of the sides.

Drill three countersunk pilot holes each through the top scallop and the back brace. Drive No. 8 × 1¼-inch wood screws through the pilot holes into the top.

After all this has been done, fill the screw holes with a colored wood filler which is approximately the same color you plan to stain or a little bit darker. For some reason, darker filler seems less noticeable.

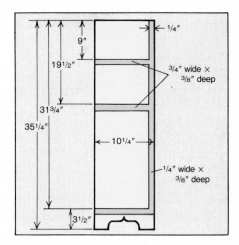

DETAIL A
SIDE LAYOUT

STEP 11
ADDING THE BACK
Install the back when the finish on the bookcase is dry and polished. Fit the back into position and fasten to the sides and shelves with ¾-inch brads. The upper edge of the back fits flush against the top back brace. Use four No. 8 × ¾-inch flathead wood screws, evenly spaced, to secure the back to the brace. This will provide added stability.

LARGE STORAGE CABINET

MATERIALS LIST

A Sides (2), 3/4" × 16 1/4" × 70"
B Lower top (1), 3/4" × 16 3/4" × 36"
C Lower shelf (1), 3/4" × 16" × 33 3/4"
D Bottom (1), 3/4" × 15 1/4" × 33 3/4"
E Upper top (1), 3/4" × 10 1/8" × 36 3/4"
F Upper shelves (2-3), 3/4" × 9 1/8" × 33 3/4"
G Lower top side braces (2), 3/4" × 1 1/8" × 13 3/4"
H Upper top cross member (1), 3/4" × 1 1/4" × 33"
J Lower top cross member (1), 3/4" × 1 5/8" × 33"
K Back braces (2), 3/4" × 1 1/4" × 33"
L Bottom cross member (1), 3/4" × 1 3/4" × 33"
M Front foot (1), 3/4" × 3 1/2" × 36"
N Side feet (2), 3/4" × 3 1/2" × 17"
P Lower back (1), 1/4" × 25 3/4" × 33 3/4"
Q Upper back (1), 1/4" × 33 3/4" × 40 3/4"
R Molding, 3/8" × 3/4" × 54 3/4" (total)

DOORS

S Stiles (4), 3/4" × 2 1/4" × 24 1/4"
T Rails (4), 3/4" × 2 1/4" × 12 7/8"
U Panels (2), 3/4" × 12 5/8" × 20 1/4"

HARDWARE

3/8" offset cabinet door hinges (2 pair)
Magnetic catches (2)
Door pulls (2)
Record dividers (optional)
No. 8 × 1 1/4" flathead wood screws
4d finishing nails.

This storage cabinet can solve space problems in the children's bedroom, in the living room, or in the family room. Its rather simple, straight lines allow the cabinet to blend with many other furniture styles. The design can also be easily altered to suit your individual needs. You can build the upper cabinet with two, three, or more shelves. The shelf in the lower cabinet can be raised or lowered to accept stereo equipment, records, or any other item you wish to store.

The amount of machining involved and the considerable surface area to be sanded make this project somewhat time-consuming. Be sure to allow plenty of shop space for assembling this large cabinet.

STEP 1
MACHINING THE SIDES
Cut the parts for each of the two

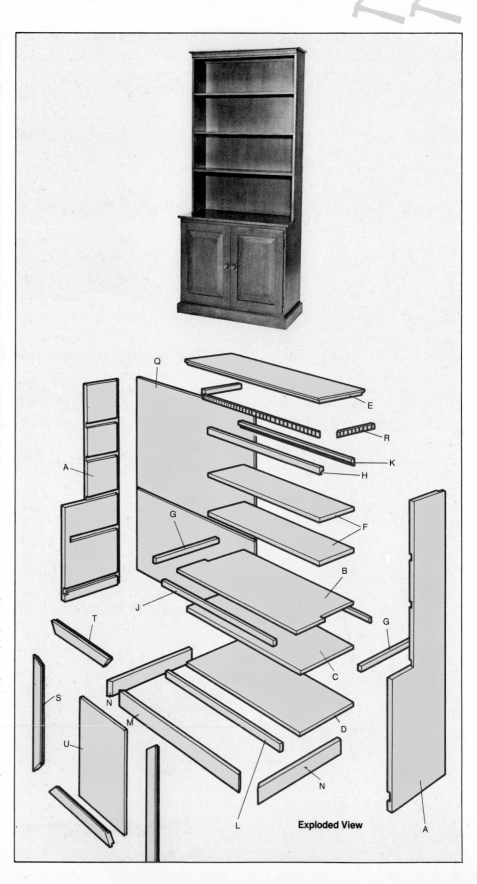

Exploded View

sides and glue them up in the configuration shown in Detail A. See the Gluing section, pages 11-12, for details on gluing these boards together. After the glue has dried, cut the standard shelf grooves, flush shelf grooves, drawer brace grooves, and flush-back grooves in the inside surfaces in the locations shown in Detail A. See specifications #4, #7, and #5, pages 17 and 18, for details on these cuts. They can be made with a table saw, radial arm saw, or router.

STEP 2
MACHINING THE CABINET TOP, UPPER TOP, SHELF, AND BRACE

The top of the cabinet section is notched on each side with a saber saw or band saw, as shown in Detail B. Round the leading and short side edges with a ⅜-inch quarter round bit in the router.

The shelf is notched with standard flush cuts, as shown in Detail C. See specification #3, page 17, for information on making this cut.

If you plan to use the lower cabinet for record storage, drill holes for the standard A-shaped record dividers in the cabinet bottom; see Detail B on page 74 for details on the exact placement of these holes. (It is a good idea to drill these even if you don't intend to use the cabinet for record storage—you may change your mind someday.)

Rout a ⅜-inch-radius cove in the upper top along the edges of two ends and one long side. This cove will complement the molding fitted just under it. Also, rout a ⅜-inch cove along the lower front edge of the top back brace, as shown in Detail D.

Note: The upper back will show through the open shelves and should be of a complementary piece of wood or the same type.

STEP 3
MACHINING THE FEET

The foot arrangement wraps around the cabinet, and so 45° miter joints are cut on the front and side feet. The front foot has two 45° cuts. The two side feet have one 45° angle each to mate with the front foot. If a decora-

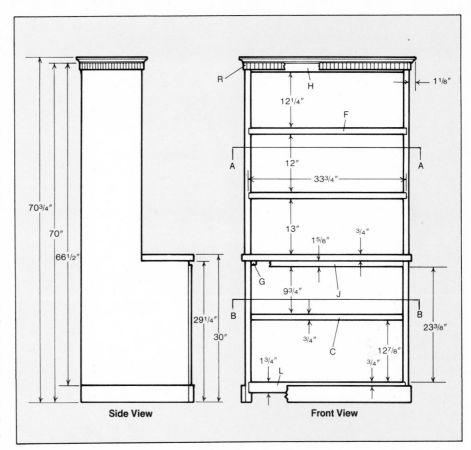

Side View   **Front View**

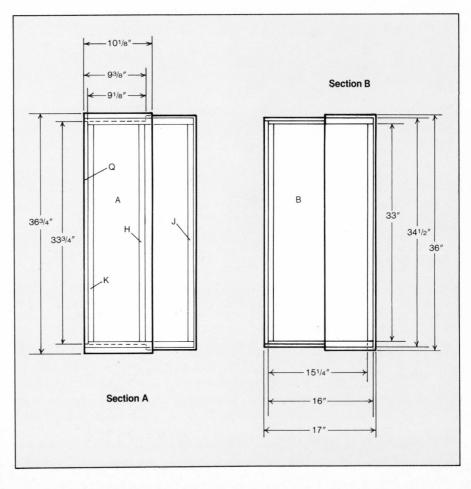

Section A   **Section B**

tive or rounded edging is desired on the leading edge of the foot, then it should be machined onto the foot boards before they are mitered. The foot design is left to the builder.

STEP 4
MACHINING THE MOLDING
Molding wraps around the top of the cabinet just like the foot arrangement. Be careful how you miter this molding. The cuts should be symmetrical so that the design appears continuous. For details on making these cuts, see specification #15, page 20.

STEP 5
MAKING THE DOORS
To construct the two standard frame doors for the cabinet section, see pages 19 and 20 for details of machining the door components.

The two doors require four A stiles and four rails. The material and style of the C panel is left to the builder: a flat plywood panel or a raised panel section must be machined according to directions given in specification #13, page 20. Rout a ⅜- × ⅜-inch rabbet around the top, bottom, and outside edges of the door to form a lip.

STEP 6
SANDING
Rough- and finish-sand the sides, upper top, and upper shelves on both sides. Sand each side's front edge only between the grooves where the lower top and first upper shelf will fit. You can skip the finish sanding on the inside surfaces of the sides hidden by the closed doors. Rough- and finish-sand the top surface and routed edges of the lower top. The bottom and the lower shelf, along with its front edge, need only be rough-sanded. Top braces are not sanded at all. Rough- and finish-sand the top and bottom cross members' forward and inside edge surfaces; do the same to the top back brace and feet. Plywood backs and moldings do not usually need sanding. The sanding of door parts is explained in detail in the Assembly section.

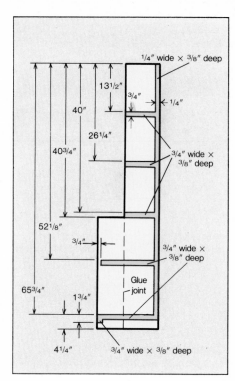

DETAIL A
SIDE LAYOUT

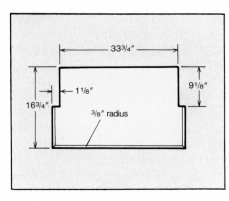

DETAIL B
LOWER TOP LAYOUT

STEP 7
ASSEMBLING THE CABINET
Complete instructions for assembling this cabinet and installing the doors are given in the Assembly section on pages 25-32. Here is the sequence for this project:

(1) Construct the doors. (2) Attach top braces to each side. (3) Insert all shelves, the lower top, and the bottom into the sides and secure with 4d finishing nails. (4) Install the top and bottom cross members and top back brace. (5) Attach the feet. (6) Attach the top by nailing or screwing down

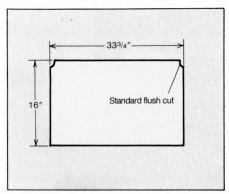

DETAIL C
LOWER SHELF LAYOUT

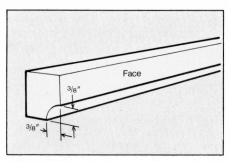

DETAIL D
TOP BACK BRACE DETAIL

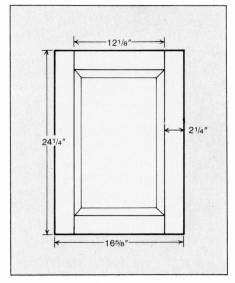

DETAIL E
DOOR LAYOUT

through the top. (7) Attach the lower back. (8) Attach the doors. (9) Apply the desired finish to the cabinet when the process is complete, and finally, (10) attach the upper back.

HALL CABINET

MATERIALS LIST

A Top (1), 1¼″ × 13″ × 30″
or
A-1 Center top (1), ¾″ × 13″ × 30″
A-2 Leaves (2), ¾″ × 11″ × 30″
A-3 Leaf braces (4), ¾″ × 2″ × 13″
B Front foot (1), ¾″ × 4½″ × 30″
C Side feet (2), ¾″ × 4½″ × 13″
D Top cross member (1), ¾″ × 1¼″ × 27¾″
E Bottom cross member (1), ¾″ × 1¾″ × 27¾″
F Middle cross member (1), ¾″ × 1¼″ × 27¾″
G Sides (2), ¾″ × 12¼″ × 29¼″
H Top back brace (1), ¾″ × 1¼″ × 27″
J Top braces (2), ¾″ × 1¼″ × 10″
K Drawer runners (2), ¾″ × 1¼″ × 11¼″
L Shelf (1), ¾″ × 11¼″ × 27¾″
M Adjustable shelf (1), ¾″ × 11¼″ × 27″
N Drawer front (1), ¾″ × 6¼″ × 27¾″
P Drawer back (1), ¾″ × 5⅜″ × 25½″
Q Drawer sides (2), ¾″ × 5⅜″ × 12″
R Drawer bottom (1), ¼″ × 11⅝″ × 26″
S Door stiles (4), ¾″ × 2″ × 16¾″
T Door rails (4), ¾″ × 2″ × 10⅝″
U Door panels (2), ¾″ × 10⅜″ × 13¼″
V Back (1), ¼″ × 27¾″ × 29¼″

HARDWARE

Offset cabinet hinges (4)
Magnetic catches (2)
Sewing-cabinet hinges (4)
Brass knob with backplate (1 set)
Drawer pulls (2)
Drawer glides (4)
Adjustable shelf pegs (4)
4d finishing nails

Useful both as a decorative storage piece and as a server for the dining room, this cabinet will fit nicely in most halls because it is only 13 inches wide. If you choose to build the flip-top version, it will provide a full 13- × 60-inch of serving area.

Because of the several woodworking techniques used in completing this project, it is moderately difficult, which makes it a good one for the craftsperson who wishes to show off his or her talent. The machining for the sewing-cabinet hinges and the fitting of the lift lids, doors, and drawer will provide a challenge even for the experienced cabinetmaker.

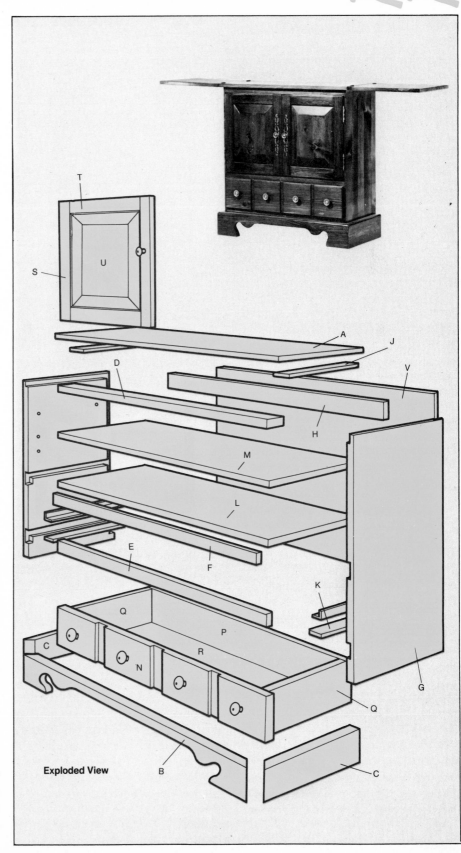

Exploded View

STEP 1
MACHINING THE TOP

This cabinet may be made with either of two tops: a flat, plain top that provides a very useful hall-cabinet surface, or a flip-lid top that is more versatile and provides a 5-foot serving area.

The flip top has a center section and two leaves. Cut a ¼- × ¼-inch groove in both ends of these leaves, as shown in Detail A, and along one edge of each of the four leaf braces, as shown in Detail B. These cuts are easily machined on a table saw with a dado cutter head. The leaf braces are joined to the leaves with four birch or maple splines.

Using plenty of glue, insert the splines into both ends of the leaves, attach leaf braces, and clamp until dry. These leaves will eventually fold down flat on the center section of the cabinet top.

STEP 2
MACHINING THE SIDES

Cut the sides to size and then machine them with the standard shelf, back, and drawer-brace grooves in addition to the standard shelf-peg holes, as shown in Detail C. See specifications #2, #4, and #5, on page 17, for details on the grooves and peg holes.

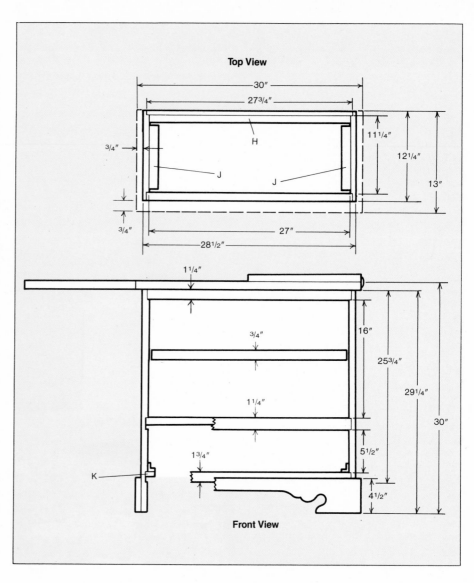

Top View

Front View

STEP 3
MACHINING THE SHELVES

Cut the two shelves to size. The adjustable shelf is best made from ¾-inch plywood or a composition material to avoid the possibility of warpage. The bottom shelf may be cut from any suitable material. The front edges of the shelves may be faced with flexible wood trim. Or you can use screen molding for a different edge treatment; see specification #28, page 23, for details on facing a shelf edge with screen molding.

STEP 4
MACHINING THE FEET

The feet wrap around two sides and the front of the cabinet and have 45° miters machined in both ends of the front foot and one end of each side foot to make the corners.

Round the leading edge of the pieces with a ⅜-inch quarter round router bit before cutting the miters. The choice of a front-foot cutout design is left to you. See specification #31, page 24, for suggested designs.

STEP 5
MACHINING THE DRAWER

The cabinet has one hand-fitted drawer with an overlap front. To construct the drawer, use the dimensions given in the Materials List and see specifications on pages 21 and 22 for details.

You can leave the drawer front plain, in which case round the leading edge with a ⅜-inch quarter round router bit. For a somewhat fancier appearance, make apothecary cuts in the front, as shown in Detail D.

STEP 6
MACHINING THE DOORS

The cabinet has two 4/4 stock frame-and-panel doors which overlap the cabinet opening. To construct these doors, use the dimensions given in the Materials List and see specifications on pages 19 and 20 for details.

STEP 7
SANDING THE PARTS

Rough- and finish-sand the upper face and three machined or exposed edges of the top. Since the two leaves and the center section of the alternate top selection must be fitted together, it is important that all three top parts are the same thickness after they have been rough- and finish-sanded. Sand the two leaf assemblies to finish quality on both faces and on all edges.

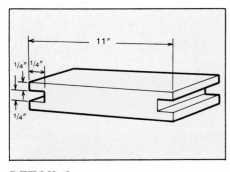

DETAIL A
LEAF JOINERY

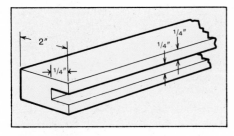

DETAIL B
LEAF BRACE JOINERY

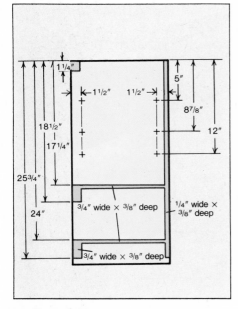

DETAIL C
SIDE LAYOUT

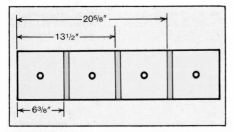

DETAIL D
APOTHECARY DRAWER LAYOUT

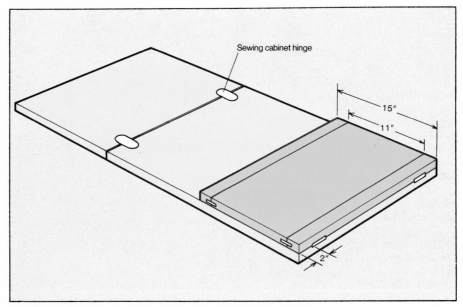

Sewing cabinet hinge

DETAIL E
FLIP-TOP ISOMETRIC VIEW

Rough- and finish-sand the upper face of the center top section and all edges. Care should be taken to mate the leaves to the end edges of the center section to accommodate assembly later. Rough- and finish-sand the outside faces of the sides, and the top edges and front faces of the foot section. However, only rough sanding need be done on the inside faces of the sides; the adjustable shelf; the top, middle, and bottom cross members; and the bottom shelf. Sand the door and drawer parts.

Plywood backs, drawer runners, and top braces never need sanding. In this case, do not bother sanding the top back brace either.

STEP 8
ASSEMBLING THE BASE
Follow the cabinet assembly directions given in the Assembly section, pages 25-27, and attach the drawer runners to the sides with glue and 4d finishing nails. Then attach the bottom shelf; the top, middle, and bottom cross members; and the top back brace. Next attach the wraparound foot assembly according to the Assembly section.

STEP 9
ATTACHING THE TOP
If you are building the flip-top cabinet, use a straight fluted bit to rout a groove that will accommodate the sewing-cabinet hinge in each of the leaves and the center section, as shown in Detail E. The leaves of the hinge should be flush with the wood surface.

STEP 10
ASSEMBLING THE DOORS AND DRAWER
Assemble and install the doors and drawer according to the directions given on pages 27-32 in the Assembly section. Attach the back after the cabinet has been finished.

SQUARE-EDGE BUFFET

MATERIALS LIST
A Top (1), 1¼″ × 19″ × 66″
B Doors (4), ¾″ × 15″ × 19¼″
C Back (1), ¼″ × 29¼″ × 65¼″
D Sides (2), ¾″ × 17⅛″ × 32″
E Shelf (1), ¾″ × 16⅞″ × 65¼″
F Bottom (1), ¾″ × 16⅞″ × 65¼″
G Front foot (1), ¾″ × 4″ × 66″
H Top back brace (1), ¾″ × 1″ × 64½″
J Top cross member support (1), ¾″ × 1″
  × 64½″
K Top cross member (1), ¾″ × 1″ × 64¼″
L Top braces (2), ¾″ × 1⅛″ × 14″
M Drawer brace (1), ¾″ × 1½″ × 64¼″
N Bottom cross member (1), ¾″ × 1½″ ×
  64¼″
P Right and left vertical cross members
  (2), ¾″ × 1⅞″ × 28″
Q Vertical cross members (2), ¾″ × 1¾″
  × 28″
R Center vertical cross member (1), ¾″ ×
  1¾″ × 21½″

SMALL DRAWERS*
S Fronts (2), 1¼″ × 6¼″ × 15″
T Sides (4), ¾″ × 5¼″ × 16¾″
U Backs (2), ¾″ × 5¼″ × 11¾″
V Bottoms (2), ¼″ × 12¼″ × 16⅛″

LARGE DRAWER*
W Front (1), 1¼″ × 6¼″ × 31″
X Sides (2), ¾″ × 5¼″ × 16¾″
Y Back (1), ¾″ × 5¼″ × 27¾″
Z Bottom (1), ¼″ × 28¼″ × 16⅛″

*Dimensions of drawer parts will change
depending on drawer-roller hardware.

HARDWARE
18″ drawer slides (6)
Drawer-slide brackets (6)
Magnetic catch (4)
Self-closing cabinet hinges (4)
Drawer pulls (4)
Door pulls (4)
No. 8 × 1¼″ flathead wood screws
No. 8 × 1½″ flathead wood screws
4d finishing nails
1″ brads

At 66 inches in length, this piece offers a tremendous amount of storage space. Although initially designed as a buffet, it works equally well as a media cabinet in a living room (its 16¾ inches of usable depth will accommodate most stereo and video equipment), or as a storage cabinet in a bedroom or sewing room. The clean lines harmonize with most furniture styles.

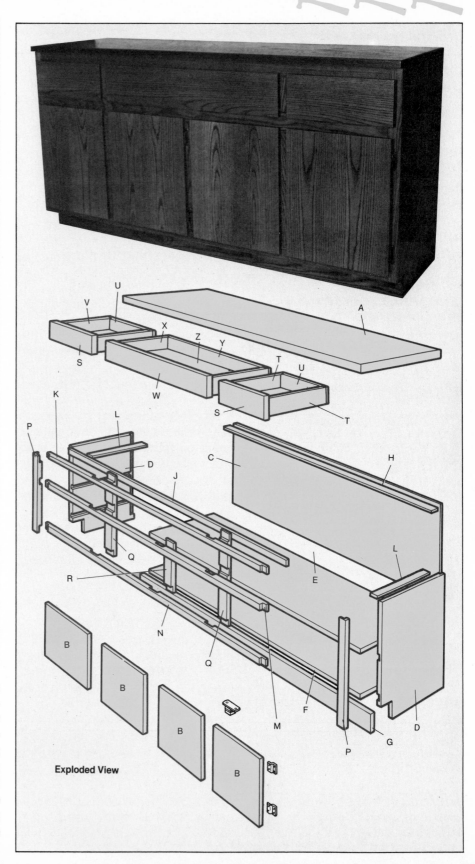

Exploded View

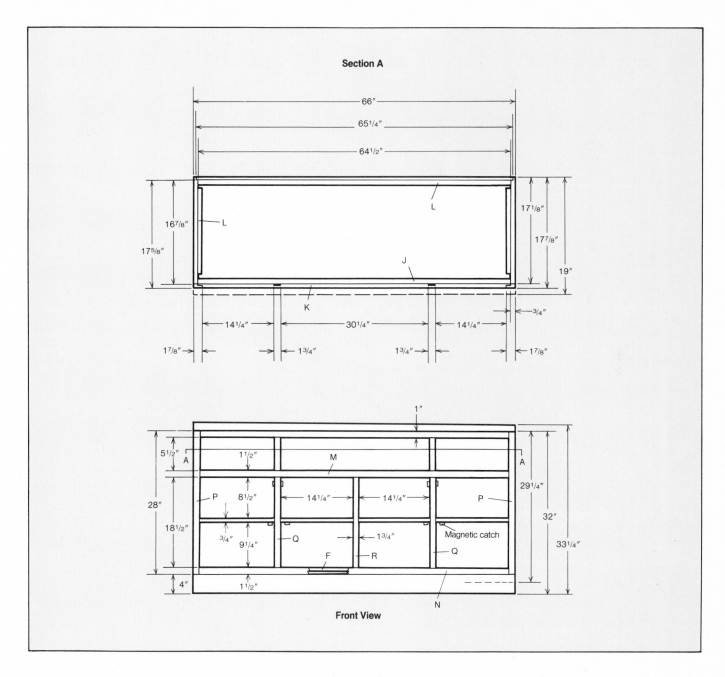

Section A

Front View

The number of pieces requiring precise machining makes the project moderately challenging, but the construction principles are simple.

STEP 1
CREATING THE TOP AND SHELVES
If you have to glue up stock for the top or shelves, see the Gluing section, pages 11-12, for details. The top has square edges and requires no further machining.

STEP 2
MACHINING THE SIDES
Cut two plywood sides to size and machine a mirror-image pair with standard shelf and back grooves, as shown in Detail A; see specifications #4 and #3, page 17, for details on these grooves.

STEP 3
MACHINING THE CROSS MEMBERS AND BRACES
Cut the cross members and braces, label them to avoid confusion, and then cut the various lap joints, as shown in Details B-F. These pieces form the grille on which the doors hang and through which the drawers pass. The joints must be cut with precision; use a dado head on a table

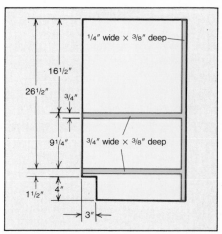

1/4" wide × 3/8" deep

3/4" wide × 3/8" deep

DETAIL A
SIDE LAYOUT

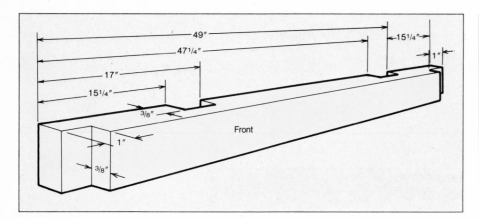

DETAIL B
TOP CROSS-MEMBER JOINERY

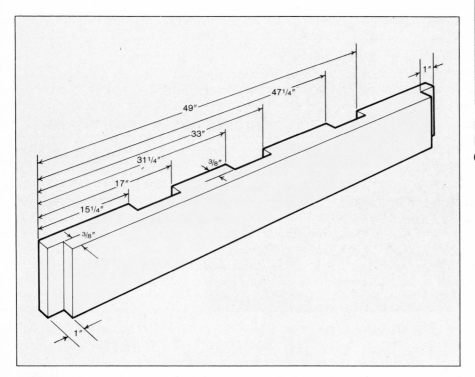

DETAIL C
DRAWER BRACE AND BOTTOM CROSS-MEMBER JOINERY

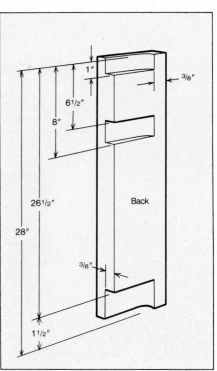

DETAIL D
RIGHT AND LEFT VERTICAL
CROSS-MEMBER JOINERY

saw or radial arm saw, or use a router. The radial arm saw is preferred for this job.

STEP 4
CUTTING THE DRAWER PARTS
The cabinet has three drawers (two the same size, one larger) with overlap fronts for use with drawer roller systems. See specifications #18 and #19, page 21, for details on cutting these parts. Use the dimensions given in the Materials List for this project.

The drawer fronts require the addi-tional machining of fingerhold grooves in the lower lip, as shown in Detail G. Use a router to make the cuts.

STEP 5
CUTTING THE DOORS
The four cabinet doors are simple panels of ¾-inch plywood. Use lumber-core plywood to avoid the need for finishing the edges of the panels. Cut the door panels to size and rout fingerholds in the backs, as shown in Detail H.

STEP 6
SANDING
Rough- and finish-sand the front, side edges, and top surface of the top. Because the top is cut ⅛ inch longer than the actual cabinet length, you can sand as much as necessary without fear of ending up with a short top.

The plywood should not need sanding (touch up, if necessary). The shelf and bottom need only rough sanding on the top surfaces and leading edges. Rough- and finish-sand the face and ends of the front foot. The top braces and top cross-member supports do not need any sanding.

The various grille components should not be sanded until after they have been assembled, and then only on edges which will be conspicuous when the doors are opened: for instance, the top edge of the bottom cross member, which should be rough- and finish-sanded. Sand the other components surrounding the door openings to your satisfaction.

The plywood back will not need sanding unless it is extremely rough,

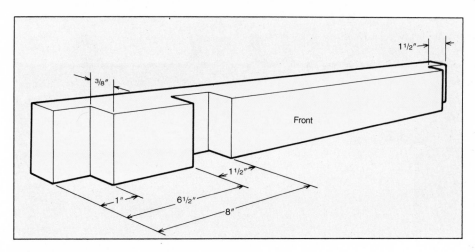

DETAIL E
VERTICAL CROSS-MEMBER JOINERY

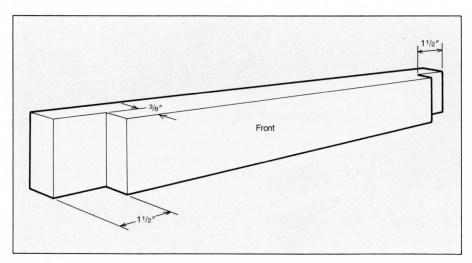

DETAIL F
CENTER VERTICAL CROSS-MEMBER JOINERY

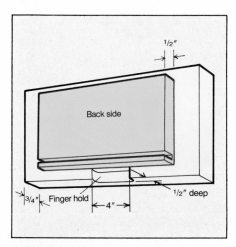

DETAIL G
DRAWER FRONT DETAIL

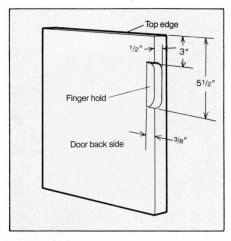

DETAIL H
DOOR DETAIL

in which case rough sanding is all that is necessary.

Sand the drawer parts as directed in the Assembly section, page 28. Rough- and finish-sand the edges of the lumber-core door panels.

STEP 7
ASSEMBLING THE BUFFET
See the Assembly section, pages 25-27, for detailed information on assembling this kind of cabinet. The sequence of steps for this cabinet follows. Refer to the plans (Section A and Front View) as you work.

(1) Assemble the entire grille: top cross members, drawer brace, bottom cross member, and center, right, and left vertical cross members. (2) Attach the bottom and shelf into the dados in the sides with glue and 4d finishing nails driven from beneath the pieces into the sides. (3) Glue the top cross-member support and rear top brace in place, clamp, and secure with 4d finishing nails driven through the sides into these members. (4) Assemble the drawers according to the directions given in the Assembly section, pages 29-31. (5) Rough- and finish-sand the grille assembly as necessary, and then (6) attach it to the cabinet subassembly with 4d finishing nails, after having applied glue to the front edge of the sides and bottom and the front face of the top cross-member support. (7) Attach the front foot with glue and 4d finishing nails, and then clamp. (8) Attach the back with ¾-inch brads. (9) Place the top upside down on a padded surface and invert the cabinet onto it, flush with the back and sides. Attach the cabinet to the top with No. 8 × 1½-inch flathead wood screws driven at a slight angle through the top braces (three at either end and four along the front and back). Finally, (10) install the drawers and doors.

FOUR-DOOR BUFFET

MATERIALS LIST
A Top (1), 1¼″ × 18¾″ × 66″
B Sides (2), ¾″ × 17″ × 32⅜″
C Shelf (1), ¾″ × 16¾″ × 63¼″
D Bottom (1), ¾″ × 16¾″ × 63¼″
E Back (1), ¼″ × 27⅝″ × 63¼″
F Back brace (1), ¾″ × 1⅛″ × 62½″
G Side braces (2), ¾″ × 1⅛″ × 14″
H Front brace (1), ¾″ × 1⅛″ × 62½″
J Upper grille rail (1), ¾″ × 1″ × 60½″
K Center grille stiles (3), ¾″ × 2″ × 29⅝″
L Grille outside stiles (2), ¾″ × 2¾″ × 29⅝″
M Front foot (1), ¾″ × 4½″ × 65½″
N Side feet (2), ¾″ × 4½″ × 18½″
P Middle grille rail (1), ¾″ × 1½″ × 60½″
Q Bottom grille rail (1), ¾″ × 2¾″ × 60½″

DRAWERS*
R Drawer fronts (4), ¾″ × 5¼″ × 13⅞″
S Drawer sides (8), ¾″ × 4¼″ × 16⅝″
T Drawer backs (4), ¾″ × 4¼″ × 10⅝″
U Drawer bottoms (4), ¼″ × 11⅛″ × 16″

*Dimensions of drawer parts will change depending on drawer-roller hardware.

DOORS
V Door stiles (8), ¾″ × 2″ × 20⅝″
W Door rails (8), ¾″ × 2″ × 10⅝″
X Door panels (4), ¾″ × 10⅜″ × 17⅛″

HARDWARE
Offset cabinet hinges (4 pair)
Magnetic catches (4)
18″ drawer-roller systems with brackets (4 sets)
1½″ brass knob with backplate (4 sets)
Drawer pulls of your choice (4)
No. 8 × ¾″ flathead wood screws
No. 8 × 1¼″ flathead wood screws
No. 8 × 1½″ flathead wood screws
4d finishing nails
1″ brads

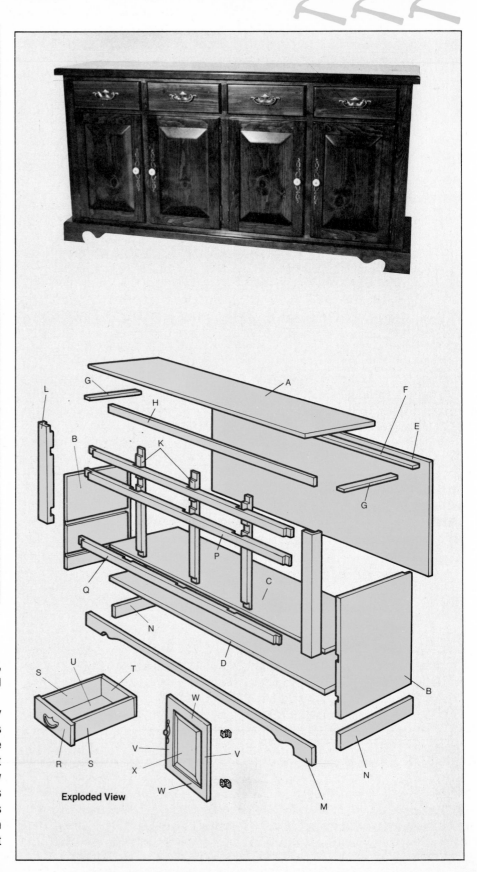

Exploded View

Much like the square-edge buffet, this is a spacious cabinet for dining room or living room.

Attention to machining precisely and to keeping assemblies square as you fasten them is the way to make this and any other cabinet come out right. This project will show off how well you make doors and drawers, as there are four of each. Spend as much time on the finish as you do on the construction, and this cabinet will be a prized piece.

Section A

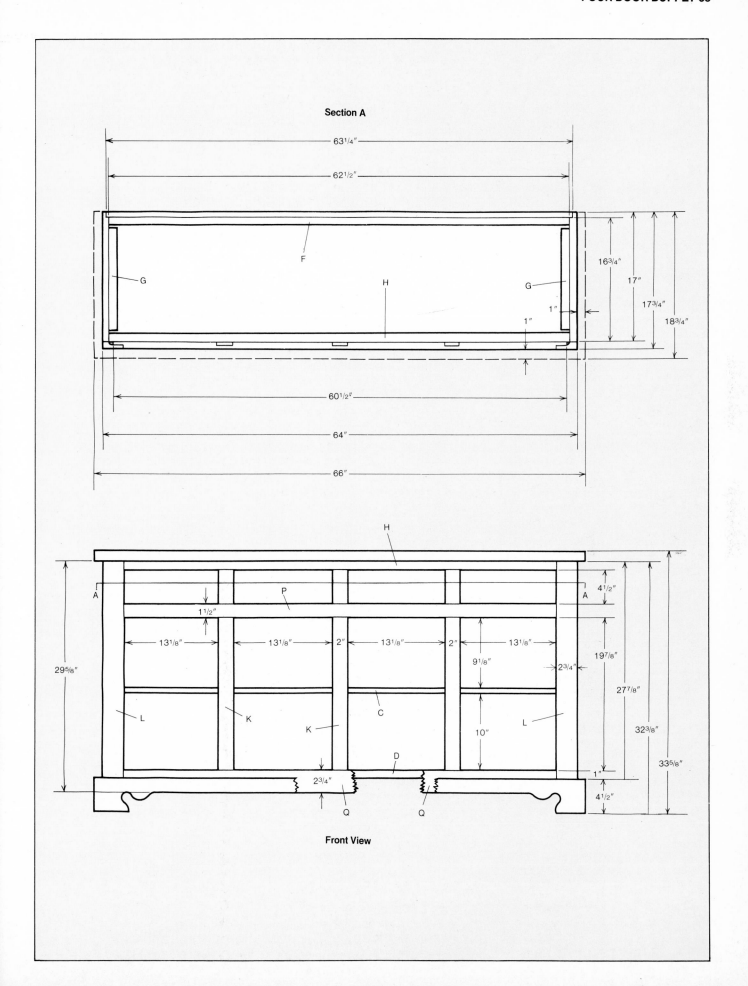

Front View

STEP 1
MACHINING THE TOP
The top must be glued to width. See the Gluing section, pages 11-12, for specific directions. When the glue has set, round three edges with a ½-inch quarter round router bit.

STEP 2
MACHINING THE FEET
The feet wrap around the buffet on three sides. The front foot has a 45° miter cut at each end. The side feet have one 45° miter cut each, which will mate with the mitered ends of the front foot. If you wish to round or shape the leading edge with a router, do it before machining the miter cuts. The design of the foot section is left to you; see specification #31, page 24, for a selection of designs.

STEP 3
MACHINING THE SIDES
Cut the sides from ¾-inch plywood faced with the same wood you are using for the rest of the cabinet surfaces, or from glued-up stock. The sides have standard back and shelf rabbets and dadoes, which are located as shown in Detail A; see specifications #1 and #4, page 17, for details on these joints. Note that the left and right sides are mirror images of each other.

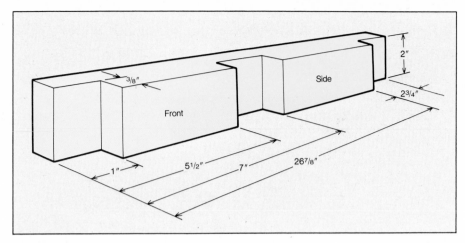

DETAIL B
CENTER GRILLE STILE JOINERY

STEP 4
MACHINING THE BOTTOM, SHELF, AND SUPPORT PIECES
A bottom and a shelf are cut from glued-up ¾-inch stock. Three vertical stile pieces are dadoed on a table or radial arm saw or with a router, as shown in Detail B. The radial arm saw is the best choice.

The right and left outside stiles are grooved (dadoed or routed) on the back face, as shown in Detail C, to accommodate the top and bottom cross-member pieces and the drawer brace; see specification #5, page 17, for details on the standard drawer-brace dado. Note: these two pieces are mirror images of each other.

The top grille rail, middle rail, and bottom rail are all dadoed or routed alike, as shown in Detail D.

STEP 5
MACHINING THE DRAWERS
The cabinet has four drawers with overlap fronts designed for use with roller systems. See specifications on page 21 for details on cutting the parts for these drawers.

If you wish, rout a ⅜-inch-radius rounded edge all the way around the leading edge of the drawer fronts.

STEP 6
MACHINING THE DOORS
The cabinet has four frame-and-panel doors that overlap the opening. See specification #16, page 20, for details on cutting the door parts.

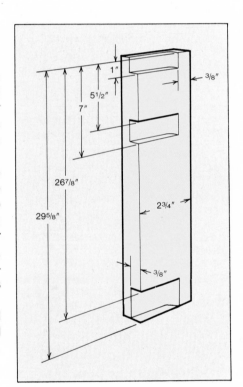

DETAIL C
OUTSIDE GRILLE STILE JOINERY

You can use either a flat or raised panel (the C section of the door). If you wish to add door-rail moldings to flat plywood panel doors, they should be cut to fit after the doors are assembled.

STEP 7
SANDING THE PIECES
Rough- and finish-sand the routed

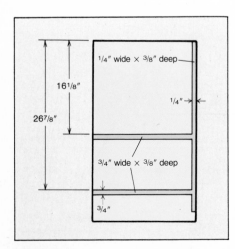

DETAIL A
SIDE LAYOUT

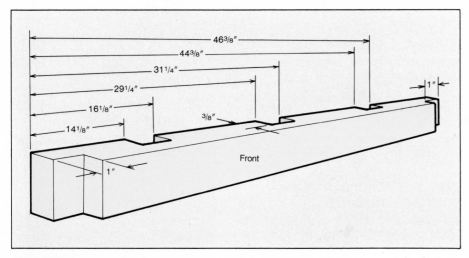

DETAIL D
GRILLE RAIL JOINERY

edges and top edge of the feet and the front face.

If the sides of the buffet are of plywood, they will not need sanding. If they are cut from solid wood, sand the outside face to a rough and then a finish level; sand the inside surface to the rough stage only.

The top surface of the bottom and shelf, as well as the leading edge of the shelf, need only be rough-sanded.

Since the top braces are never seen, do not sand them. Rough-sand the edges of the grille parts only where they will show when the doors are open. Sand the other surfaces as explained on page 32 of the Assembly section.

Sanding of drawer and door parts is explained in detail in the Sanding section, pages 13-15.

STEP 8
ASSEMBLING THE GRILLE FRAMEWORK
Every assembly step for this cabinet is explained in the Assembly section, pages 25-27. The sequence of steps for this cabinet follows.

(1) Lay out the parts of the grille and join with glue. Check for square and level. This face frame of the buffet cannot be out of alignment or warped, or the doors and drawers will not fit properly. Clamp, check for square again, and allow the glue to set up. (2) Assemble the doors and drawers following the specific instructions given on pages 28-32 in the Assembly section for these pieces. Rout a cabinet lip all around the outside edges of the doors and drawer fronts. (3) Following the Assembly directions on pages 25-27, install the bottom and the shelf into the sides. Next install the back and the top braces. Check for square. (4) Install the grille and top front brace on the buffet cabinet. (5) Turn the cabinet upside down (you will need help with this) and attach the feet with glue, nails, and screws, as described on page 27. (6) Place the top upside down on a padded surface, place the cabinet upside down on it with the back edges of the sides flush against the back edge of the top, and attach the cabinet with No. 8 × 1½-inch wood screws driven through the top braces. (7) Turn the cabinet right side up and install the doors and drawers as described on pages 28-32 in the Assembly section.

DRY SINK

Offering both beauty and large storage capacity, this dry sink has a drawer tucked under one side and shelves behind its doors. It can be used as a bar, for display (perhaps with plants seated in the well), or simply for elegant storage.

This project will be a showpiece for the craftsperson who builds it. The precise machining require-

ments, the variety of woodworking techniques, and the subassemblies involved make the project one for an experienced craftsperson.

STEP 1
CUTTING THE PARTS

Cut and label all the parts given in the Materials List except the top and bottom cross members, which will

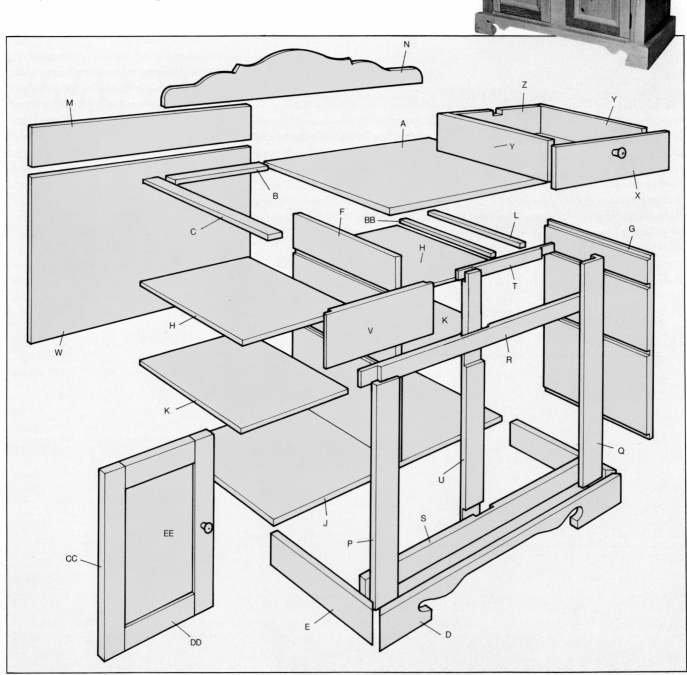

MATERIALS LIST

A Right top (1), 1¼" × 18" × 20⅝"
B Back top (1), 1¼" × 1¾" × 17⅜"
C End top (1), 1¼" × 2½" × 18"
D Front foot (1), ¾" × 4½" × 40"
E Side feet (2), ¾" × 4½" × 17¾"
F Center divider (1), 1¼" × 16" × 27½"
G Sides (2), ¾" × 16¼" × 33"
H Well bottom (1), ¾" × 16" × 19⅝"
J Bottom (1), ¾" × 16" × 37¾"
K Shelves (3), ¾" × 16" × 19⅝"
L Drawer guide (1), ¾" × 1" × 16"
M Upper back (1), ¼" × 5⅜" × 37¾"
N Top scallop (1), ¾" × 5⅝" × 36½"
P Left vertical cross member (1), ¾" ×
　3¼" × 24¼"
Q Right vertical cross member (1), ¾" ×
　3¼" × 29¼"
R Top cross member (1), ¾" × 1½" ×
　34½"
S Bottom cross member (1), ¾" × 1¾" ×
　34½"
T Topmost cross member (1), ¾" × ¾" ×
　17⅞"
U Center vertical cross member (1), ¾" ×
　3¼" × 29¼"
V Well front (1), 1¼" × 5" × 19⅝"
W Lower back (1), ¼" × 23⅛" × 37¾"

DRAWER AND DOORS

X Front (1) 1¼" × 5" × 15⅛"
Y Sides (2), ¾" × 4" × 16"
Z Back (1), ¾" × 4" × 13⅝"
AA Bottom (1), ¼" × 14⅛" × 15¼"
BB Drawer leveler (1), ¾" × 1" × 16"
CC A stiles (4), ¾" × 2" × 21¾"
DD B rails (4), ¾" × 2" × 11⅞"
EE C panels (2), ¾" × 11⅝" × 18¼"
FF Rail molding for panels (optional)

HARDWARE

Self-closing cabinet hinges (2 pair)
Magnetic catches (2)
Backplates (2)
Brass knobs (2)
Drawer pull (1)
Drawer glides (2)
Stock rail molding
No. 8 × 1¼" flathead wood screws
No. 8 × 2" flathead wood screws
4d finishing nails
6d finishing nails
1" brads

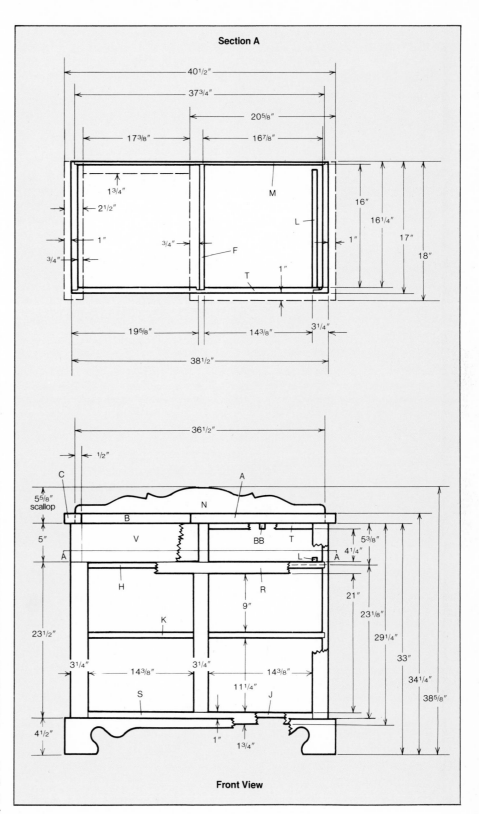

Section A

Front View

be machined as one piece and then cut into two parts. The front foot has 45° miter cuts at both ends, and each of the two side feet has a 45° miter cut at one end.

STEP 2
MACHINING THE FRONT FOOT AND TOP SCALLOP

Select a design from specification #31, page 24, and cut it out of the front foot (the dry sink shown here has a standard Bennington design). Mark the pattern of the top scallop as given in Detail A, cut it out, and rout a ⅜-inch-radius rounded edge along the front top edge of the pattern.

STEP 3
MACHINING THE SIDES, CROSS MEMBERS, AND WELL PARTS

Cut the rabbets, notches, and dadoes specified in Details B-H.

The center vertical cross member requires two cuts, as shown in Details F and G. The top and bottom cross members (Detail D) are easiest to groove simultaneously: from ¾-inch stock, cut a board 3½ inches wide, cut the joinery as specified, and then cut the board into the two cross members (the top one is 1½ inches wide, and the bottom one is 1¾ inches wide).

STEP 4
MAKING THE DRAWER AND DOORS

Build a hand-fitted drawer with overlap front from the plans given in specification #23, page 22. Use the dimensions given in the Materials List for this project.

Build two frame-and-panel construction doors from the plans given in specification #10, page 19. Use the dimensions given here.

STEP 5
SANDING THE PARTS

Because the sink top is made up of three pieces, it should be laid out before sanding to find the most attractive grain pattern. Mark the top and edges to be rough- and finish-sanded; do not sand edges that will be glued together.

Rough- and finish-sand the top edges and outside faces of the feet, one wide face of the center divider, the face with the rounded edge of the top scallop, and one face of the upper back and well bottom.

The inside surface of the left side will be visible above the top shelf groove, and so rough- and finish-sand that area; then rough- and finish-sand the outside faces of the sides. The inside surface of the sides (with the exception already noted) need only be rough-sanded. Rough-

and finish-sand both sides and the top edge of the well front. Rough-sand the edges of the grille parts; the

grille as a whole will be face-sanded after assembly.

For information on sanding the

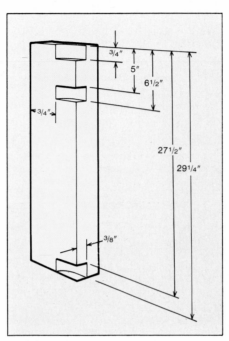

DETAIL B
RIGHT VERTICAL
CROSS-MEMBER JOINERY

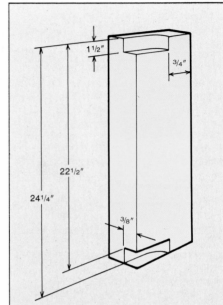

DETAIL C
LEFT VERTICAL
CROSS-MEMBER JOINERY

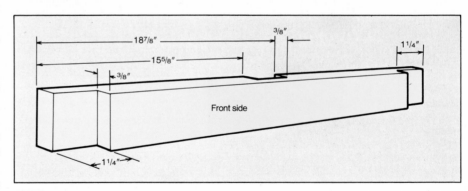

DETAIL D
TOP AND BOTTOM CROSS-MEMBER JOINERY

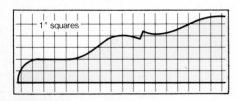

DETAIL A
SCALLOP PATTERN

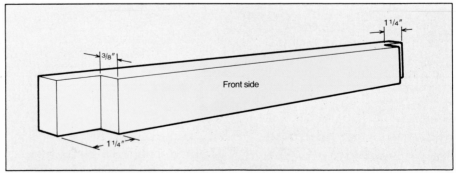

DETAIL E
TOPMOST CROSS-MEMBER JOINERY

door and drawer parts, see the Sanding section, pages 13-15.

STEP 6
ASSEMBLING THE DOORS, DRAWER, AND GRILLE
See the instructions on pages 25-32 of the Assembly section for information on assembling these parts.

STEP 7
ASSEMBLING THE TOP
Spread glue on both ends of the top back and glue all three top pieces together. Clamp the parts together on plywood to hold the pieces flat.

After the glue has set up, rout a 3/8-inch-radius rounded edge around the top edge of the assembled top except along the back. Finish-sand by hand.

STEP 8
ASSEMBLING THE BASIC CABINET
Install the shelf and well bottom in the sides according to the instructions in the Assembly section, page 26-27. Then attach the upper back to the side/bottom/shelf assembly, using glue and 4d finishing nails. (Note that the lower edge of the upper back should cover half the back edge of the well bottom.)

STEP 9
INSTALLING THE GRILLE
Rough- and finish-sand the outside face of the grille. Attach the grille to the cabinet with glue and 4d finishing nails driven through the face. Use pipe or bar clamps to hold the grille in place. The top edges of the bottom and top cross members should line up flush with the top surfaces of the bottom and the well bottom, respectively.

Attach the drawer guide with three No. 8 × 1¼-inch wood screws. Check to make sure that the drawer moves in and out easily before attaching the guide.

STEP 10
INSTALLING THE WELL FRONT AND CENTER DIVIDER
Hand-sand all edges of the well front and the part of the grille with which it

will come into contact. After gluing, use 4d finishing nails to nail through the face of the well front into the edge of the side and the front of the center divider.

STEP 11
INSTALLING THE FEET
Sand the edges of the grille flush with the sides; then attach the wraparound feet, following the instructions on page 27 of the Assembly section.

STEP 12
FINAL ASSEMBLY
Attach the drawer leveler to the underside of the top with glue and

No. 8 × 1¼-inch wood screws. Screw the top scallop to the back edge of the top assembly with No. 8 × 2-inch wood screws. Use 6d finishing nails to nail through the face of the top to attach it to the cabinet.

Insert the drawer glides according to the Assembly section, pages 30-31. Check the fit and movement of the drawers. Install the doors following the instructions given on pages 27-29 of the Assembly section. Do this before staining and finishing so that you can be sure the fit is correct. Take the doors off for finishing. Stain and finish the cabinet as you please, and then attach the back with glue and 1-inch brads.

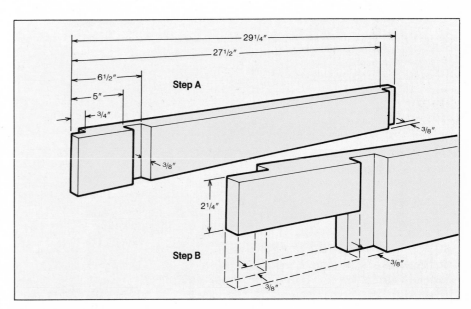

DETAILS F AND G
CENTER VERTICAL CROSS-MEMBER JOINERY

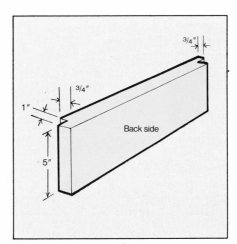

DETAIL H
WELL-FRONT JOINERY

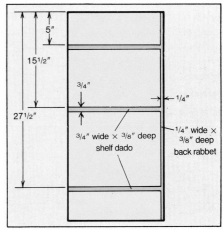

DETAIL J
SIDE LAYOUT

RECORD CABINET

MATERIALS LIST
A Top (1), 3/4″ × 16″ × 18″
B Sides (2), 3/4″ × 15¼″ × 24¾″
C Bottom (1), 3/4″ × 14¼″ × 15¾″
D Front foot (1), 3/4″ × 3½″ × 18″
E Side feet (2), 3/4″ × 3½″ × 16″
F Top cross member (1), 3/4″ × 1″ × 15¾″
G Bottom cross member (1), 3/4″ × 2″ × 15¾″
H Top back brace (1), 3/4″ × 1″ × 15″
J Top side braces (2), 3/4″ × 1″ × 12″
K Back (1), ¼″ × 15¾″ × 22″
L Door (1), 3/4″ × 15¾″ × 19¾″

HARDWARE
Hinges (1 pair)
Magnetic catch (1)
Drawer pulls (3)
A-shaped record dividers (3)
No. 8 × 3/4″ flathead wood screws
No. 8 × 1¼″ flathead wood screws
No. 8 × 1½″ flathead wood screws
4d finishing nails
1″ brads

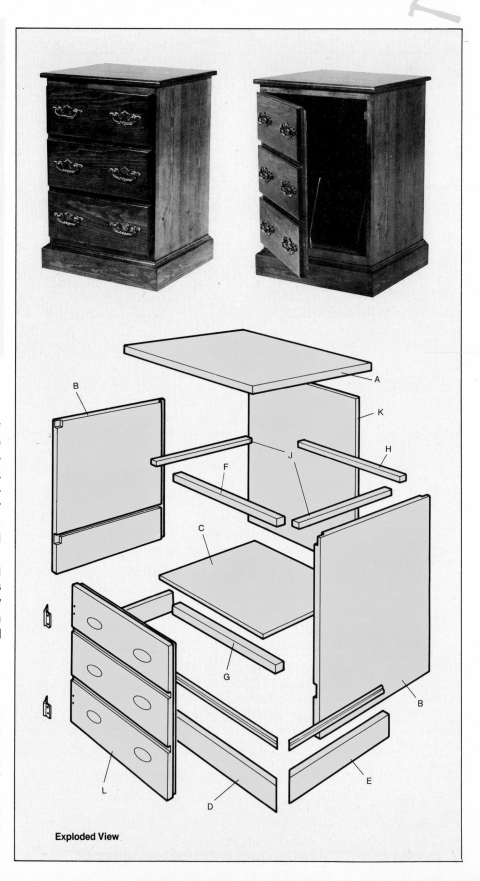

Exploded View

This convenient record cabinet may surprise your friends. The three drawers are actually decorative facings on the door, which conceal a spacious record-storage area. A-shaped record dividers make for tidy storage of several types of records—they can be omitted if your record collection completely fills the case.

While many typical woodworking techniques are used to build this cabinet, none of them is particularly difficult. The beginning craftsperson should find this a satisfying and instructive project.

STEP 1
MACHINING THE TOP
The entire cabinet is constructed from 3/4-inch stock except where noted. If pieces must be glued to create the size required for the top, see the Gluing section, pages 11-12, for directions.

Cut the top to size and rout with a 3/8-inch quarter round radius bit around one long and two short edges.

STEP 2
MACHINING THE SIDES

The two sides are mirror images of each other. Use a table saw with dado cutter or, preferably, the radial arm saw to produce the standard back, shelf, and drawer brace grooves indicated in Detail A. See specifications, page 17, for details on cutting these grooves.

STEP 3
MACHINING THE BOTTOM

The bottom has holes drilled into it for standard A-shaped record dividers, as shown in Detail B.

STEP 4
MACHINING THE FEET

The foot of the cabinet will wrap around the unit. Cut 45° miters at each end of the front foot and at one end of each side foot. If you wish, round the top edge of the feet with a 3/8-inch quarter round radius router bit—do this before cutting the miters. If you wish to have a cutout design on the feet, see specification #31, page 24, for a selection of designs.

STEP 5
MACHINING THE DOOR

The door, which looks as if it were three drawers, is easy to make from one piece of 3/4-inch lumber-core plywood faced with the kind of wood you are using for the rest of the project (or faced with a contrasting wood, if you wish). Veneer-core plywood or a solid wood door, braced to prevent warpage, can be substituted for lumber-core plywood.

Cut the piece to size. Machine a 3/8 × 3/8-inch-deep standard cabinet lip around the back of the piece to accommodate 3/8-inch offset hinges.

STEP 6
MACHINING THE DRAWER FRONTS

Cut the decorative fake drawer fronts by cutting shallow dadoes, just 1/4-inch deep, in the front surface of the door, as shown in Detail C. Use a table saw with a dado cutter.

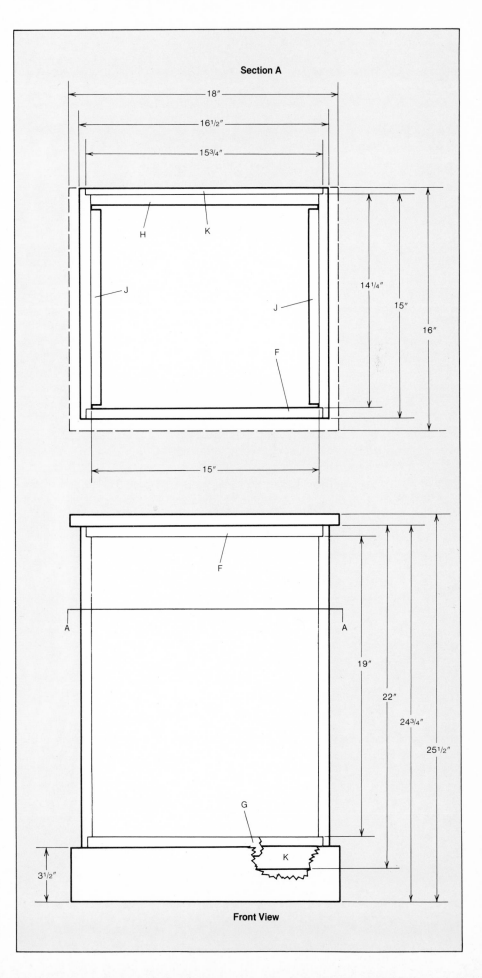

Section A

Front View

STEP 7
SANDING THE PIECES
Rough- and finish-sand the routed edges and upper face of the top, as well as the exposed face of each side piece. The inside surfaces of the sides, the upper face of the bottom, the feet, and the top and bottom cross members need only be rough-sanded.

Rough- and finish-sand the fake drawer fronts on the front surface and all edges. Plywood parts usually need not be sanded, and the top braces can be left unsanded.

STEP 8
INSTALLING THE BOTTOM
Check the fit of the bottom into the grooves on the sides. Glue and nail the bottom into place with 4d finishing nails and use pipe or bar clamps to hold it in place and square until the glue is set.

STEP 9
INSTALLING THE CROSS MEMBERS AND BACK
Attach the cross members to the

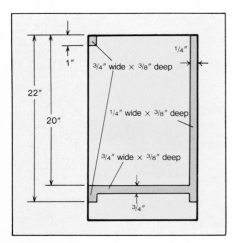

DETAIL A
SIDE LAYOUT

sides as shown in the Exploded View with glue and 4d finishing nails driven through the sides. Be sure that the nails are spaced sufficiently so as to avoid splitting the cross member; angle them slightly to bite into several layers of grain.

Glue and use 1-inch brads driven through the back into the sides to attach the back. Check the cabinet for square and clamp until dry.

STEP 10
INSTALLING THE TOP BRACES
Drill pilot holes in the top braces and attach to the cabinet with No. 8 × 1½-inch flathead wood screws. Two braces should be attached to the sides and one to the back, as shown in the plans.

STEP 11
INSTALLING THE FEET
To install the feet, follow the specific directions on page 27 of the Assembly section.

STEP 12
INSTALLING THE TOP
Place the top on a padded work surface with the underside of the finished top face up. Place the assembled cabinet on the top. Align the back of the base unit with the back edge of the top.

Drive 3d finishing nails through the top braces just into the top. Check the unit for square and adjust as necessary. See the Assembly section, pages 26-27, for details on cabinet squaring. When the unit is square, attach the top with No. 8 × 1½-inch flathead wood screws.

STEP 13
INSTALLING THE DOOR
Position the two hinges 2¼ inches from the top and bottom of the door.

Check the door for fit and install the hinges and a magnetic catch.

When the door is properly hinged, and you are certain that everything is working correctly, remove the door, mark the location of the hinges, and finish the cabinet surface.

Reinstall the door when the finishing process is complete.

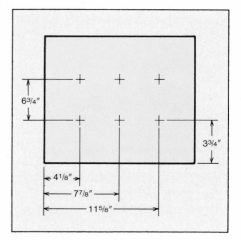

DETAIL B
BOTTOM LAYOUT

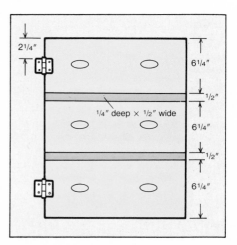

DETAIL C
DOOR LAYOUT

LARGE DRESSER

MATERIALS LIST

A Top (1), $1\frac{1}{2}$" × 20" × 68"
B Front foot (1), $1\frac{1}{2}$" × $4\frac{1}{2}$" × 68"
C Side feet (2), $1\frac{1}{2}$" × $4\frac{1}{2}$" × 20"
D Sides (2), $\frac{3}{4}$" × $17\frac{3}{4}$" × 31"
E Center vertical cross member (1), $\frac{3}{4}$" × $2\frac{1}{2}$" × $27\frac{1}{4}$"
F Outside top cross member (1), $\frac{3}{4}$" × $1\frac{1}{4}$" × 62"
G Outside bottom cross member (1), $\frac{3}{4}$" × $1\frac{3}{4}$" × 62"
H Upper drawer brace (1), $\frac{3}{4}$" × $1\frac{3}{4}$" × 62"
J Lower drawer brace (1), $\frac{3}{4}$" × $1\frac{3}{4}$" × $32\frac{1}{4}$"
K Vertical cross member (inner frame) (1), $\frac{3}{4}$" × $2\frac{5}{8}$" × $18\frac{1}{2}$"
L Vertical cross member (inner frame) (1), $\frac{3}{4}$" × $1\frac{1}{8}$" × $18\frac{1}{2}$"
M Horizontal cross members (inner frame) (2), $\frac{3}{4}$" × 2" × $30\frac{1}{4}$"
N Middle horizontal cross member (inner frame) (1), $\frac{3}{4}$" × $1\frac{3}{4}$" × $30\frac{1}{4}$"
P Left vertical cross member (1), $\frac{3}{4}$" × $2\frac{1}{2}$" × 31"
Q Right vertical cross member (1), $\frac{3}{4}$" × $2\frac{1}{2}$" × 31"
R Top braces (2), $\frac{3}{4}$" × $1\frac{1}{8}$" × $14\frac{1}{2}$"
S Back braces (top and bottom) (2), $\frac{3}{4}$" × $1\frac{1}{8}$" × $63\frac{1}{2}$"
T Top cross-member support (1), $\frac{3}{4}$" × $1\frac{1}{8}$" × $63\frac{1}{2}$"
U Spacer (1), $1\frac{3}{4}$" × $1\frac{1}{4}$" × $16\frac{3}{4}$"
V Spacer (1), $1\frac{3}{4}$" × $1\frac{1}{4}$" × $30\frac{1}{4}$"
W Back (1), $\frac{1}{4}$" × $27\frac{1}{4}$" × $64\frac{1}{4}$"
X Center wall (1), $\frac{3}{4}$" × $17\frac{1}{2}$" × $18\frac{1}{2}$"

UPPER DRAWERS
Y Fronts (2), $1\frac{1}{4}$" × $6\frac{3}{4}$" × $29\frac{1}{2}$"
Z Sides (4), $\frac{3}{4}$" × $5\frac{3}{4}$" × $17\frac{3}{4}$"
AA Backs (2), $\frac{3}{4}$" × $5\frac{3}{4}$" × $26\frac{1}{4}$"

MIDDLE DRAWER
BB Front (1), $1\frac{1}{4}$" × $7\frac{3}{4}$" × $29\frac{1}{2}$"
CC Sides (2), $\frac{3}{4}$" × $6\frac{3}{4}$" × $17\frac{3}{4}$"
DD Back (1), $\frac{3}{4}$" × $6\frac{3}{4}$" × $26\frac{1}{4}$"

LOWER DRAWER
EE Front (1), $1\frac{1}{4}$" × $8\frac{1}{2}$" × $29\frac{1}{2}$"
FF Sides (2), $\frac{3}{4}$" × $7\frac{1}{2}$" × $17\frac{3}{4}$"
GG Back (1), $\frac{3}{4}$" × $7\frac{1}{2}$" × $26\frac{1}{4}$"
HH Bottoms (4), $\frac{1}{4}$" × 17" × $26\frac{3}{4}$"

TRAY-FRONT DRAWERS
JJ Fronts (2), $1\frac{1}{4}$" × $7\frac{1}{8}$" × $27\frac{1}{4}$"
KK Sides (4), $\frac{3}{4}$" × $6\frac{1}{8}$" × $15\frac{3}{4}$"
LL Backs (2), $\frac{3}{4}$" × $6\frac{1}{8}$" × 24"
MM Bottoms (2), $\frac{1}{4}$" × 15" × $24\frac{1}{2}$"

OVERLAP DOORS
NN A stiles (4), $\frac{3}{4}$" × 2" × $17\frac{1}{4}$"
PP B rails (4), $\frac{3}{4}$" × 2" × $11\frac{1}{2}$"
QQ C panels (2), $\frac{3}{4}$" × $11\frac{1}{4}$" × $13\frac{3}{4}$"
Rail molding (cut to fit after doors are assembled; optional), approximately 10'

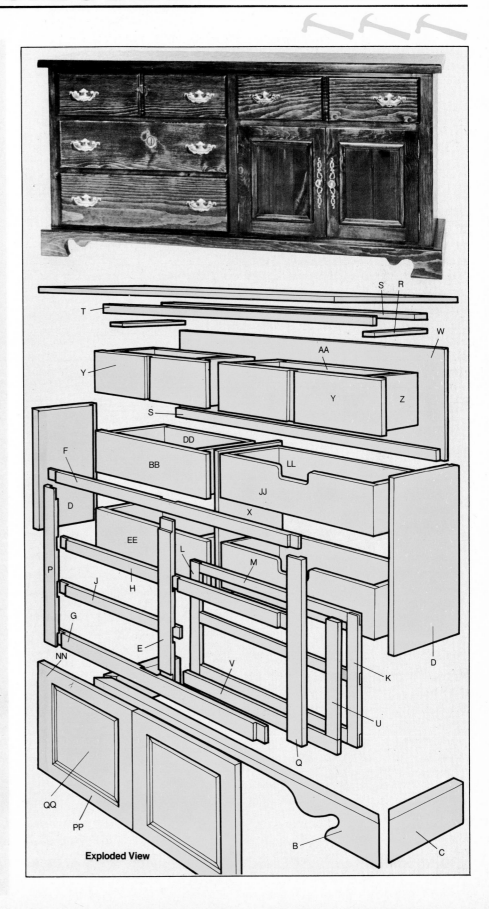

Exploded View

HARDWARE
Hinges (2 pair)
Magnetic catches (2)
16″ drawer roller systems (2 pair)
18″ drawer roller systems (4 pair)
Brackets (12)
Drawer pulls (4)
Knobs (4)
Brass knob with 8″ backplate (1 pair)
No. 8 × 1¼″ flathead wood screws
No. 8 × 1½″ flathead wood screws
4d finishing nails
1″ brads

With its six drawers, this dresser is very spacious as well as handsome. It will easily accommodate stacks of bulky items such as sweaters. The doors covering two of the drawers give the dresser an elegant appearance in addition to keeping dust out.

STEP 1
MACHINING THE TOP
Glue up stock to make a piece wide enough for the top; see the Gluing section, pages 11-12, for details. When the top has been glued and cut to size, round the front and side edges with a ½-inch-radius quarter round router bit.

STEP 2
MACHINING THE FEET
The front foot requires 45° miters on each end to join the side feet; each side foot has a 45° miter at one end to mate with the front. If you want the leading edge of the feet rounded, do it with a ⅜-inch-radius quarter round router bit before cutting the miters. Any foot-cutout design is left to you; see specification #31, page 24, for design suggestions.

STEP 3
MACHINING THE SIDES
The sides may be cut from ¾-inch plywood or from ¾-inch stock glued up to size. Cut standard back grooves, ¼ inch wide × ⅜ inch deep, in both pieces, as shown in specification #1, page 17.

STEP 4
MACHINING THE GRILLE COMPONENTS
The grille components—the parts to which doors are attached and

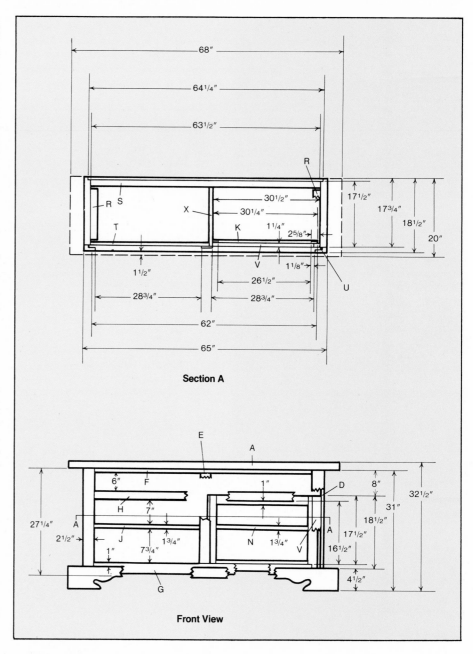

Section A

Front View

against which drawers rest when closed—are all of ¾-inch stock. All grille components must be dadoed and rabbeted to mate with other components; see Details A-E. This machining may be done on a radial arm (preferred) or table saw or with a router.

Because this cabinet has drawers located behind doors, an inner grille frame is needed to accommodate them. This frame is of ¾-inch stock and joined exactly like the components of the exterior grille; see Details F and G.

The left and right vertical cross members are dadoed alike, except

where shown in Detail A. With that exception, these pieces are mirror images. For details of the required drawer-brace groove, see specification #5, page 17.

STEP 5
MACHINING THE DRAWERS
For details on cutting the parts for the six overlap-front drawers to be equipped with the roller systems, see page 21. Use the dimensions given in the Materials List for this project. The dimensions of the drawer parts may change depending on the hardware used to mount the drawers.

Also see specification #24, page

22, for details on making the apothecary cuts and standard drawer-tray cutouts. The apothecary cuts are for decoration for the 6¾-inch-wide drawer fronts only.

Cut all the 1¼-inch-stock drawer fronts at the same time.

STEP 6
MACHINING THE DOORS
The dresser has two frame-and-panel doors that overlap the cabinet opening when closed. For details on machining the parts for these doors, see specification #10, page 19. Use the dimensions here.

STEP 7
SANDING THE PARTS
Rough- and finish-sand the top surface and routed edges of the top, and the outside faces and leading edges of the foot unit. If the sides are made of plywood, they need not be sanded. If the sides are of solid wood, rough- and finish-sand the outside faces.

Rough-sand the grille parts on the edges and faces that will show when the doors are open—these are the bottom, center vertical, and right vertical cross members. Do not sand the bottom edge of the drawer brace which is over the door opening, since this edge is never seen. The rest of the outer and inner grille or frame members do not require any sanding. Rough-sand the two spacer pieces on the 1¼-inch edge (which will be seen when the doors are opened). You need not sand the top braces, bottom back brace, top cross-member support, plywood back, or center wall. For detailed instructions on sanding the drawer and door parts, see Sanding section, pages 13-15.

STEP 8
ASSEMBLING THE INNER AND OUTER GRILLES
First check to see that all grille parts join perfectly square; then fasten the grilles with glue. Clamp the sections, recheck for square, let glue set.

STEP 9
ASSEMBLING THE DOORS AND DRAWERS
See Doors and Drawers (pages 27-

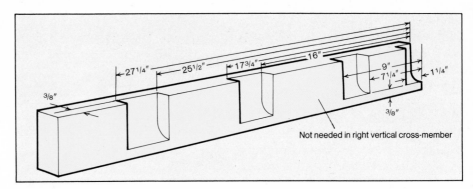

DETAIL A
LEFT AND RIGHT VERTICAL CROSS-MEMBER JOINERY

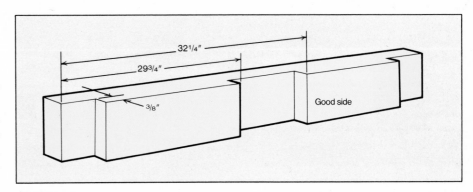

DETAIL B
UPPER DRAWER-BRACE JOINERY

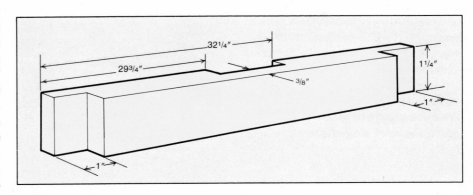

DETAIL C
OUTSIDE TOP CROSS-MEMBER JOINERY

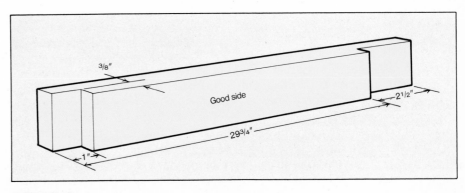

DETAIL D
LOWER DRAWER-BRACE JOINERY

31), in the Assembly section for detailed instructions on assembling these pieces.

STEP 10
ASSEMBLING THE CABINET

Attach the grille to the sides with glue. Clamp and check for square. Nail the top cross member into position with 4d finishing nails driven at a slight angle and offset a little so the nails bite into different areas of the end grain of the top cross member.

Attach the back with glue, and clamp when you have checked for square. Recheck when you have pulled the clamps tight. Adjust the clamps if necessary. Attach the top brace with No. 8 × 1¼-inch wood screws through the back.

STEP 11
ASSEMBLING THE INNER COMPONENTS

Use glue, 4d finishing nails and/or No. 8 × 1¼-inch wood screws to secure the spacers, the inner grille, and the center wall in this order. Screw spacers to inside of outer grille; set the center wall in place and secure it in the cabinet with nails; and finally, attach the inner grille to the spacers and center wall with wood screws.

The grille, inner wall, and one side will support the weight of the tray-style drawers, and so these components must be very secure.

STEP 12
ATTACHING THE FOOT ASSEMBLY

Attach the two side feet to the cabinet with No. 8 × 1½-inch wood screws after C-clamping the front foot section into place. Position the side feet carefully before screwing them into place. Countersink the screws and cover with screw plugs, or fill the holes with wood putty.

Remove the C clamps and spread glue on the mitered ends of the front and side feet. Use a bar clamp to draw the ends together. Use 4d finishing nails in the corners, countersunk and filled, to assure permanent positioning while the glue dries.

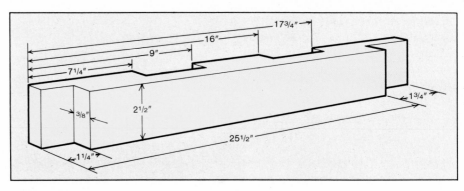

DETAIL E
CENTER VERTICAL CROSS-MEMBER JOINERY

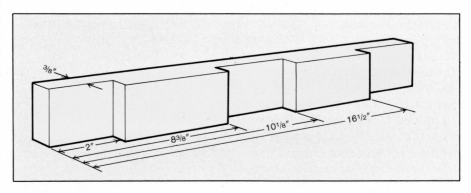

DETAIL F
INNER FRAME VERTICAL CROSS-MEMBER JOINERY

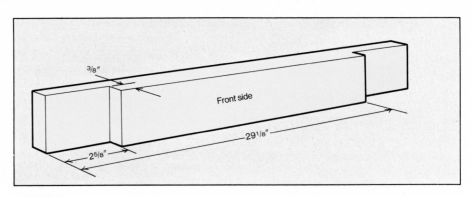

DETAIL G
INNER FRAME HORIZONTAL CROSS-MEMBER JOINERY

STEP 13
ATTACHING THE TOP

Place the top upside down on a padded surface. Invert the cabinet unit onto the top (this may require a second pair of hands). Attach the top with No. 8 × 1½-inch wood screws driven through the top braces and top cross member support. Be sure to check for square. If the unit is slightly out of square, you can pull it square with the top. Use 4d nails through the brace and cross member support to hold the top and cabinet in position while you secure the top with the screws.

STEP 14
COMPLETING THE UNIT

Install the drawers and doors. Attach the doors with appropriate hinges and magnetic catches; see page 29 in the Assembly section.

Use drawer roller systems to mount the drawers in position. Choose appropriate drawer pulls before finishing.

WALL UNIT

MATERIALS LIST

A Upper top (1), $3/4'' \times 15 3/4'' \times 31 1/2''$
B Left/middle sides (2), $3/4'' \times 15 3/4'' \times 57 5/8''$
C Wall #1 (1), $3/4'' \times 15 3/4'' \times 27 1/2''$
D Wall #2 (1), $3/4'' \times 15 3/4'' \times 13 1/2''$
E Wall #3 (1), $3/4'' \times 15 3/4'' \times 11 1/2''$
F Shelf #1 (1), $3/4'' \times 15 3/4'' \times 15 3/4''$
G Shelf #2 (1), $3/4'' \times 15 3/4'' \times 30 1/2''$
H Shelf #3 (1), $3/4'' \times 15 3/4'' \times 30 1/2''$
J Left bottom (1), $3/4'' \times 15'' \times 30 1/2''$
K Top cross member (1), $1/2'' \times 3/4'' \times 30 3/4''$
L Drawer brace (1), $3/4'' \times 3/4'' \times 15 3/4''$
M Bottom cross member (1), $3/4'' \times 1 1/2'' \times 81 1/4''$

TV-DESK SECTION

N Lower top (1), $3/4'' \times 15 3/4'' \times 50 3/4''$
P Right side (1), $3/4'' \times 15 3/4'' \times 41 1/8''$
Q Wall #4 (1), $3/4'' \times 15 3/4'' \times 40 3/4''$
R Amplifier shelf (1), $3/4'' \times 15'' \times 24 1/2''$
S Middle bottom (1), $3/4'' \times 15'' \times 24 1/2''$
T TV shelf (1), $3/4'' \times 15'' \times 25 1/2''$
U Right bottom (1), $3/4'' \times 15'' \times 25 1/2''$
V Lower top cross member (1), $3/4'' \times 1'' \times 50 1/4''$
W Desk cross member (1), $3/4'' \times 1 1/4'' \times 24 1/2''$
X TV cross member (1), $3/4'' \times 1 1/4'' \times 25 1/2''$
Y Desk-top support (horizontal) (1), $3/4'' \times 2 1/2'' \times 23 3/8''$
Z Desk-top support (vertical) (1), $3/4'' \times 3'' \times 23 3/8''$
AA Desk-top support (diagonal) (1), $3/4'' \times 2 1/4'' \times 33''$
BB Adjustable shelves (2), $3/4'' \times 12 1/2'' \times 23 3/8''$
CC Desk top (1), $3/4'' \times 23 3/4'' \times 24 1/2''$
DD Doors (2), $3/4'' \times 12 3/8'' \times 13 7/8''$

DRAWER PARTS*

EE Front (1), $3/4'' \times 3 7/8'' \times 15 1/8''$
FF Sides (2), $3/4'' \times 3 7/8'' \times 14 1/2''$
GG Back (1), $3/4'' \times 3 7/8'' \times 12 5/8''$
HH Front (1), $3/4'' \times 6 1/8'' \times 15 1/8''$
JJ Sides (2), $3/4'' \times 6 1/8'' \times 14 1/2''$
KK Back (1), $3/4'' \times 6 1/8'' \times 12 5/8''$
LL Bottoms (2), $1/4'' \times 13 1/8'' \times 13 1/2''$

*Dimensions of drawer parts will change depending on the hardware used to mount the drawers.

HARDWARE

Roller systems (2 sets)
Piano hinges (3), $1 1/2'' \times 24''$
Brass knobs (2)
Flush pull (1)
Adjustable shelf strips (2 sets), 24"
Brass butt hinges (3), 2"
Flexible wood trim, 18' (Note: If your project will be made entirely of plywood, then 60' will be needed.)

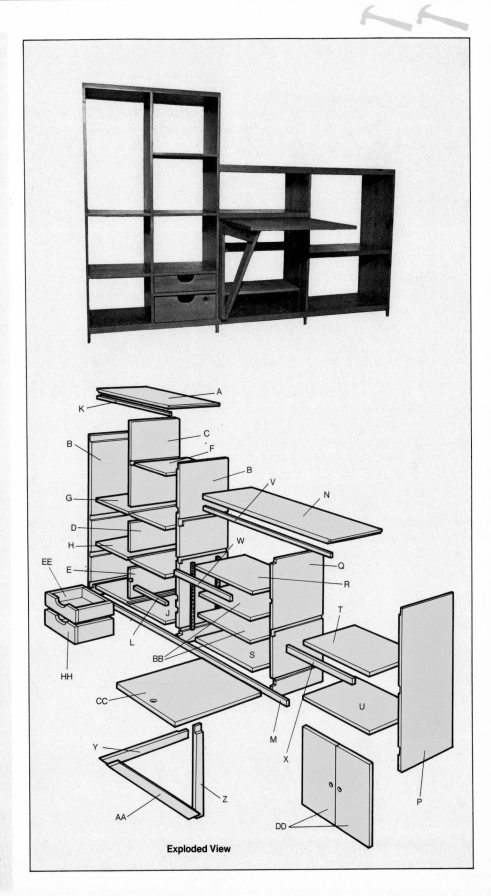

Exploded View

A wall unit with shelves, compartments, drawers, a fold-away desk top, and a place for the television would be a functional, attractive addition to anyone's bedroom. The plans given here can be adjusted to suit the size of the space available.

You will use basic cabinetmaking skills to put together the wall unit. The cuts are simple, so don't let the size of the project daunt you. Once you have completed this unit, you'll wonder how you got along without it. In fact, why not build another for the living room or family room?

STEP 1
GLUING BOARDS TO WIDTH
A number of parts for this project are wider than the lumber generally available. If this is the case for you, gluing is necessary to obtain the width desired. Refer to the Gluing section, pages 11-12, for specific directions.

STEP 2
MACHINING THE PARTS FOR THE RECORD STORAGE SECTION
Cut the upper top and dado or rout ⅜-inch wide × ⅜-inch deep rabbets in each end on the bottom face, as shown in Detail A. The left and middle sides are the same size, but they are machined quite differently, as shown in Details B and C. See specifications on page 17 for details on cutting these grooves. Wall No. 1 is notched with a saber saw and machined as shown in Detail D. Wall No. 2 is plain, and center wall No. 3 is notched and grooved as shown in Detail E. Shelf No. 1 is plain, and shelves No. 2 and No. 3 have ¾- × ¼-inch-deep grooves on both face sur-

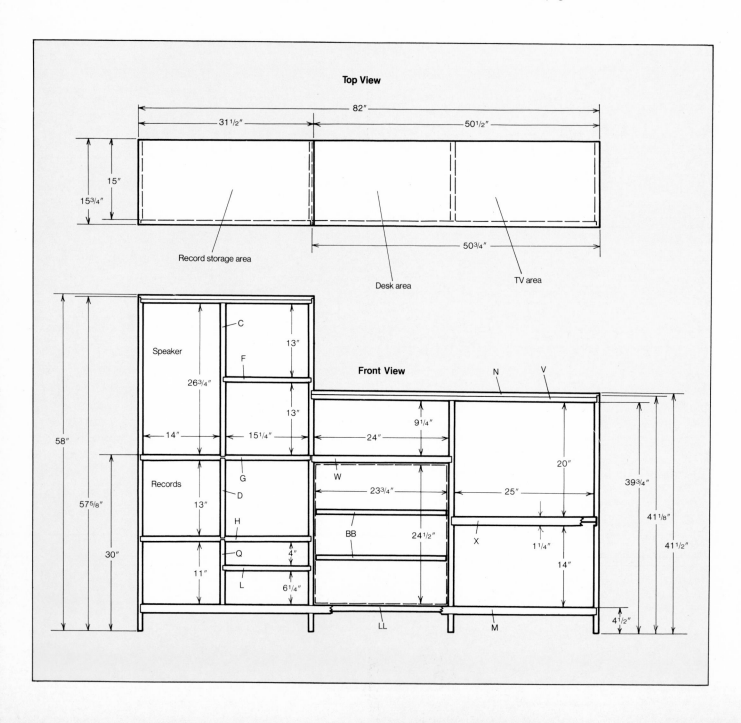

faces 14⅜ inches from the left end, as shown in Detail F. The left bottom is grooved, as shown in Detail G.

STEP 3
MACHINING PARTS FOR THE TV AND DESK SECTION
The lower top for the TV and desk sections extends the length of both. It has a ⅜- × ⅜-inch rabbet routed into the underside, as shown in Detail H. The right side is dadoed on the inside face, as shown in Detail J, and the wall No. 4 is machined on both faces, as shown in Detail K. The notches on both pieces are best cut with a saber saw. After cutting the desk top, drill a 1-inch-diameter hole through it at the location shown in Detail L.

Cut the three parts of the desk-support subassembly according to the specifications given in Details M, N, and P.

STEP 4
MACHINING THE DRAWER PARTS
The wall unit has two drawers with flush fronts to be mounted on rollers. See specification #22, page 21, for details on cutting these drawer parts; see specification #26, page 22, for instructions on making the tray cutout in the drawer fronts.

STEP 5
SANDING
Every face surface of every piece must be both rough- and finish-sanded. Only the undersides of the bottom pieces need not be sanded at

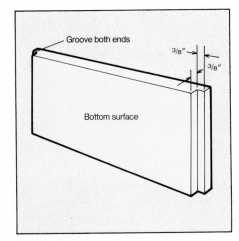

DETAIL A
UPPER TOP JOINERY

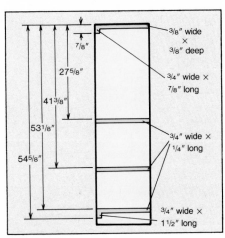

DETAIL B
LEFT SIDE JOINERY

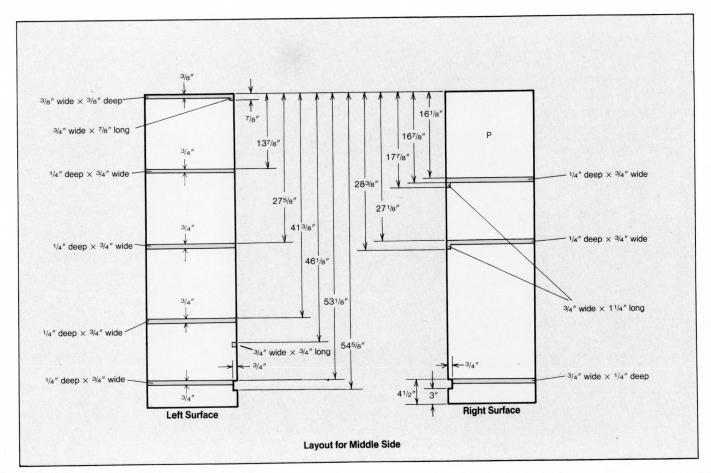

Layout for Middle Side

DETAIL C
MIDDLE SIDE JOINERY

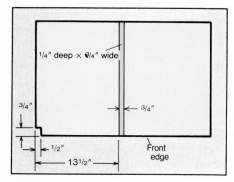

DETAIL D
WALL #1 JOINERY

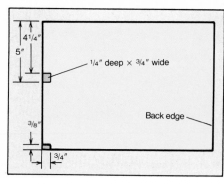

DETAIL E
WALL #3 JOINERY

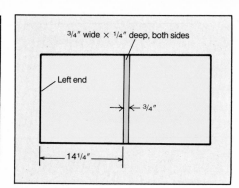

DETAIL F
SHELF #2 AND #3 JOINERY

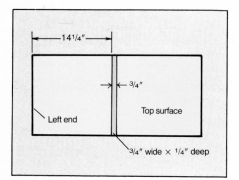

DETAIL G
LEFT BOTTOM JOINERY

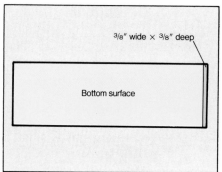

DETAIL H
LOWER TOP JOINERY

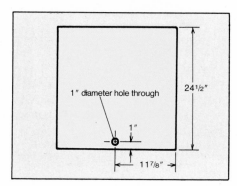

DETAIL L
DESK TOP DETAIL

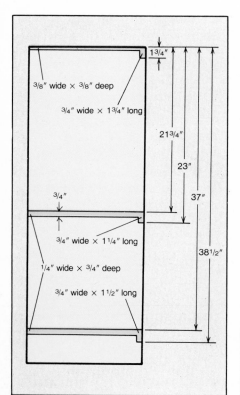

DETAIL J
RIGHT SIDE JOINERY

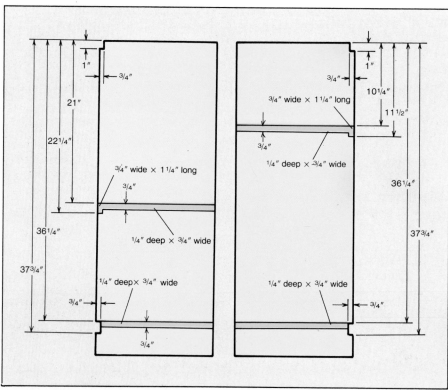

DETAIL K
WALL #4 JOINERY

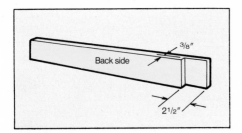

DETAIL M
VERTICAL DESK TOP
SUPPORT JOINERY

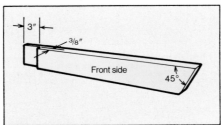

DETAIL N
HORIZONTAL DESK
TOP SUPPORT JOINERY

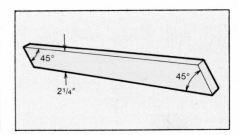

DETAIL P
DIAGONAL DESK TOP
SUPPORT JOINERY

all because they will never be seen. If you have used plywood instead of solid wood, there shouldn't be any need for sanding, but check the pieces for scratches and use 120-grit sandpaper to sand them out. All front edges will be sanded after assembly. In addition, rough- and finish-sand all surfaces of the three desk-top-support pieces.

STEP 6
ASSEMBLY

Before beginning construction of this project, review the procedures on pages 25-32 of the Assembly section. These provide the necessary information for assembling this cabinet's major sections, such as the case, drawers, and drawer roller system. The following lists the order in which the construction should take place, with additional tips on particular procedures required specifically for this project.

(1) Assemble the record-storage section of the cabinet. (2) Assemble the TV area. (3) Attach the record-storage section to the TV cabinet, thereby creating the central desk area. It is imperative that these cabinet sections are assembled square. (4) Assemble the drawers. (5) Assemble the desk-top support. (6) Finish-sand the front or leading edges of the cabinet, thus readying it for the drawers, desk top, and doors. (7) Install the adjustable shelf strips,

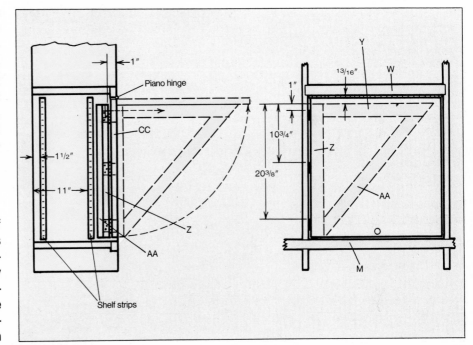

DETAIL Q
DESK TOP SUPPORT DETAIL

using the screws that accompany them in the package. Position these strips where shown in Detail Q. (8) Install the desk-top support assembly, using three 2-inch butt hinges and the appropriate flathead screws, as shown in Detail Q.. (9) Install the desk top using a 1½- × 24-inch piano hinge and the appropriate flathead wood screws that usually accompany it. (10) Install the two drawers, using roller systems. (11) Install the two doors which cover the

TV area. Use the same type of piano hinge as used for the desk top, cut to fit the doors. The doors may need to be trimmed to fit. Do the trimming with a table saw. (12) Attach flexible wood trim to the edges of all plywood components to hide the laminated layers. Follow the instructions which accompany each package of wood trim. (13) Install the two brass knobs on the doors and the flush pull on the desk top, positioning them to suit your own taste.

ARMOIRE

MATERIALS LIST

BOTTOM SECTION

A Top (1), 1 1/4" × 21 3/4" × 42 1/4"
B Front foot (1), 1 1/4" × 4 1/2" × 42 1/4"
C Side feet (2), 1 1/4" × 4 1/2" × 21 3/4"
D Sides (2), 3/4" × 19 3/4" × 22 3/4"
E Top back brace (1), 3/4" × 1 1/8" × 38 1/4"
F Top cross-member support (1), 3/4" × 1 1/8" × 38 1/4"
G Bottom bracket brace (1), 3/4" × 1 1/8" × 38 1/4"
H Top braces (1), 3/4" × 1 1/8" × 17 1/4"
J Top cross member (1), 3/4" × 1 1/4" × 36 3/4"
K Drawer brace (1), 3/4" × 2" × 36 3/4"
L Bottom cross member (1), 3/4" × 2" × 36 3/4"
M Side vertical cross members (2), 3/4" × 2 1/2" × 22 3/4"
N Back (1), 1/4" × 19 1/4" × 39"

BOTTOM SECTION DRAWERS*

P Fronts (2), 1 1/4" × 7 3/4" × 35 1/2"
Q Sides (4), 3/4" × 6 3/4" × 19 1/4"
R Backs (2), 3/4" × 6 3/4" × 32 1/4"
S Bottoms (2), 1/4" × 18 1/2" × 32 3/4"

*Dimensions of drawer parts will change depending on the type of hardware used to mount the drawers.

TOP SECTION

T Top (1), 1 1/4" × 42 1/4" × 21 3/4"
U Sides (2), 3/4" × 18 5/8" × 37 3/4"
V Top back brace (1), 3/4" × 1 1/8" × 36"
W Bottom back brace (1), 3/4" × 1 1/8" × 36"
X Top side braces (2), 3/4" × 1 1/8" × 13 3/4"
Y Bottom side braces (2), 3/4" × 1 1/8" × 17 1/4"
Z Vertical spacers (2), 1 1/4" × 1 3/4" × 26 1/4"
AA Top spacer (1), 1 1/4" × 1 1/2" × 36"
BB Bottom spacer (1), 1 1/4" × 1 1/2" × 36"
CC Center vertical cross member (1), 3/4" × 1 3/8" × 7 3/4"
DD Drawer brace (1), 3/4" × 1 1/2" × 34 1/2"
EE Top cross member (1), 3/4" × 3 3/4" × 34 1/2"
FF Bottom cross member (1), 3/4" × 2 1/8" × 34 1/2"
GG Side vertical cross members (2), 3/4" × 2 1/2" × 37 3/4"
HH Top cross member (inner frame) (1), 3/4" × 4 3/4" × 36"
JJ Drawer braces (inner frame) (2), 3/4" × 1 1/2" × 36"
KK Bottom cross member (inner frame) (1), 3/4" × 2 1/4" × 36"
LL Side vertical cross members (inner frame) (2), 3/4" × 3 1/4" × 31"
MM Front bed molding (1), 3/4" × 1 1/2" × 39"

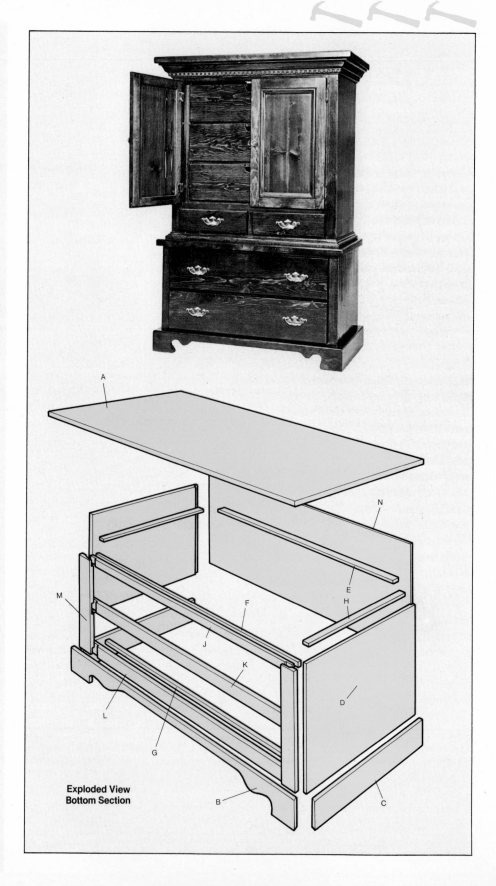

**Exploded View
Bottom Section**

NN Side bed moldings (2), 3/4" × 11/2" × 221/2"

PP Front crown molding (1), 11/4" × 23/4" × 40"

QQ Side crown moldings (2), 11/4" × 23/4" × 205/8"

RR Front dentil molding (optional) (1), 3/8" × 3/4" × 40"

SS Side dentil molding (optional) (2), 3/8" × 3/4" × 205/8"

TT Back (1), 1/4" × 363/4" × 373/4"

LOWER DRAWERS, TOP SECTION*

UU Fronts (2), 11/4" × 47/8" × 165/16"
VV Sides (4), 3/4" × 37/8" × 181/4"
WW Backs (2), 3/4" × 37/8" × 131/16"
XX Bottoms (2), 1/4" × 139/16" × 171/2"

UPPER DRAWERS, TOP SECTION*

YY Fronts (3), 11/4" × 73/4" × 311/4"
ZZ Sides (6), 3/4" × 63/4" × 161/4"
AAA Backs (3), 3/4" × 63/4" × 27"
BBB Bottoms (3), 1/4" × 151/2" × 271/2"

*Dimensions of drawer parts will change depending on the type of hardware used to mount the drawer.

DOORS

CCC A stiles (4), 3/4" × 2" × 27"
DDD B rails (4), 3/4" × 2" × 133/8"
EEE C panels (2), 3/4" × 131/8" × 231/2"

HARDWARE

Offset cabinet hinges (2 pair)
Door pulls (2)
Drawer pulls (6)
Drawer rollers and channels (14)
No. 8 × 11/4" flathead wood screws
4d finishing nails
1" brads

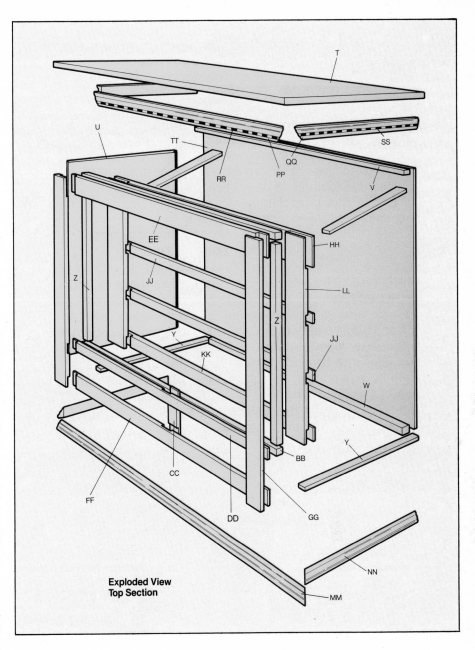

Exploded View
Top Section

This spacious armoire is constructed in two parts. The bottom section is truly a separate cabinet. The last assembly step is to marry the top and bottom sections. The two sections can most efficiently be machined, sanded, and assembled at the same time since common tools, sanding, and assembly setups will be used. Plan to have a second set of strong hands available for lifting when you assemble the armoire.

STEP 1
GLUING UP THE TOP: BOTTOM SECTION
Glue up stock for the top, following directions in the Gluing Section, pages 11-12. Rout the upper edges with a 1/2-inch-radius quarter round router bit.

STEP 2
MACHINING THE FEET
Miter a 45° angle at both ends of the front foot and at one end of each of the two side feet. If you wish to round the leading edge of the feet, use a 3/8-inch router bit. Do this before cutting the miter joints. The foot cutout design is left to you; for a selection of other patterns, see specification #31, page 24.

STEP 3
MACHINING THE SIDES: BOTTOM SECTION
The two sides can be cut from either 3/4-inch solid stock or 3/4-inch ply-

wood. Each has a standard back rabbet, 1/4 inch wide × 3/8 inch deep, as shown in specification #1, page 17 of the Machining section.

STEP 4
MACHINING THE GRILLE PIECES AND CROSS MEMBERS: BOTTOM SECTION
For location of the joinery on the top cross member, the drawer brace, and the bottom cross member, see Detail A. All these parts are notched on the front, or good, side. Two vertical cross members are machined the same (mirror images of one another) for the left and right sides of the front

grille, but with the dadoes on the back side; see Detail B.

STEP 5
MACHINING THE DRAWERS: BOTTOM SECTION
Build two drawers with overlapping fronts according to the plans given in specifications #17- #20, page 21. Use roller systems to mount these drawers. The dimensions in the Materials List in this project may change depending on the mounting hardware used.

STEP 6
MACHINING THE TOP AND SIDES: TOP SECTION
Cut the top to size and round the upper side and front edges with a ½-inch-radius quarter round router bit.

The two sides may be made from either ¾-inch plywood or ¾-inch solid stock. Cut a standard back rabbet, ⅜ inch wide × ⅜ inch deep, as along the entire length of the back edge of the sides.

STEP 7
OUTER GRILLE PARTS: TOP SECTION
The drawer brace and the bottom cross member are dadoed and rabbeted exactly the same; see Detail C. The two vertical cross members are mirror images of each other; see Detail E. For information on standard drawer-brace grooves, see specification #5, page 17.

STEP 8
INNER GRILLE PARTS: TOP SECTION
The horizontal inner grille parts are machined as shown in Detail G. The top cross member, drawer braces, and bottom cross member of the inner grille are all exactly the same. The vertical cross members on the sides of the inner grille are machined as shown in Detail H.

STEP 9
MOLDING: TOP SECTION
Bed molding surrounds the sides

and front of the foot of the top section. This must be mitered at 45° on both ends of the front piece and one end of each of the side pieces.

The underside of the top is likewise surrounded by a combination of moldings, mitered the same as the molding around the foot. See specifications #14 and #15, page 20, for details on creating this molding combination.

STEP 10
DRAWERS: TOP SECTION
Build three large drawers and two smaller ones of the same type used in the bottom section. See the plans in specifications #17- #20, page 21, for details; use the dimensions given in the Materials List for this project.

The two smaller drawer fronts are cut to a standard rectangular shape, while the three larger ones have a drawer-tray cutout, as shown in specification #26, page 22. Round all front edges with a ⅜-inch-radius quarter round router bit.

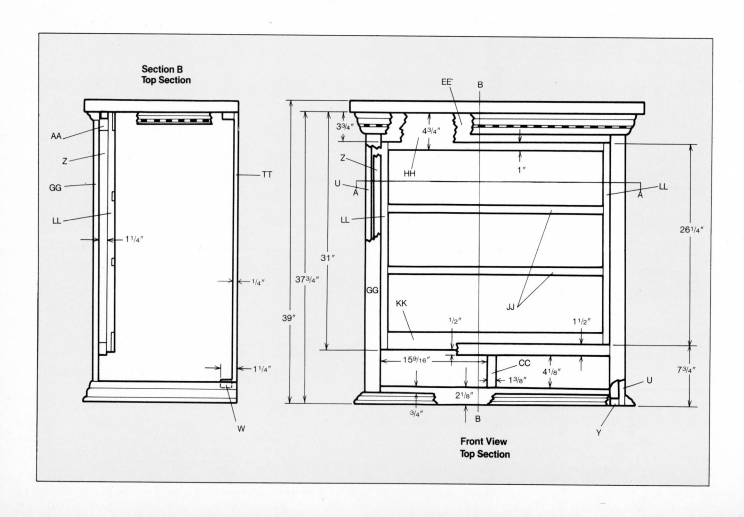

Front View
Top Section

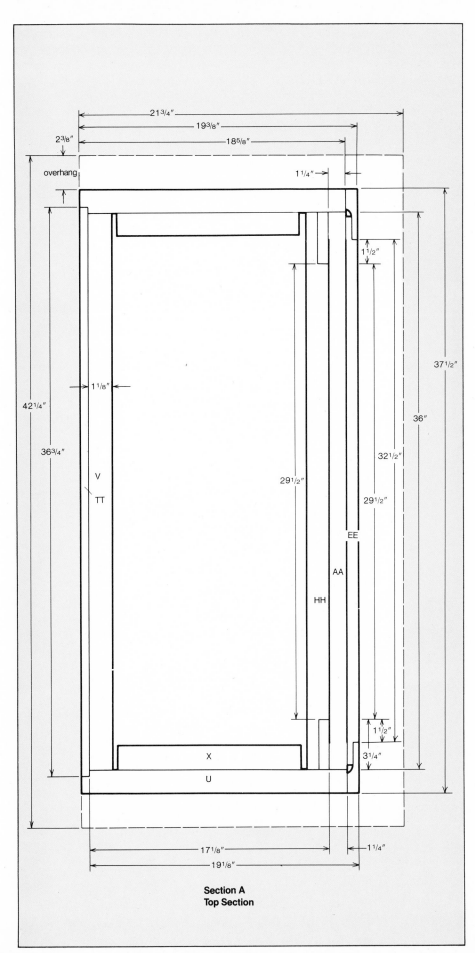

Section A
Top Section

STEP 11
MACHINING THE DOOR: TOP SECTION

Follow the plans given in specification #16, page 20, to make the doors for this project. They have 3/8-inch wide cabinet lips that overlap the cabinet opening.

You will need four A stiles and four B rails cut to the dimensions given in the Materials List. The choices for the C panel section include a 1/4-inch plywood panel or a 3/4-inch thick raised panel, machined to the design given in specification #13, page 20. If you wish to use rail molding with a plywood panel door, it must be cut to fit after the doors are assembled.

STEP 12
SANDING

Rough- and finish-sand the upper surface of the bottom section only about 2 inches in from the routed edges (on three sides), since the upper cabinet will hide the rest. Also, the routed edges need to be sanded to this level. For the upper cabinet, rough- and finish-sand the upper surface, routed edges, and approximately 2 inches back from the three routed edges on the underside of the top. If the sides of both sections are of plywood, usually no sanding is required.

Rough- and finish-sand the outside faces of both outside grilles. Do not bother sanding either section's top or bottom braces, bottom side braces, top cross-member supports, backs, or any grille or frame parts except the edges of those grille parts that will show when doors are opened. (The top cross member, drawer brace, and the outer edges of the two side vertical cross members will be visible when the doors are opened.) Since there are no doors on the bottom section, the inside edges of the grille parts need not be sanded. Note that there are no doors attached to the upper section's inner grille parts, and so do not sand them either. Rough-sand one edge of each of the four spacers. Rough- and finish-sand the front face and upper routed edge of the feet. The moldings usually do not need to be sanded at this time.

Sanding drawer parts is covered in detail in the Sanding section, pages 13-15. Likewise, the door parts are to be sanded according to the sanding directions on page 28.

STEP 13
ASSEMBLING THE CABINET

Every assembly step for this cabinet is explained in detail in the Assembly section, pages 25-32. The steps should be completed in this order.

(1) Assemble the grilles for the top and bottom sections. (2) Assemble the inner frame (grille) of the top section. (3) Assemble the doors. (4) Assemble the drawers. (5) Attach the spacers to the backside of the top section. (6) Attach the outer grille and inner frame to the spacers. (7) Attach the top section's back, top braces, and bottom braces to its sides. (8) Attach the top section's outer grille assembly to its sides and back. (9) Attach the top to the upper section. (10) Attach the combination molding (while the upper cabinet is upside down on the work table). (11) Attach the entire top section to the top of the bottom section. (12) Attach the bed molding. (13) Install the drawers. (14) Install the doors. (15) Assemble the bottom section's sides, back, top braces, and bottom back brace. (16) Attach the bottom section's grille to this assembly. (17) Attach the wraparound foot assembly. (18) Attach the top. (19) Install the drawers.

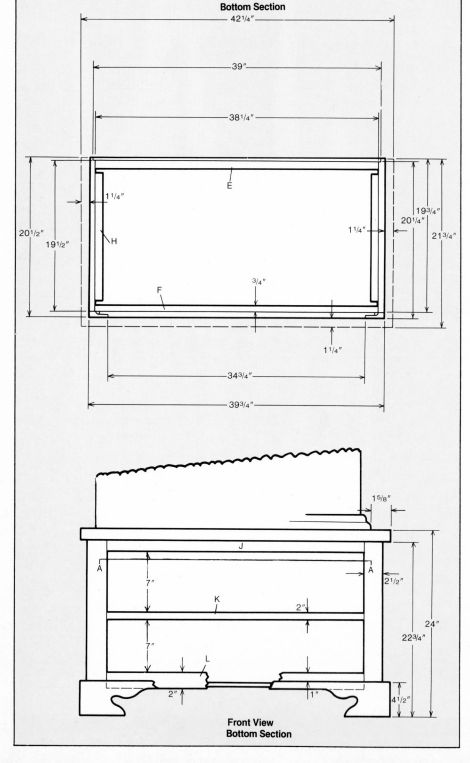

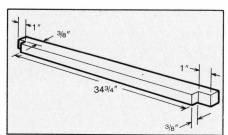

DETAIL A
LOWER SECTION CROSS-MEMBER AND DRAWER-BRACE JOINERY

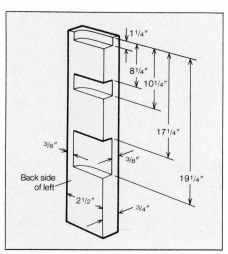

DETAIL B
LOWER SECTION SIDE VERTICAL CROSS-MEMBER JOINERY

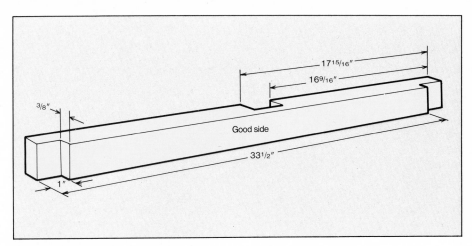

DETAIL C
DRAWER BRACE AND BOTTOM
CROSS MEMBER JOINERY

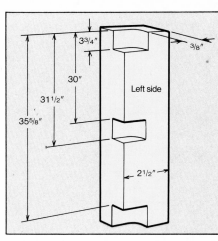

DETAIL E
SIDE VERTICAL CROSS-MEMBER
JOINERY

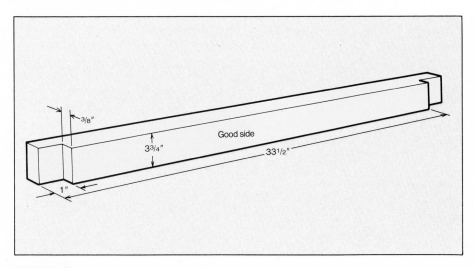

DETAIL D
TOP CROSS-MEMBER JOINERY

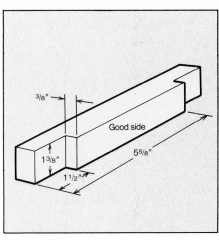

DETAIL F
OUTER GRILLE CENTER VERTICAL
CROSS-MEMBER JOINERY

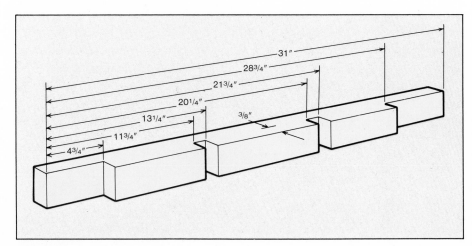

DETAIL H
INNER FRAME SIDE VERTICAL
CROSS-MEMBER JOINERY

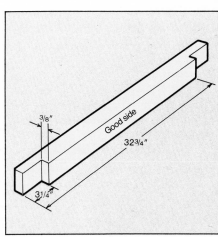

DETAIL G
INNER FRAME CROSS-MEMBER
AND DRAWER-BRACE JOINERY

NIGHTSTAND

MATERIALS LIST

A Top (1), 3/4″ × 151/2″ × 20″
B Sides (2), 3/4″ × 143/4″ × 261/4″
C Bottom (1), 3/4″ × 133/4″ × 173/4″
D Top cross member (1), 3/4″ × 1″ × 173/4″
E Drawer brace (1), 3/4″ × 11/4″ × 173/4″
F Drawer brace (1), 3/4″ × 11/4″ × 173/4″
G Bottom cross member (1), 3/4″ × 13/4″ × 173/4″
H Top brace (1), 3/4″ × 11/8″ × 17″
J Side braces (2), 3/4″ × 11/8″ × 121/2″
K Back (1), 1/4″ × 173/4″ × 261/4″
L Back braces (2), 3/4″ × 11/8″ × 17″
M Front foot (1), 3/4″ × 23/4″ × 20″
N Side feet (2), 3/4″ × 23/4″ × 151/2″

DRAWERS

P Fronts (2), 3/4″ × 41/2″ × 173/4″
Q Sides (4), 3/4″ × 31/2″ × 131/2″
R Backs (2), 3/4″ × 31/2″ × 141/2″
S Bottoms (2), 1/4″ × 127/8″ × 15″

DOORS

T A stiles (4), 3/4″ × 2″ × 121/4″
U B rails (4), 3/4″ × 2″ × 55/8″
V C panels (2), 3/4″ × 53/8″ × 83/4″

HARDWARE

Offset cabinet hinges (2 pair)
Magnetic catches (2 sets)
Monorail roller systems (2 sets)
Brass knobs (2)
Decorative drawer pulls (4)
No. 8 × 3/4″ flathead wood screws
No. 8 × 11/4″ flathead wood screws
No. 8 × 11/2″ flathead wood screws
4d finishing nails
1″ brads

The drawer-and-door combination in a nightstand is very popular. Certainly it is versatile and attractive. At 27 inches, this small cabinet is just the right height for a lamp table.

The project is a little harder than its size may suggest. With two drawers and two doors, this cabinet contains all the machining and assembly demands of a dining-room buffet, scaled down in size! Accuracy in machining as well as patience during assembly will help you to turn out a good job.

STEP 1
MACHINING THE TOP AND SIDES

With the exception of a few pieces of plywood, this project is made entirely of 3/4-inch stock. Glue up

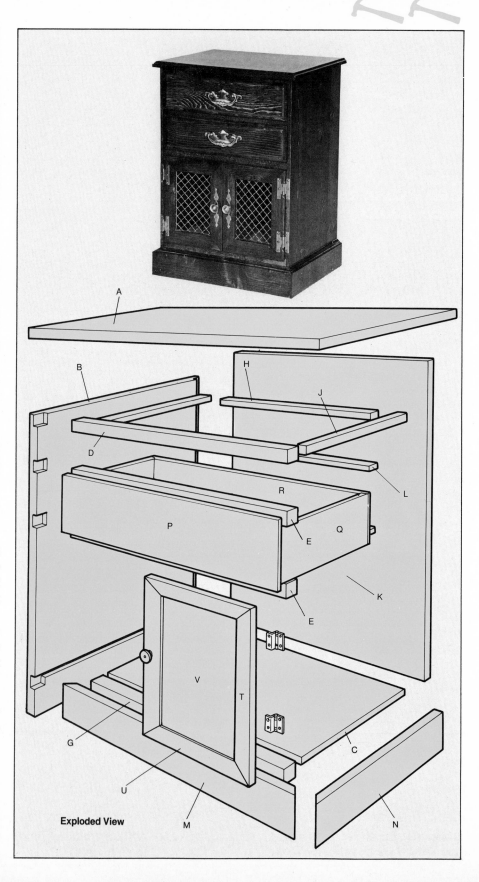

Exploded View

stock to make a piece wide enough for the top if necessary. See the Gluing section, pages 11-12, for details. Round the front and side edges of the top with a ⅜-inch-radius quarter round router bit. Cut the sides to size, and cut the dadoes and rabbets shown in Detail A; see specifications on page 17 for directions. The sides are mirror images of each other.

STEP 2
MACHINING THE FEET
The feet wrap around the base of the cabinet, and so the front foot requires two 45° miter cuts to mate with the side feet, which have one 45° miter cut each. If you wish to cut a decorative pattern into the feet, machine it before cutting the miters. See specification #31, page 24, for a selection of foot designs.

STEP 3
MACHINING THE DRAWERS
The drawers for this project have ⅜-inch lips that overlap the nightstand front and are designed for use with a monorail drawer system. See specifications #18 and #19 on page 21 for details on cutting the parts.

Remember that the dimensions given in the Materials List may change, depending on hardware.

STEP 4
MACHINING THE DOORS
See the information on cutting the parts for the raised-panel doors in specification #13, page 20, as well as

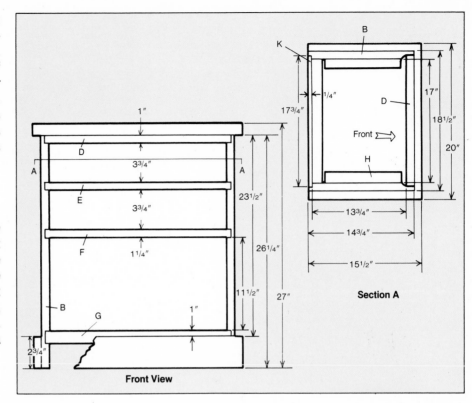

Front View

Section A

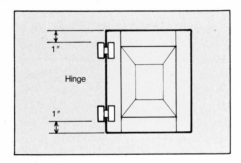

DETAIL B
DOOR LAYOUT

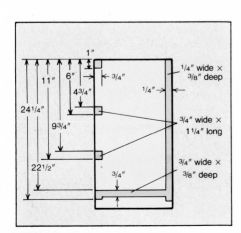

DETAIL A
SIDE LAYOUT

machining instructions on the cabinet lip cut for doors in specification #16, on page 20. Like the drawers, the doors have ⅜-inch cabinet lips that overlap the front of the nightstand.

STEP 5
SANDING THE PARTS
Rough- and finish-sand the top and the outside faces of the sides. The inside faces of the sides and the upper face of the bottom need only be rough-sanded, since they will not show. The top cross member, bottom cross member, and drawer braces need only be rough-sanded at this time. They will be finish-sanded after

construction. Be sure to rough-sand the upper edge of the bottom cross member because it will show when the doors are opened. Top braces are not sanded. The feet need rough sanding only on the front face, and rough- and finish-sanding on the upper or leading edge. Since the back will most likely never be seen, don't bother sanding at all. For detailed information on sanding door and drawer parts, see the Sanding section, pages 13-15.

STEP 6
ASSEMBLING THE CABINET
Complete instructions for assembling the components of this cabinet are outlined in the Assembly section, pages 25-27. The order of construction, however, is as follows:

(1) Attach the bottom, top, and bottom cross members and drawer braces to the two sides with glue and 4d finishing nails. (2) Construct the drawers. (3) Construct the doors. (4) After finish sanding the partially assembled cabinet, attach the top braces, the top, and then the feet. (5) Attach the back. (6) Install the drawers and the doors. (7) Install the knobs and pulls.

PEDESTAL END TABLE

MATERIALS LIST
A Top (1), 1 1/4" × 22" diameter
B Feet (2), 2 1/2" × 5 3/4" × 18"
C Leg (1), 16 5/8" × 7" diameter
D Top braces (2), 1" × 4 3/4" × 14"

HARDWARE
No. 8 × 1 1/2" flathead wood screws
No. 10 × 3" flathead wood screws

This project requires that you either have a lathe or can get a piece turned for you by someone who does. The pedestal that supports the ample top of this table is turned from a block of glued-up stock.

The table is perfect next to a comfortable chair or a couch. It is designed to be sturdy. Take care with the lap cuts on the feet and braces so the fit will be snug for strength.

STEP 1
MACHINING THE TOP
The top most likely will have to be glued up from several pieces to obtain the necessary width. See the Gluing section, pages 11-12, for details. When the glue has thoroughly dried, use a band or saber saw to cut out the round shape. You can also cut out a hexagonal shape, as shown in the photo here. Round with a 3/8-inch-radius quarter round router bit all the way around the top edge.

STEP 2
MAKING THE FEET
The two feet can be machined from 2 3/8-inch-thick stock, or the thickness may be obtained by gluing up pieces of thinner stock and then jointing or planing them. See Detail A for dimensional details for machining the two feet.

Use a jointer or band saw to cut the relief on the bottom surface of each foot. The angular cuts on the top face are best made with a band saw. After cutting the two feet, fit them together and set them on a flat

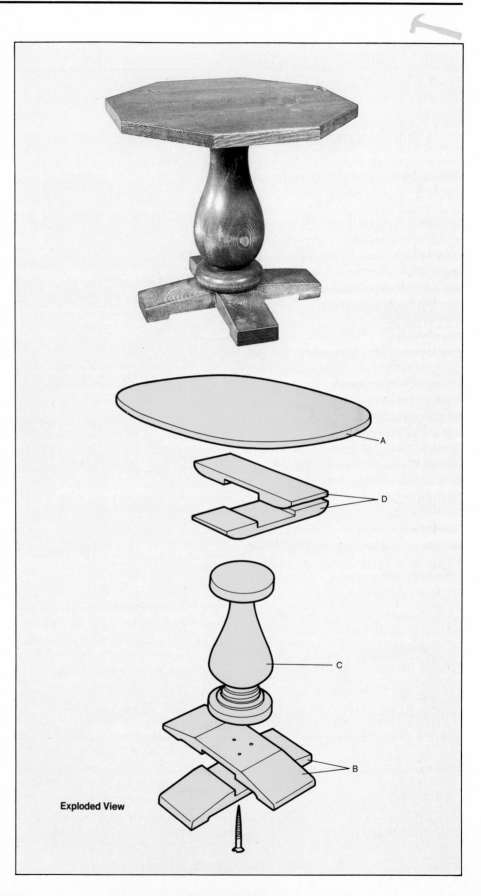

Exploded View

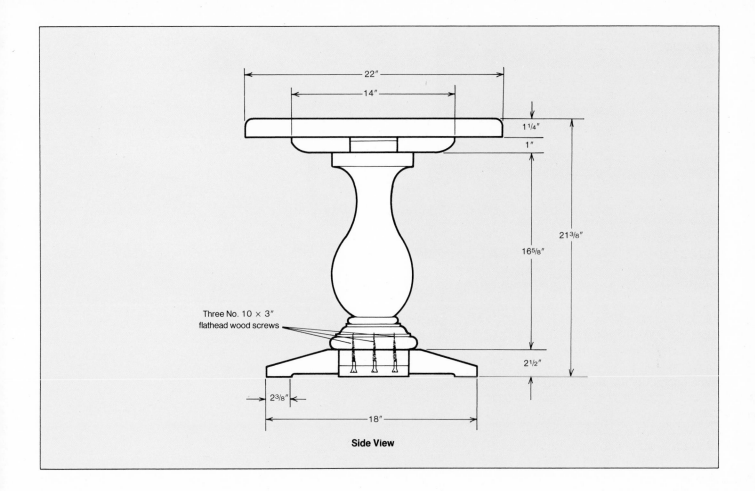

Three No. 10 × 3″
flathead wood screws

Side View

surface to make sure that they are level. A table-saw top is perfect for this. If the feet don't sit flat, the finished pedestal will wobble. If the pieces aren't flat, carefully inspect them for the problem and cut one or both again, correcting your mistake.

STEP 3
MAKING THE PEDESTAL
Glue up stock to obtain the 7-inch-thick blank from which to turn the pedestal. Allow some extra stock because the four pieces will shift slightly while you are gluing. Also, allow a little extra wood at each end of the blank to attach to a lathe for turning. See Detail B for the pedestal design and specifications.

STEP 4
CUTTING THE TOP BRACES
Cut the interlocking top braces with a band saw as shown in Detail C. Use oak if you can get it. Be sure to check the interlocking lap joints for a proper fit before starting assembly.

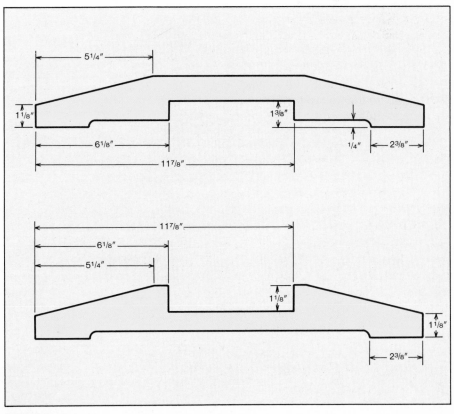

**DETAIL A
FEET LAYOUT**

STEP 5
SANDING
Rough- and finish-sand the upper surface and edges of the top. Rough- and finish-sand the feet, except on the bottom, taking special care not to loosen the fit of the pieces. The top braces need only be rough-sanded since they will not be seen. The pedestal leg should be finish-sanded on the lathe.

STEP 6
ASSEMBLING THE FEET AND PEDESTAL
Glue and clamp the feet together and set them aside to set up. Next, join the top braces with glue, and immediately glue and screw the unit to the top of the pedestal leg. Use No. 10 × 3-inch wood screws through pilot holes; take care to center the top brace assembly on the pedestal.

STEP 7
COMPLETING THE ASSEMBLY
Attach the top by screwing through pre-drilled pilot holes in the top braces into the top with No. 8 × 1½-inch flathead screws. Do not use glue between the top brace and the top!

After the feet have thoroughly set up, round the top edges with a ⅜-inch-radius quarter round router bit; touch up or smooth out with a hand sander. Secure the feet to the bottom of the pedestal leg with a bit of glue and three No. 12 × 3-inch wood screws driven through pre-drilled pilot holes. Break, or slightly round, all hard edges of the feet and the top with a hand sander to ensure a good surface for finishing.

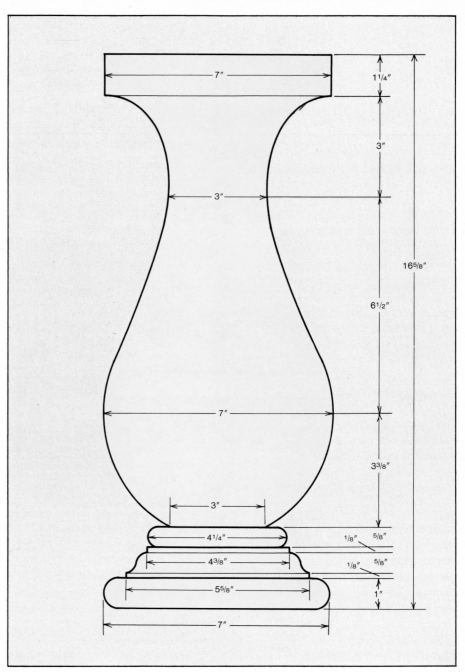

DETAIL B
LEG LAYOUT

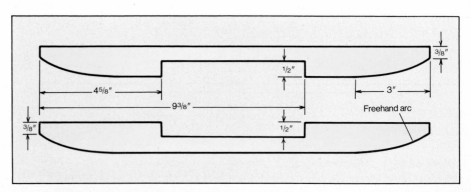

DETAIL C
TOP BRACE LAYOUT

CANDLESTAND

MATERIALS LIST
A Top (1), 1¹/₄″ × 24″ diameter
B Feet (2), 1¹/₄″ × 7″ × 20″
C Top brace (1), ³/₄″ × 4³/₄″ × 21″
D Pedestal leg* (1), 21¹/₂″ × 3¹/₂″ diameter

*May substitute a commercially-turned post.

HARDWARE
No. 8 × 1¹/₄″ flathead wood screws
No. 10 × 3″ flathead wood screws

This is an easy project that nonetheless requires some precision in cutting. Machining the few pieces so that they mate snugly is the secret to a satisfactory job.

Really an all-purpose table, this candlestand can be used as lamp table, nightstand, end table, plant stand, and/or smoking stand. You can vary the size of the top to suit your taste.

STEP 1
MACHINING THE TOP

Glue up 1¹/₄-inch stock from which to cut a 24-inch-diameter circle; see the Gluing Section, pages 11-12, for details. Cut the top with a band saw or saber saw. Sand the edge smooth, then round the upper edge with a ³/₈-inch radius quarter round bit on a router.

STEP 2
CUTTING THE LEG

You can turn a pedestal for this table if you have a lathe, or you can cut one from a pre-turned table leg like the one shown in Detail A. When the leg has been cut to size, make the additional cuts shown in Detail B with a band saw. Make these cuts in several steps: (1) Cut straight down one side to corner A and back the blade out. (2) Cut down the other side to corner B and back the blade out halfway. (3) Make a curved cut in toward corner A, as shown by the dotted line in Detail B. (4) Remove the waste and square the cut, cutting back toward

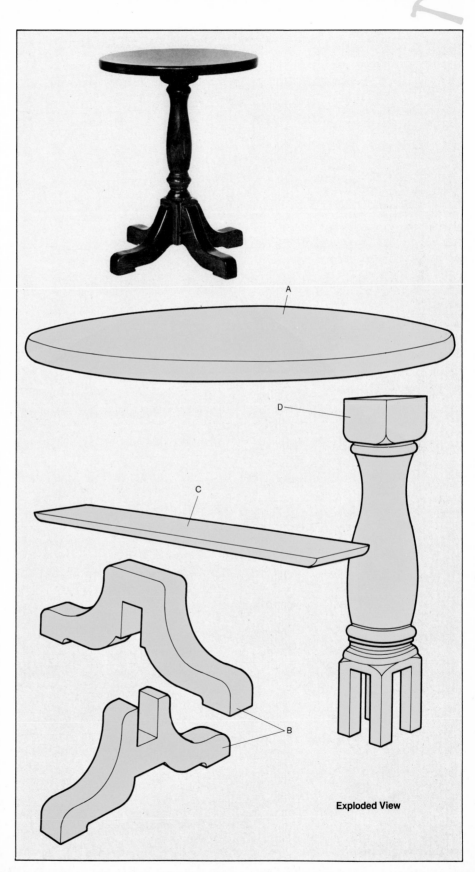

Exploded View

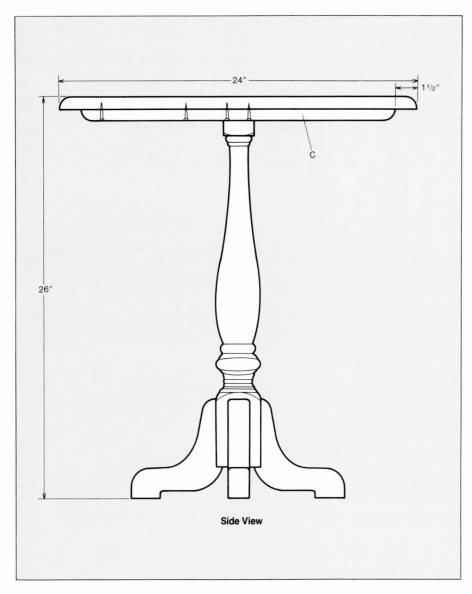

Side View

DETAIL A
PEDESTAL LEG LAYOUT

corner B. (5) Turn the pedestal 90° and repeat steps 1 through 4.

STEP 3
MACHINING THE FEET
Transfer the patterns given in Detail C to 7-inch-wide 2-inch stock. Make the cuts for the lap joints where the feet will join in the same manner as you cut the joinery on the bottom of the pedestal leg. Then cut out the patterns with a band saw. After cutting the feet, rout the top edges using a ³⁄₈-inch quarter round router bit and the bottom edges using a ¹⁄₄-inch bit.

STEP 4
MACHINING THE TOP BRACE
The top brace may be cut from any ³⁄₄-inch hardwood such as maple, birch, or oak. Rout a ³⁄₈-inch-radius curve on the two end edges, as shown in Detail D.

Drill seven pilot holes in the brace; three are near the center of the brace where it will be attached to the pedestal leg. The other four pilot holes are spaced so as to provide for secure attachment of the brace to the top.

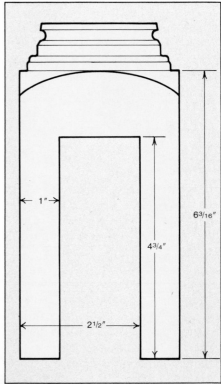

DETAIL B
PEDESTAL LEG BASE JOINERY

STEP 5
SANDING THE PARTS

Rough- and finish-sand the top and feet; however, the top brace need only be rough-sanded. If you have used a pre-turned pedestal leg, it will most likely need only a minimal amount of touching up because it came from the manufacturer already finish-sanded.

STEP 6
ASSEMBLING THE FEET

Apply a modest amount of glue, fit the feet together, and place feet down on a perfectly flat surface to correct for any tilt. (If you can't correct the tilt, you'll have to recut the legs.) Wait until the glue has set thoroughly (overnight) before continuing with the assembly.

STEP 7
ADDING THE LEG

After the feet are completly set, fit the pedestal leg over the foot assembly; make sure that it is at right angles to the floor and that the top end is level. When the fit is exact, glue and set aside carefully. Again, wait until the glue sets up. Make sure, throughout the gluing procedure, that the pedestal stands at exact right angles to a level floor; otherwise the tabletop won't be level.

STEP 8
ADDING THE TOP BRACE

Apply a generous amount of glue to the top brace and drive three No. 10 × 3-inch flathead wood screws into the top of the pedestal through pilot holes in the top brace. Note, once again, that it is critical to make sure that the brace is level with the floor before securing it. If the brace is not level, the top will not be level with the floor.

STEP 9
ATTACHING THE TOP

Attach the top with four No. 8 × 1¼-inch flathead wood screws driven into the top through pilot holes in the top brace. Do not glue the top to the brace. Orient the top so that its grain runs at right angles to the brace below. Again, check to see that the top is level with the floor. If it is not, loosen the screws slightly, check again for level, and tighten the screws slightly to adjust until the top is level.

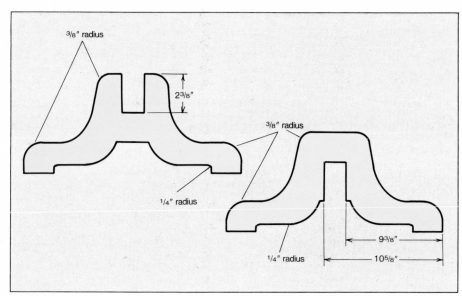

DETAIL C
FEET LAYOUT

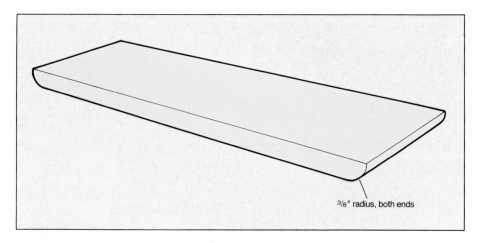

DETAIL D
TOP BRACE DETAIL

DINING TABLE

MATERIALS LIST
A Top halves (2), 1¼″ × 24″ × 48″
B Long aprons (2), 1¼″ × 3″ × 24″
C Short aprons (4), 1¼″ × 3″ × 11¹⁵/₁₆″
D Top braces (2), ¾″ × 9″ × 20″
E Pedestal (1), 6″ diameter × 25⁷/₈″
F Legs (2), 3¼″ × 3¼″ × 30″
G Leaves (2), 1¼″ × 12″ × 24″
H Alignment pins (9), ⅜″ diameter × 2″

HARDWARE
Tabletop lock
Adjustable table glides (4)
Equalizer single pedestal slides (2)
Lag bolts (3), 6″ × ¼″
Lag bolts (3), 4″ × ¼″
No. 10 × 1¾″ flathead wood screws
No. 10 × 2½″ flathead wood screws

A dining table is one of the most popular projects for any woodworker. This 48-inch-diameter round table extends to 6 feet in length when its two 12-inch leaves are in place. This table is designed with adjustable table glides built into each leg for stability and a tabletop lock to prevent the top from separating when the leaves are not in use. The plans call for 1¼-inch stock for both the top and aprons for strength.

STEP 1
MACHINING THE TOP AND LEAVES
The top is cut most easily from two pieces at least 25 × 49 inches. The type of the wood is up to you; your selection should be based upon the desired appearance of the table, not on sturdiness. The final size of the two halves of the tabletop will be 24 × 48 inches. See the Gluing section, pages 13-14, for detailed information on how to create pieces this wide. When you have glued up stock for the two halves of the top, cut them into two half circles with either a band saw or saber saw.

Cut the two leaves ¼- to ½-inch longer than specified in the Materials List. This will give you room to fit them in the top.

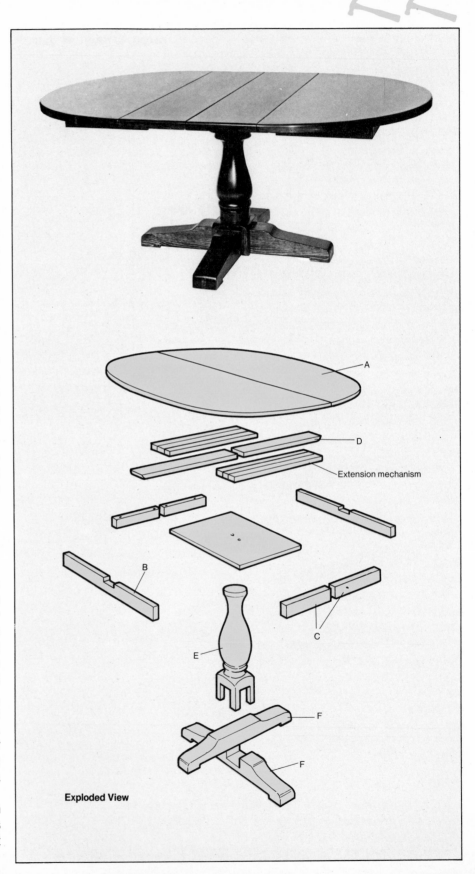

Extension mechanism

Exploded View

STEP 2
MACHINING THE APRONS

The aprons on this table do not support the top. Instead, they simply add rigidity and help keep the top from warping. Cut the apron parts from 1¼-inch thick stock, then drill and counterbore them as shown in Details A and A-2, to be attached to the underside of the table top.

STEP 3
MACHINING THE LEGS AND PEDESTAL

Using the pattern in Detail B, cut out two legs from 3¼-inch thick stock. Use a band saw for this operation, if you have one. It takes a great deal of time and a special deep cut blade to cut stock this thick with a saber saw.

Make a lap joint where the two legs cross each other, as shown in the working drawings. This joint is easiest to make on a band saw.

Glue up stock for the pedestal, 6 inches thick, 6 inches wide, and 28 inches long. Allow the glue to dry at least twenty-four hours, then band saw the joint in the bottom of the pedestal that straddles the leg. To make this joint, cut the shape in one face, temporarily tape the waste stock back to the board, and cut the shape in the second face. This technique can be called a compound cut.

Turn the pedestal on a lathe, following the pattern in Detail C. If you don't have a lathe, you may opt to cut the pattern on a band saw with a compound cut, described above.

STEP 4
MACHINING THE TOP BRACES

Two top braces have an arc, as shown in Detail D, that you can either cut freehand on a band saw or grind over on a portable or table belt sander.

STEP 5
SANDING THE PIECES

The top and leaves are rough-sanded on the top surfaces and edges. (Finish sanding will be done after the table has been completely assembled.) Rough-sand and finish-sand the aprons on the face that will show when the table is assembled. The lower edge of the apron need only be

rough-sanded. The top braces need only be rough-sanded. Sand the top and the sides of the legs, but not the bottom. The pedestal should be sanded on the lathe to get it ready for finishing.

STEP 6
ASSEMBLING THE LEGS AND PEDESTAL

Glue the legs together at the lap joint, then assemble them to the pedestal so that the bottom of the pedestal straddles the legs, as shown in the working drawings. Use plenty of glue and wipe away any excess. Secure the legs to the pedestal with three 6-inch × ¼-inch lag bolts, countersunk into the leg bottom.

Attach the mounting plate to the top of the pedestal with glue and three 4-inch × ¼-inch lag bolts. It's not necessary to countersink the top bolts.

Section A

Extension mechanism

Extension mechanism

1/8″

1/8″

48″

3″

Attach to top

A

A

28¼″

29½″

Side View

STEP 7
ASSEMBLING THE TOP

Drill three ⅜-inch-diameter by ¾-inch-deep holes for the alignment pegs into the straight edge of one of the halves of the top which mates to the other half. Locate two of these holes 4 inches in from each end, and one directly in the center. Center the holes on the thickness of the wood.

Use dowel centers to locate the holes in the other half of the tabletop. Do not locate or drill these holes in the leaves at this time.

Insert three alignment pegs into one of the halves of the top, but do not glue them in yet. Place the two halves, mated, upside down on top of a work table.

STEP 8
ATTACHING THE LEG ASSEMBLY

Following the plans (Top View), attach the top braces to the top with No. 10 × 1¾-inch flathead wood screws. Do not glue the braces to the top. Mount the aprons over the braces and secure them to the top with No. 10 × 2½-inch screws through the pre-drilled holes.

Attach the slide mechanisms to the top, following the manufacturer's directions. You must use equalizer single pedestal slides for this project. Ordinary table extension slides will not work. (Equalizer slides are available from most sources that sell furniture hardware.) Attach the table-top lock.

Mount the leg assembly to the tabletop assembly by screwing the mounting plate to the equalizer slides, as per the manufacturer's directions. Install adjustable table glides in the bottom of the legs.

STEP 9
COMPLETING THE LEAVES

Turn the table upright on a smooth, level surface and install the leaves. Use dowel centers to determine locations for alignment pegs, as described in Step 7 for the two halves

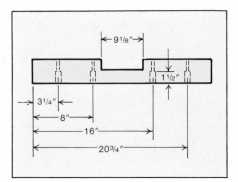
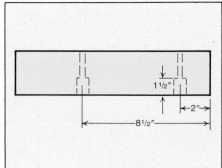

DETAIL A
LONG AND SHORT APRON LAYOUTS

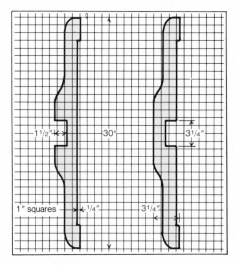

DETAIL B
LEG PATTERN

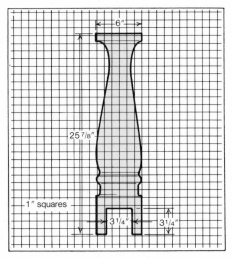

DETAIL C
PEDESTAL PATTERN

of the tabletop, and install but do not glue.

The leaves will need to be trimmed to the exact width of the table. This trimming can be done with a table or radial arm saw; do not trim, however, until after both leaves have been fitted into the table.

Trim or cut the leaves to proper length. Number the leaves so that they will always go into the table in the same sequence. This will assure a constant, good fit.

STEP 10
FINISHING THE SANDING

Rough-sand the top edge of the table while the leaves are still in place.

Then remove the leaves, close the top, and rough- and finish-sand the entire top completely.

STEP 11
COMPLETING THE TABLE

After sanding once again, check to make sure that the leaves and top halves line up and that the top is level. When you are sure that the alignment is exact, glue the alignment pegs or table pins in place permanently.

Finally, use a hand sander to break, or slightly round, the edges between the leaves and the two halves of the top so that they have no sharp edges.

DROP-LEAF TRESTLE TABLE

MATERIALS LIST
A Top (1), 1¼″ × 22″ × 60″
B Leaves (2), 1¼″ × 10″ × 60″
C Trestle cross member (1), 1¼″ × 4¾″ × 38½″
D Top braces (2), 1¼″ × 1¾″ × 20″
E Center top brace (1), 1½″ × 1¾″ × 2″
F Legs (2), 1½″ × 15½″ × 25½″
G Feet (2), 2½″ × 3″ × 27½″
H Pins (2), ¾″ × ¾″ × 3″
J End caps (2), 1¼″ × 1¾″ × 3¾″

HARDWARE
Drop leaf supports (2 pair)
Brass butt hinges (3 pair)
No. 10 × 2″ flathead wood screws
No. 10 × 3″ flathead wood screws
6d finishing nails

If you make this handsome but simple table, you will probably want to make two of the trestle benches shown in the next project to go with it. This table is 5 feet long and 22 inches wide when folded; with its leaves up, it is a comfortable 42 inches wide.

Be choosy when picking wood for the top and leaves. The beauty of the table depends on a good top. When you glue up stock for the top, make sure that the pieces are a good match and that the seams are tight and the pieces flat. If you don't have a wide belt sander, consider having the top sanded or planed professionally to make it perfectly smooth.

STEP 1
MACHINING THE TOP
You will have to glue up 1¼-inch stock to make a piece of sufficient width for the top; see the Gluing section, pages 11-12, for details on gluing up stock.

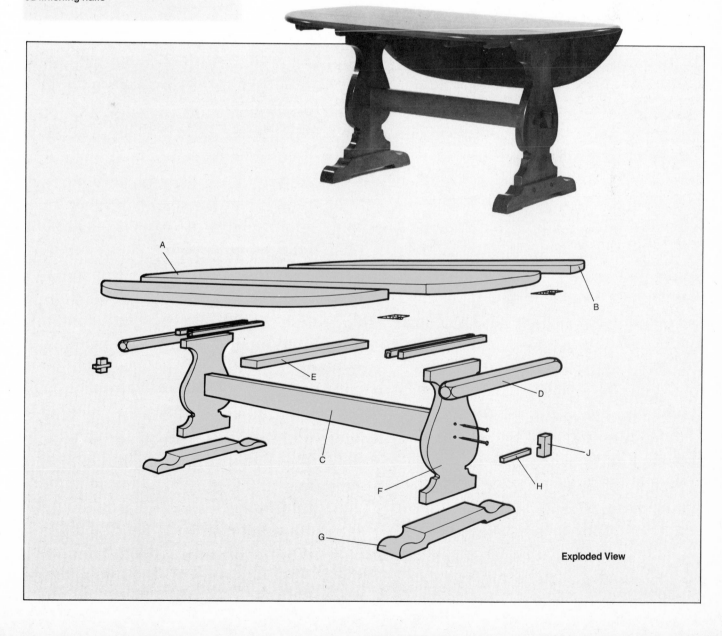

Exploded View

STEP 2
CUTTING THE TRESTLE END PIECES

The table is given stability by the trestle cross member from which it takes its name. To give the appearance that this trestle passes through the legs and is held in place by pins, caps with pins are fashioned to attach to the legs opposite the ends of the trestle cross member. Cut these end pieces from 1¼-inch stock, and notch, as shown in Detail A. The pins fit into these slots and sit against the legs.

STEP 3
MACHINING THE TOP AND CENTER BRACES

The tabletop is braced in three places: along the outside of each leg, and in the center. All three braces are the same size, but the two top braces (which sit outside the legs) are further shaped, as shown in Detail B. Make the cuts with a saber saw or, preferably, a band saw.

STEP 4
MACHINING THE LEGS

If you have to glue up stock to obtain boards of sufficient width to make the legs, cut the individual boards to 25¾ inches before gluing and trim to 25½ inches afterward. Copy and transfer the pattern given in Detail C to the two legs and cut them out with a saber saw or band saw.

STEP 5
MACHINING THE FEET

The feet can be cut either from 2½-inch thick stock or, if you can't obtain stock that thick, from two pieces of 1¼-inch stock glued up. Cut the feet to size; then copy and transfer the pattern given in Detail D, taking care to mark the drill holes indicated on the pattern. Drill the two ⁵/₁₆-inch holes where indicated. To avoid ragged edges on the holes, drill just through the board, and then turn it over and complete the hole from the other side. After drilling the holes, complete cutting out the pattern with a saber saw or, far more easily, with a band saw.

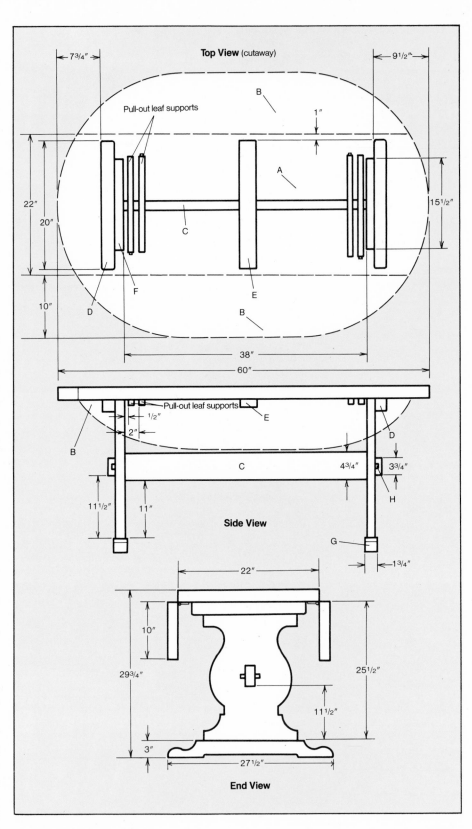

STEP 6
SANDING THE PARTS

Rough- and finish-sand the top on the upper surface and edges. Since all surfaces of the leaves will be visible, all should be rough- and finish-sanded; the same is true for the trestle cross member, trestle end pieces, pins, and legs. The two outside top braces need only be sanded on the surfaces that will show when the table is completed. The top center

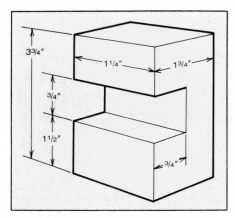

DETAIL A
END CAP LAYOUT

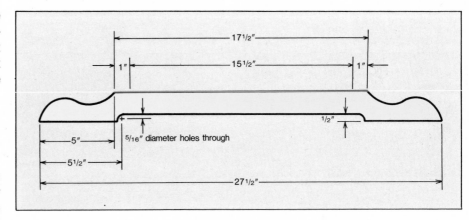

DETAIL B
TOP BRACE DETAIL

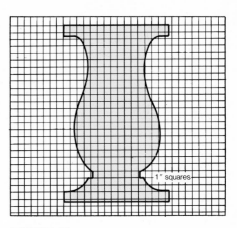

DETAIL C
LEG PATTERN

1" squares

brace will not show and need not be sanded at all. Finally, rough- and finish-sand all the surfaces of the feet except the bottoms, which need not be sanded until a later stage in the project.

STEP 7
ATTACHING THE LEGS TO THE FEET
Apply a small amount of glue to the bottoms of the legs and then center the legs on the feet, securing these assemblies with bar clamps. Drill two pilot holes through the bottom of each foot into the leg at slight angles to the perpendicular so that the screws that fasten the foot to the leg will penetrate slightly across the grain and thus hold more surely. Attach the feet to the legs with No. 10 × 3-inch flathead wood screws.

STEP 8
ATTACHING THE BRACES
Attach the two top braces to the outside of the legs, flush with the top edge, with two No. 10 × 2-inch flathead wood screws for each brace, driven through pilot holes. Next, center the center top brace on the underside of the top and attach it with two of the same size screws.

STEP 9
ATTACHING THE LEAVES
With the top upside down, set the leaves against it on either side, their ends squared up with the ends of the top. Attach three 3- × 2-inch brass butt hinges between each leaf and

DETAIL D
FOOT LAYOUT

the top, using the brass screws supplied with the hinges. Position two hinges 3 inches in from each end and one in the center.

STEP 10
ATTACHING THE TRESTLE CROSS MEMBER
Attach one end of the trestle cross member to the center of each leg, 11 inches above the bottom end of the leg, as shown in the plan (Side View). The procedure for positioning and squaring up the cross member is given in Step #8 of the directions for building the trestle bench. When the cross member has been attached, position the trestle end pieces on the legs opposite the ends of the trestle cross member, as shown in the plan (Side View). Drill two pilot holes for each, apply a small amount of glue, and attach them with 6d finishing nails.

STEP 11
COMPLETING THE TABLE
With the top and leaf assembly face down on a work surface, set the leg and cross-member assembly upside down on it. Center the legs on the main section of the top, and attach with four No. 10 × 2-inch flathead wood screws driven through each top brace. Finally, install four pullout-type drop-leaf supports on the top in the positions shown in the Side View.

STEP 12
FINAL SANDING
Stand the table upright. Raise the leaves and pull out the leaf supports to hold them up. Use a belt sander to correct any unevenness between the ends of the leaves and the end of the tabletop. If you wish, round the perimeter edges of the entire top (with leaves extended) with a 1/2- or 3/8-inch radius quarter round router bit.

TRESTLE BENCH

MATERIALS LIST
A Seat (1), 1¼" × 14" × 60"
B Legs (2), 1¼" × 11" × 16¾"
C Braces (2), 1¼" × 1¾" × 11"
D Cross member (1), 1¼" × 4" × 42"
E End caps (2), 1¼" × 1¾" × 3"
F Pins (2), ¾" × ¾" × 3"

HARDWARE
Lag screws (4), ⅜" × 4"
No. 10 × 2" flathead wood screws
6d finishing nails

This easy-to-build bench with simple lines complements the trestle table shown in the previous project. You can make it whatever length you like, depending on the stock you use. Its sturdiness is assured by the trestle.

The appearance is of a trestle that pierces the legs and is pinned in place, but this effect is simulated by making a few easy cuts in scrap.

A trestle table with two of these benches makes a handsome addition to any country kitchen.

STEP 1
MACHINING THE SEAT

To give the bench a balanced appearance, the seat should be 14 inches wide. If you have to glue up stock to make this width, see the Gluing section, pages 11-12, for details. The length is determined by you. If you are building a pair of benches for a trestle table (see page 101), the length of bench should match that of the table. You may wish to make the seats slightly thicker than shown in the plans, particularly if the overall length is more than 60 inches. However, matching the thickness of the tabletop gives the set a nice unity. If you use 1¼-inch stock, and if the length is greater than 72 inches, the bench should be braced along its full length with a 1¼- × 3-inch board attached along its narrow edge to the bottom of the bench. If you use thicker stock, the bench needs no additional bracing for lengths up to 96 inches.

After you cut the seat to size, round the top edge all the way

around with a ½-inch-radius quarter round router bit.

STEP 2
MACHINING THE LEGS

If you save scrap pieces, you may be able to find some from which to cut the legs. Because they are only 9½ inches wide, you probably won't have to glue up stock to obtain boards of sufficient width. Cut the legs to size, and then copy and trace the pattern from Detail A onto the pieces and cut out the outline with a band saw. Round the side edges of the legs (the edges cut out by the band saw) with a ¼-inch-radius router bit.

STEP 3
CUTTING THE BRACES AND CROSS MEMBER

Cut the two braces from 1¼-inch scrap wood. The cross member provides the bench with stability so that a person sitting at one end won't cause the other end to rise. The length of the cross member depends on the length of the bench. The plan shows a bench 60 inches long, to

match the table in the previous chapter. Cut the piece to size and round the four long edges with a ¼-inch-radius quarter round router bit.

STEP 4
MACHINING THE CROSS-MEMBER END PIECES

In order to simulate the appearance of the cross member passing through the legs, two end caps are attached to the outside of the legs, opposite the ends of the cross member.

Cut the end caps as shown in Detail B. Cut out the two pins, fit them into the cross-member end pieces, and attach with 6d finishing nails.

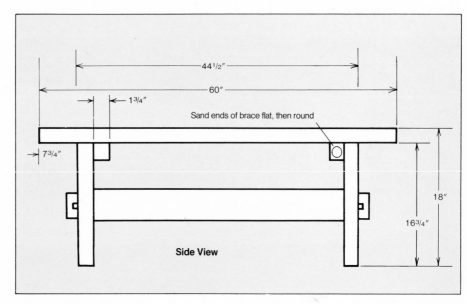

Side View

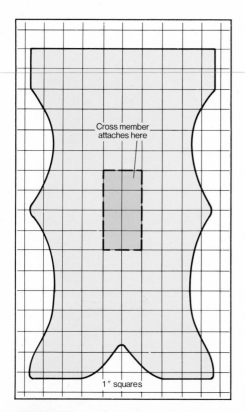

DETAIL A
LEG PATTERN

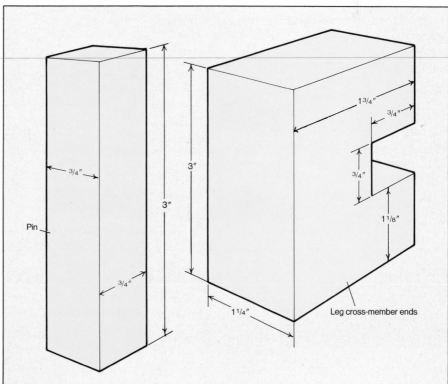

DETAIL B
END CAP LAYOUT

STEP 5
SANDING THE PIECES

Rough- and finish-sand all the parts. For the braces and cross-member end-cap pins, first rough- and finish-sand them square; then round over the ends, as shown in Detail C. This treatment gives those components a soft, worn look.

STEP 6
ATTACHING THE BRACES AND CROSS MEMBER

Attach the braces flush with the top of each leg with two No. 10 × 2-inch flathead wood screws.

See the leg pattern in Detail A for the position where the cross member is to be attached. Mark out the cross-section of the cross member at its attachment points and, from the outside of the legs, drill two pilot holes for the screws that will secure the cross member; as with the feet, angle these slightly to give the screws extra holding power in the ends of the cross member. Next drive two 6d finishing nails just through the legs (about ⅛ to ¼ inch) at the point of attachment so the cross member can sit on the nails for final, precise positioning as shown in Detail D. Set up the assembly shown in the detail (get some help to steady the long cross member) and set the cross member lightly on the nail points. Use a small square to position the cross member so that it is square with the foot, as shown in Detail E, and then press the cross member down on the nail points to fix its position. Lower the assembly so you can get access to the outside of the leg and drive home two ⅜- x 4-inch lag screws through the pilot holes. Drill ¾-inch holes, ⅜-inch deep in the legs to countersink the heads of the lag screws. Repeat the operation at the other end.

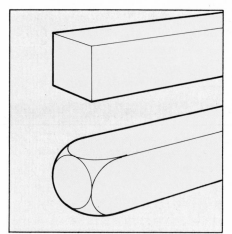

DETAIL C
BRACE END DETAIL

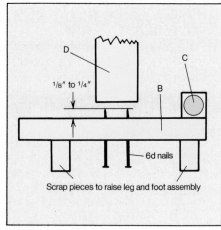

DETAIL D
LEG-TO-CROSS-MEMBER JOINERY

⅛" to ¼"

6d nails

Scrap pieces to raise leg and foot assembly

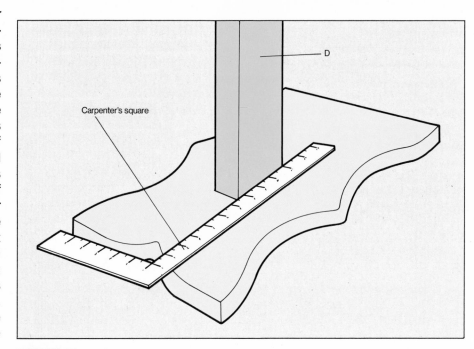

Carpenter's square

DETAIL E
SQUARING THE CROSS MEMBER TO THE LEG

STEP 7
ATTACHING THE TOP AND CROSS-MEMBER END CAPS

Place the top upside down on a padded surface and center the feet/legs/cross-member assembly on it. Attach the top by driving three No. 10 × 2-inch flathead wood screws through each brace into the top.

Finally, drill two pilot holes through each of the assembled end pieces and attach them to the legs, opposite the ends of the trestle, with 6d finishing nails.

DEACON'S BENCH

MATERIALS LIST

A Seat (1), 1¼" × 18½" × (variable)
B Back (1), 1¼" × 4½" × (variable)
C Arms (2), 1¾" × 2⁹/₁₆" × 19¼"
D Side leg braces (4), ¾" × 2¼" × 6"
E Front leg braces (4), ¾" × 2¼" × 6¾"
F Dowels (2), ½" diameter × 8¼"
G Front posts (2), 1⁵/₁₆" diameter × 9"
H Back posts (2), 1⁵/₁₆" diameter × 14⁵/₈"
J Back spindles (7–12), 1" diameter ×
   14⁵/₈"
K Legs (4), 2½" diameter × 18"

HARDWARE

Slanted mounting plates (4)
³/₈" × 3" hanger bolts (4)
No. 10 × 2" flathead wood screws
No. 8 × 1½" flathead wood screws
Screw plugs

This elegant piece of furniture takes a lot of work to build. The machining must be done to exacting standards or the spindles and arm posts will not fit properly. A drill press is essential, and you will want to knock together the simple jig shown here to aid in drilling the numerous 80° angled holes in the seat.

The availability of pre-turned legs and slanted mounting plates makes the project a little easier than it might be otherwise, and does much to ensure a nice result if you spend the time it takes to put this bench together.

STEP 1
MACHINING THE SEAT

Directions for this bench are given for five lengths, ranging from 48 to 72 inches, as shown in Detail A. The seat is 18½ inches wide, and you probably will have to edge-glue stock to make up this width. See the Gluing section, pages 11-12, for directions.

Drill-hole placements for the back spindles and arms are given in Details B and C for the five different lengths. Make a paper template of the plan appropriate to your length bench and mark the centers with an awl. Note the angle at which the

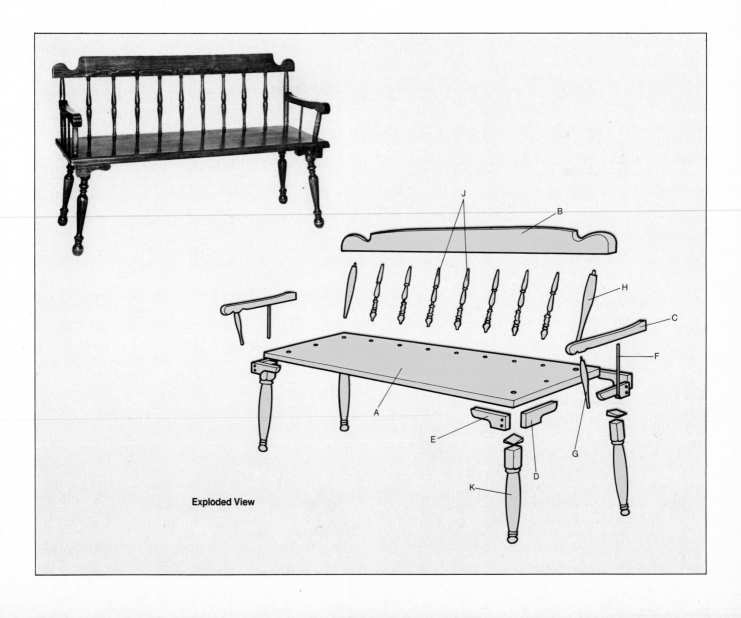

Exploded View

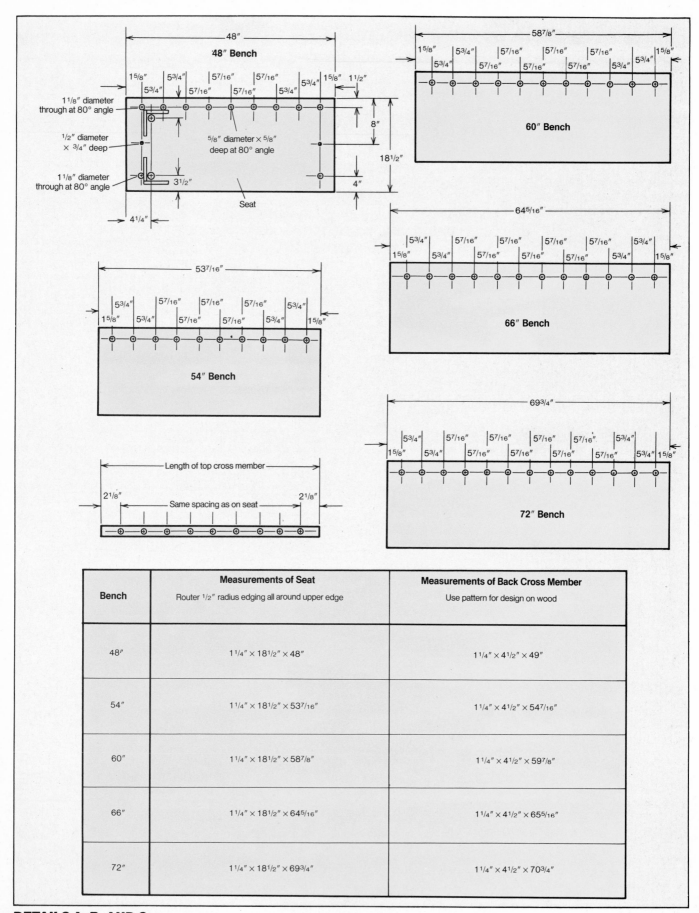

Bench	Measurements of Seat Router $1/2$" radius edging all around upper edge	Measurements of Back Cross Member Use pattern for design on wood
48"	$1^1/4$" × $18^1/2$" × 48"	$1^1/4$" × $4^1/2$" × 49"
54"	$1^1/4$" × $18^1/2$" × $53^7/16$"	$1^1/4$" × $4^1/2$" × $54^7/16$"
60"	$1^1/4$" × $18^1/2$" × $58^7/8$"	$1^1/4$" × $4^1/2$" × $59^7/8$"
66"	$1^1/4$" × $18^1/2$" × $64^5/16$"	$1^1/4$" × $4^1/2$" × $65^5/16$"
72"	$1^1/4$" × $18^1/2$" × $69^3/4$"	$1^1/4$" × $4^1/2$" × $70^3/4$"

DETAILS A, B, AND C
SEAT AND BACK SIZE CHART, SEAT AND BACK LAYOUTS

holes are to be drilled; also, check the plan (Side View) for orientation.

These holes are best drilled on a drill press with a simple jig to hold the seat at an 80° angle relative to the drill. The specifications for this jig are given in Detail D.

Position and C-clamp the jig on the drill-press table so that the drill hits the seat on the awl marks as you slide it along the jig. Drill the holes for the back spindles through the seat. Then drill the front and back post holes. For these larger holes, you should drill through one side until the bit just breaks the other surface; then flip the work over and complete the hole from the other side. Lastly, drill the perpendicular arm-support hole in each end.

To finish machining the seat, round the entire top edge with a 1/2-inch-radius quarter round router bit.

STEP 2
MACHINING THE BACK
Cut the back from 1 1/4-inch stock to the size given. Use the pattern given in Detail E to mark the cuts on either end of the back (mark one end and then flip over the pattern to mark the other). Consult Detail C for the location of the spindle holes in the bottom edge of the back, make a paper template, and mark the location of the holes. Bore the holes with a drill press before cutting the decorative ends of the back. After drilling the holes, use a band saw or saber saw to make the cuts.

STEP 3
CUTTING AND DRILLING THE ARMS
Cut the blanks for the arms from 1 1/2-inch stock to the size given in the Materials List. Make a stiff paper template to trace onto the blanks from the pattern given in Detail F. Mark the drill holes on the blanks, as shown in Detail G. Before shaping the arms, drill the holes indicated, taking care to get the angles correct. After drilling, use a band saw to cut out the arms as shown in Details F and H.

Round all the edges of the arms (except the edges of the rear drill

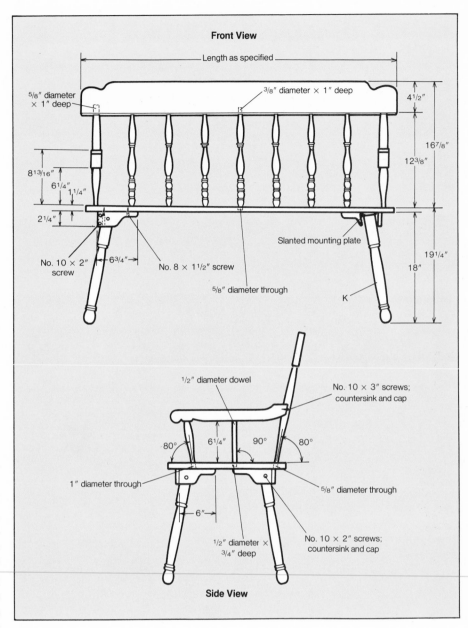

Front View

Length as specified

5/8" diameter × 1" deep

3/8" diameter × 1" deep

4 1/2"

16 7/8"

12 3/8"

8 13/16"

6 1/4"

1 1/4"

2 1/4"

No. 10 × 2" screw

6 3/4"

No. 8 × 1 1/2" screw

Slanted mounting plate

5/8" diameter through

19 1/4"

18"

K

1/2" diameter dowel

No. 10 × 3" screws; countersink and cap

80°

6 1/4"

90°

80°

1" diameter through

5/8" diameter through

6"

No. 10 × 2" screws; countersink and cap

1/2" diameter × 3/4" deep

Side View

hole) with a 1/4-inch-radius quarter round router bit.

STEP 4
MACHINING THE LEG BRACES
The bench has four sets of leg braces, whose parts should be of maple or birch. Transfer the pattern given in Detail J for side and front braces, and cut with band saw.

Mark the braces for the two holes to be drilled through the bottom of each one, and for the two holes to be drilled in the side of each front brace, as shown in Detail K. Note that all holes are countersunk pilot holes for the screws that will attach the braces to each other and to the bench.

STEP 5
TURNING THE SPINDLES AND POSTS
Each length bench requires a different number of back spindles. The critical dimensions for these spindles are given in Detail L for those who wish to turn their own. You can, of course, order the spindles pre-turned and finished.

When turning your own, start with maple or birch blanks 1 1/8 inches square by 16 inches long. The exact design of this spindle is up to you. Two 1/2-inch-diameter birch dowels 7 1/2 inches long serve as center supports under the arms.

For the front and rear posts, see

Details M and N for a suggested design and the critical dimensions. Cut the blanks from 1½-inch stock.

STEP 6
ACQUIRING THE LEGS

You will need four 2⅛-to 2½-inch-diameter 18-inch legs with hanger bolts. Lumberyards, hardware suppliers, and discount stores are good sources for legs of this type, or you can make your own. They will be attached to the bench on slanted mounting plates, as specified in the Materials List.

STEP 7
SANDING THE PARTS

Rough- and finish-sand the top and sides of the seat and all surfaces on the back. Use either a wide belt sander or a portable belt sander for the flat surfaces, and follow up with an orbital or straight-line finish sander for these parts. The bottom surface of the seat need not be sanded at all. To sand the decorative cuts in the back, use a spindle sander or drum sander attachment for your drill.

The leg braces require no sanding at this time. The back spindles, dowels, front and back posts, and legs either will have been completely sanded by the manufacturer or should be rough- and finish-sanded while in the lathe.

STEP 8
ATTACHING THE BACK AND ARMS TO THE SEAT

When gluing a spindle or dowel into a hole, it is best to place an appropriately small amount of glue into the hole by pouring it down around the sides of the hole and then spreading it around inside the hole with a matchstick or other suitable instrument. Do not place glue on the shank of the dowel, since, as the dowel enters the hole, the extra glue will rub off and spread out over the surface to be stained later.

Glue the back posts and back spindles into the back; then immediately glue them into the seat, fixing them in place with pipe or bar clamps. Also glue the ½-inch-diame-

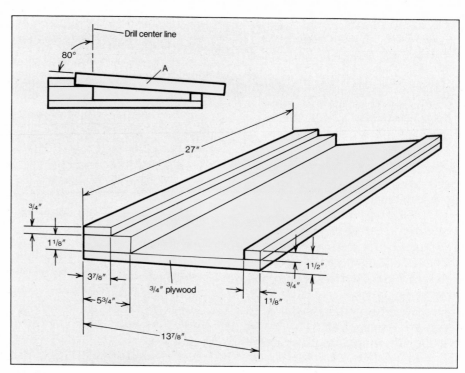

DETAIL D
DRILLING JIG

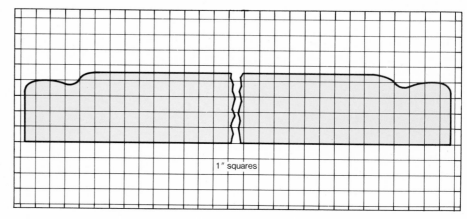

DETAIL E
BACK PATTERN

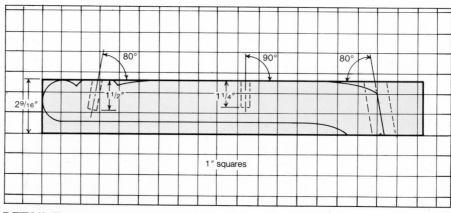

DETAIL F
ARM PATTERN

ter dowels and front posts into the arms and then into the seat at the same time. Cut several pieces of scrap wood to 12⅜ inches in length to use as temporary spacers between the seat and bottom of the back to keep the distance uniform and accurate while clamping. Cut a few more pieces of scrap to 6¼ inches and use in the same way while clamping the front and center posts.

Secure the arm to the back post with a No. 10 × 3-inch wood screw after countersinking ⅜ inch deep with a ½-inch-diameter drill bit and drilling through the back post with a 3/16-inch-diameter bit. If the arm is of pine, no pilot hole need be drilled. However, if the arm is of a hardwood, pre-drill a pilot hole into the arm the same diameter as the inside diameter of the screw thread. Before inserting screws into hardwood arms, rub soap or wax across the threads to lubricate them for easier entry. Glue in screw plugs to cover the 3-inch screws, taking care not to spread glue onto the surrounding wood which will be finished later.

STEP 9
ATTACHING THE LEGS
Remove the pipe clamps from the seat assembly after the glue has set and turn the assembly upside down on your workbench so that the legs may be installed. Position a slanted mounting plate in position, as indicated on the 48-inch seat plan in Detail B. Follow the instructions included with the plate and, using the hardware also included, fasten the plate to the bench. Fasten the other three plates in position, taking care to see that they are properly oriented. Screw hanger bolts into the top of the legs, then screw the legs into the plates. Set the bench right side up on an absolutely flat surface, and check to see whether it is level. If one leg is longer than the others, grip it firmly and twist tighter to shorten it to the length of the other three legs.

STEP 10
ADDING THE LEG BRACES
First attach the side braces to the

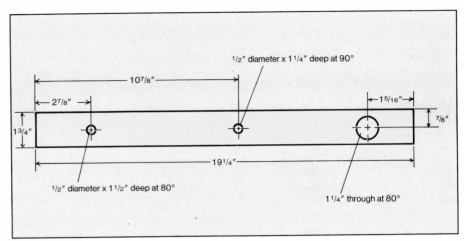

DETAIL G
ARM LAYOUT

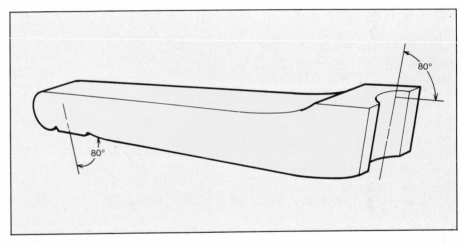

DETAIL H
ARM JOINERY

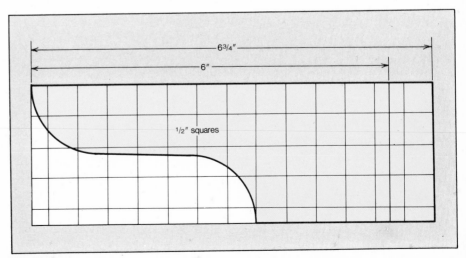

DETAIL J
LEG BRACE DETAIL

front braces, as shown in Detail K. The front leg braces overlap the side leg braces, and each joint is glued and then fastened with two No. 8 × 1½-inch countersunk screws covered with screw plugs. The joint between the side and front leg braces, along with the visible front and side surfaces, should be sanded with 120-grit sandpaper.

These assemblies are positioned as shown for the 48-inch bench in Detail B, and secured with No. 10 × 2-inch wood screws through pre-drilled holes and covered with screw plugs.

Finally secure each leg with two No. 10 × 2-inch flathead wood screws, as shown in the plan (Front View), and cover the screw heads with screw plugs. Cross-screwing the legs anchors them securely to the braces and produces a very strong, firm leg-support system, eliminating the need for stretchers or other braces running from leg to leg.

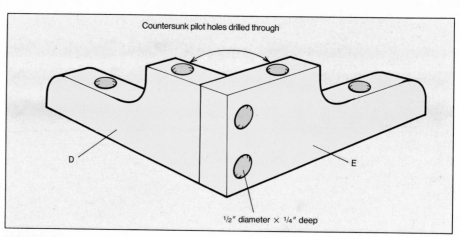

DETAIL K
LEG BRACE JOINERY

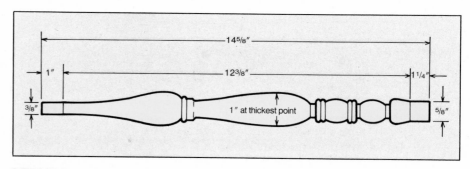

DETAIL L
BACK SPINDLE LAYOUT

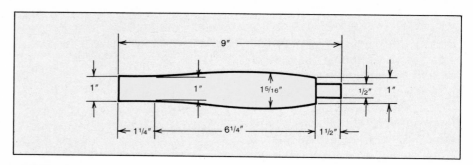

DETAIL M
FRONT POST LAYOUT

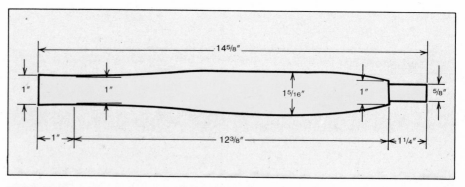

DETAIL N
BACK POST LAYOUT

LOVE SEAT

MATERIALS LIST

A Legs (2), 1¼" × 17" × 18¼"
B Seat (1), 1¼" × 17" × 48"
C Leg braces (2), ¾" × 7⅞" × 46"
D Arms (2), ¾" × 10¾" × 16"
E Back center end pieces (2), ¾" × 3⅛"
   × 4½"
F Back bottom end pieces (2), ¾" × 1½"
   × 4½"
G Spindles (7), ¾" diameter × 4⅜"
H Bottom back cross member (1), ¾" ×
   2½" × 46⅜"
J Back (1), ¾" × 8½" × 46⅜"

HARDWARE

No. 8 × 1½" flathead wood screws
No. 10 × 2" flathead wood screws
4d finishing nails

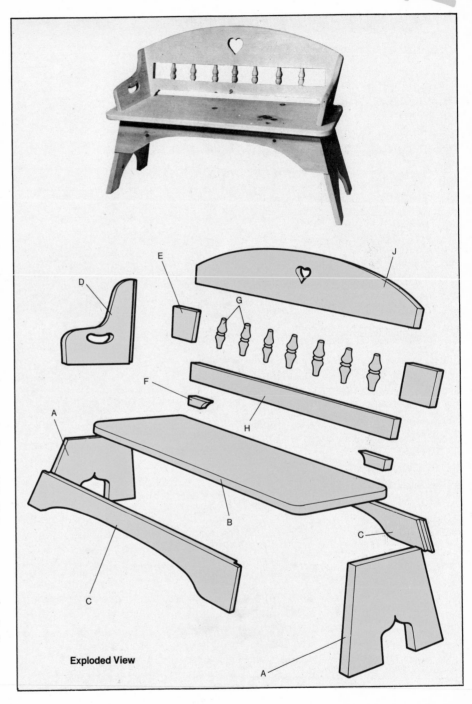

Exploded View

Although this project, when completed, shows simple lines and an uncomplicated style, the many angular cuts that must be accurately machined, as well as the many assembly steps, mean that it is a challenge. The experienced woodworker will spend at least fifteen or even twenty hours machining, sanding, and assembling the love seat. But the result is well worth the time. This piece is a handsome addition to a foyer, family room, or living room decorated in an American country style.

STEP 1
GLUING UP STOCK

Glue up stock to make boards of sufficient width for the leg section, seat, and back. See the Gluing section, pages 11-12, for more information.

STEP 2
MACHINING THE LEGS

Cut the leg section to the dimensions given in the Materials List. Both legs will be cut in the same manner, as shown in Detail A. To cut the top and bottom edge of the two legs, set the radial arm or table saw blade at a 75° angle. Lay the board flat on the table of the saw and trim the left-hand edge with the 75° angle

cut. Next cut the first leg to 18¼ inches, using the same 75° saw setting. Finally, make the last 75° angle cut to trim the second leg to 18¼ inches.

Now trim both of the legs as shown so that there is a taper to the boards, as shown on the pattern. Be

sure to maintain the 17-inch width at the bottom. The top should be 14¾ inch wide.

Transfer the leg pattern in Detail B onto the boards and cut the design with a band, jig, or saber saw. Rout with a ¼-inch-radius quarter round bit along the outside edges of the legs where indicated in Detail B, beginning 7⅞ inches below the upper edge and working all the way around the legs until reaching a point 7⅞ inches below the upper edge on the other side.

STEP 3
MACHINING THE SEAT
Cut the seat to the dimensions given in the Materials List. Drill four 3/16-inch-diameter holes exactly 2⅞ inches from each end of the board and 2 inches in from the long edge of the board, as shown in Detail C. The holes are to be drilled at an 80° angle from the outside edge toward the opposite end as shown. These are pilot holes, which are required during assembly of the unit.

Cut the corners of the seat to a 2⅜-inch radius and round them, top and bottom, to a ⅜-inch radius to give the seat a smooth, rounded appearance.

STEP 4
MACHINING THE LEG BRACES
Leg braces are cut from one board, as shown in Detail D. Set the table or radial arm saw to cut the 75°-angle ends. Transfer the pattern to the board and cut with a band, jig, or saber saw. Rout the outer side and bottom edges, and then cut the ends with a dado 1¼ inches wide by ⅜ inch deep, as shown in Detail D. (Rout the ⅜-inch radius first, and then dado to provide support for the router bit.)

STEP 5
MACHINING THE ARMS
Cut the arm sections to the dimensions given in the Materials List. Using a table saw or radial arm saw, make the two 77°-angle cuts shown in Detail E. Then set the saw blade at 80° and miter the bottom edges so that the arms are both angled away from the seat surface; mark the cuts so that the board will be 10¾ inches wide after they are made. Next, transfer the pattern given in Detail E. Cut out the two arms. Using a dado blade on a table saw or a router, machine the groove along the inside back edge of the arm section . To make the handle cutouts, drill 1⅛-inch holes at

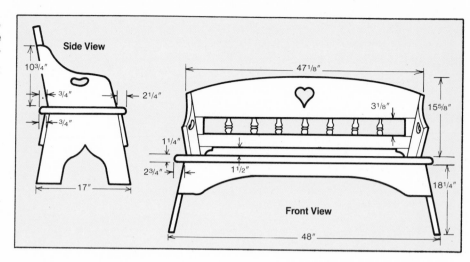

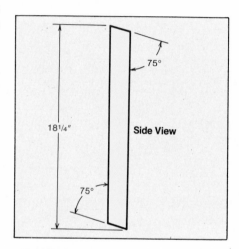

DETAIL A
LEG LAYOUT

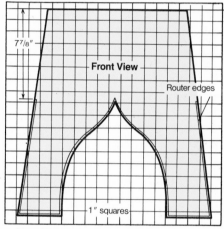

DETAIL B
LEG PATTERN

the points you have marked from the pattern—don't drill these holes all the way through the stock—and flip the board over to complete the drilling where the bit point emerges, in order to avoid splintering the wood. Use a saber or jig saw to connect the holes.

STEP 6
MACHINING THE BACK PIECES
The back assembly requires some sanding and assembly during the machining process. Cut the two ¾-inch stock center back end pieces to the dimensions given in the Materials List. The two bottom back end pieces are cut from ¾-inch stock and must have one long edge machined with a 77° angle as shown in Detail F.

The seven spindles required may

be purchased finished or hand-turned on a lathe to the specifications given in Detail G. You may be able to cut these short spindles from longer stock spindles.

Cut the top back cross member and the bottom back cross member to the dimensions given in the Materials List and drill the holes into which the spindles will be set at the locations shown in Detail H. Mark the spindle positions carefully. The first is located exactly 8 3/16 inches from the end. Measure from the same end for each hole. The size of these holes is determined by the diameter of the spindles themselves. The holes should be ⅝ inch deep.

Rough- and finish-sand the inside edges of the back assembly so that no further sanding will be required when the spindles are in place.

Glue the spindles in place, along with the center back end pieces and the bottom back end pieces, as shown in Detail J. Set in bar clamps as if you were gluing boards to width.

Once the glue is set on the back assembly, the side edges may be cut. Mark a point 5½ inches down from each of the top outside corners as shown in the plan (Front View). From these points cut each side down to the bottom edges at a 10° angle and with a 3° bevel. Do this with a table or radial arm saw. Trace the patterns on the top back cross member and the back bottom end pieces. Cut these patterns with a band, jig, or saber saw.

Mark the center of the top back cross member and drill a hole inside the heart cutout to start the saw blade. The opening will be enlarged to the shape of the heart. Cut out the heart shape with a saber saw. Rout the edge of the heart cutout with a ⅜-inch-radius quarter round bit.

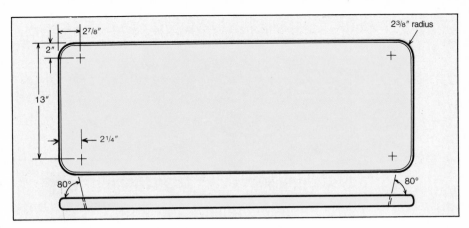

DETAIL C
SEAT LAYOUT

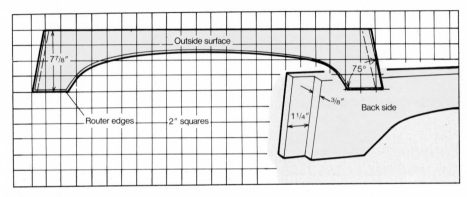

DETAIL D
LEG BRACE LAYOUT AND PATTERN

STEP 7
SANDING THE PIECES
Rough- and finish-sand the surfaces that will show, as well as the edges of the legs. The underside of the seat and the outside perimeter of the leg assembly need be rough-sanded only. Rough- and finish-sand the edges and upper surface of the seat.

The outer edges and face of the leg braces must be rough- and finish-sanded. The bottom edges may be rough-sanded if you wish. Rough- and finish-sand the back and bottom edges of the arms, as well as the entire back assembly.

STEP 8
ASSEMBLING THE BACK AND ARM UNIT
Glue and secure the arms to the back with 4d finishing nails. Use bar clamps to hold the unit square until the glue has set.

After the glue has set, rout the arm/back assembly's outside and inside upper edges with a ⅜-inch-radius quarter round bit. Finish-sand the routed edges and glue joints.

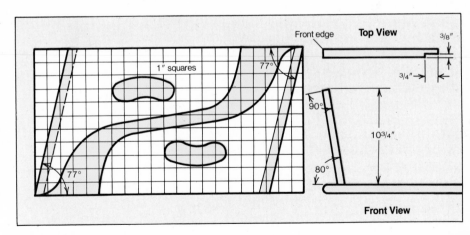

DETAIL E
ARM LAYOUT AND PATTERN

STEP 9
ASSEMBLING THE LEGS AND LEG BRACES
Glue the legs to the leg braces. Secure the joints with 4d finishing nails, clamp with bar clamps, and allow glue to set. Finish-sand the glued joints.

STEP 10
ATTACHING THE ARM/BACK ASSEMBLY TO THE SEAT
Place the arm/back assembly on a table and turn upside down. Brace the assembly so that it is secure.

Place the seat upside down on the arm/back assembly. Attach these

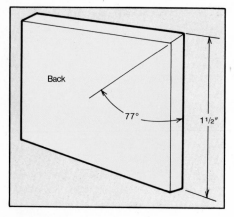

DETAIL F
BACK BOTTOM END DETAIL

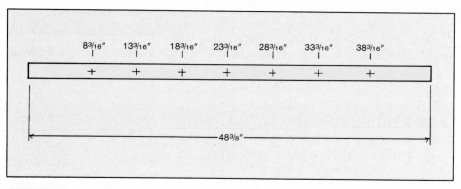

DETAIL H
SPINDLE SPACING DETAIL

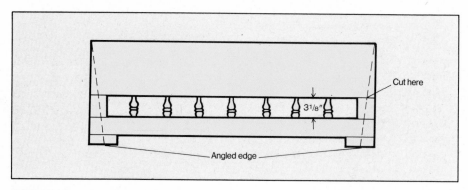

DETAIL J
BACK ASSEMBLY DETAIL

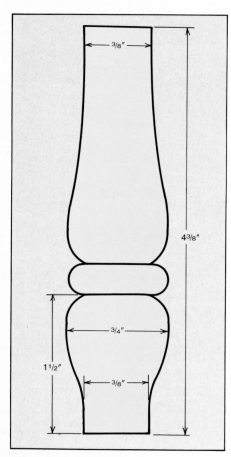

DETAIL G
SPINDLE LAYOUT

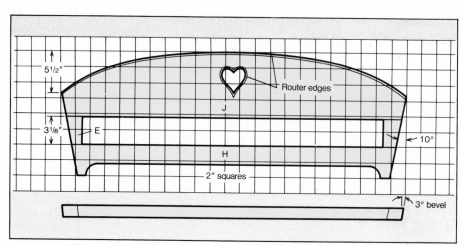

DETAIL K
BACK PATTERN

pieces with No. 10 × 2-inch screws driven through pre-drilled pilot holes.

STEP 11
ATTACHING THE LEG ASSEMBLY
Place the leg assembly upside down on the inverted seat. The back leg brace should be ¾ inch in from the back edge of the seat. The assembly should be 2¾ inches in from each side of the seat.

Drill four or five relatively evenly spaced pilot holes at a slight angle through each leg. Attach the legs to the seat with No. 8 × 1½-inch wood screws.

STEP 12
LEVELING THE LOVE SEAT
Place the love seat on a level surface, or wherever you plan to use it, and check to see whether it is level.

If the unit is not level, sand any high spots from bottom of legs.

SIMPLE BOOKCASE DESK

MATERIALS LIST

A Top (1), 3/4" × 16" × 46"
B Shelves (2), 3/4" × 15" × 23"
C Sides (2), 3/4" × 15 1/4" × 29 3/4"
D Loose side (1), 3/4" × 15 1/4" × 29 3/4"
E Drawer-enclosure back (1), 3/4" ×
    7 3/4" × 20"
F Brace (1), 3/4" × 3 1/4" × 20"
G Top cross member (1), 3/4" × 1" × 22 1/4"
H Top back brace (1), 3/4" × 1 1/8" × 22 1/4"
J Front foot (1), 3/4" × 3 1/2" × 23 3/4"
K Drawer-enclosure cross member (top)
    (1), 3/4" × 1" × 20"
L Drawer-enclosure cross members
    (bottom) (2), 3/4" × 1" × 20"
M Drawer-enclosure cross members
    (vertical) (2), 3/4" × 1" × 4"
N Top braces (3), 3/4" × 1 1/8" × 12 1/2"
P Back (1), 1/4" × 23" × 27"

DRAWER

Q Front (1), 3/4" × 4 3/4" × 18 3/4"
R Sides (2), 3/4" × 3 1/2" × 12 3/4"
S Back (1), 3/4" × 3 1/2" × 16 1/4"
T Bottom (1), 1/4" × 12 1/8" × 16 3/4"

HARDWARE

Drawer pull (1)
Monorail drawer slide
No. 10 × 2" flathead wood screws
No. 8 × 1 1/4" flathead wood screws
4d finishing nails

If you don't want as large a desk as the seven-drawer desk on page 124, try this one. It has an ample working area and its own shelves for books. This is a perfect student desk or small desk for paperwork and a telephone in the kitchen.

The techniques called for in this project are standard to all the basic cabinets in the book. The project is easy, and success with it depends on making the precise cuts called for in the directions.

STEP 1
MACHINING THE TOP

If you need to glue up boards to make the 16-inch width of the top, see the Gluing section, pages 11-12, for details.

Round the front and two side edges of the top with a 3/8-inch-radius quarter round router bit.

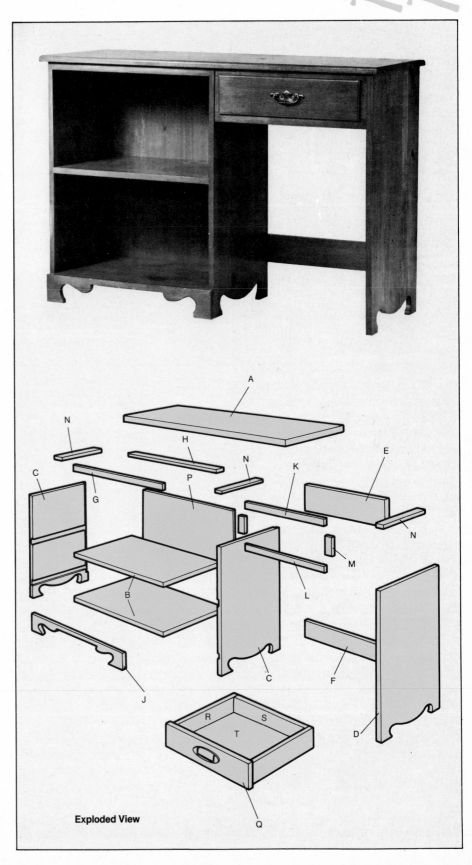

Exploded View

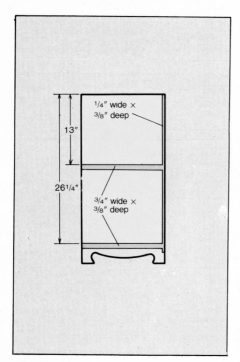

**DETAIL A
SIDE LAYOUT**

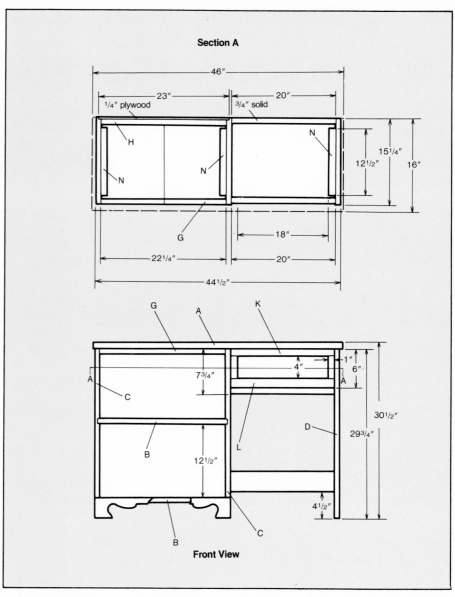

Section A

Front View

STEP 2
MACHINING THE SIDES
Machine the sides with standard back and shelf joinery, as shown in Detail A. See specifications #1 and #4, page 17, for details on these grooves. The choice of design cutouts in the front foot, at the foot of the sides, and on the loose side (the outer side) is left to you. See specification #31, page 24, for sample designs. These pieces may also be left plain if you wish.

STEP 3
CONSTRUCTING THE DRAWER
The desk has one drawer with an overlap front designed for a monorail slide system. See specifications #18 and #19, page 21, for details on the construction of this drawer. Use the dimensions given in the Materials List for this project. Round the leading edges of the front with a ⅜-inch-radius quarter round router bit.

STEP 4
SANDING
Rough- and finish-sand the top and shelves only on the top surfaces, plus the rounded edges of the top. Rough- and finish-sand the outside and inside surfaces of all the sides. The drawer-enclosure back, plywood back, and top braces do not need sanding; the top cross member, top back brace, all drawer-enclosure components, and the face and top edge of the front foot need only be rough-sanded.

For details on sanding the drawer parts, see the Sanding section.

STEP 5
ASSEMBLING THE DESK
For general information on assembling this kind of project, see pages 25–32 in the Assembly section. The specific steps are as follows:

(1) Build the drawer-enclosure grille, glue, and secure with four No. 10 × 2-inch wood screws. Clamp until dry, and then (2) insert the shelves into the sides. (3) Install the top back brace and top cross member with glue and 4d finishing nails. Use bar or pipe clamps to hold until dry. (4) Attach front foot with glue and 4d finishing nails; then sand the ends flush with the sides, using a portable belt sander and finish sander. (5) Complete sanding the drawer-enclosure grille. (6) Install the drawer-enclosure grille and back, as well as the brace between the loose side and the bookcase section. Use glue and put 4d finishing nails through the sides into these pieces; hold with a pipe clamp. (7) Attach the top braces. (8) Attach the top. (9) Install the drawer. (10) Attach the ¼-inch plywood back after finishing the unit.

SECRETARY DESK

MATERIALS LIST

DESK CABINET
A Top (1), 1¼″ × 10⅛″ × 34½″
B Sides (2), ¾″ × 18⅝″ × 38⅞″
C Front foot (1), ¾″ × 4½″ × 34½″
D Side feet (2), ¾″ × 4½″ × 19⅜″
E Drop lid (1), ¾″ × 12³/₁₆″ × 28¼″
F Drop-lid ends (2), ¾″ × 2″ × 12³/₁₆″
G Desk top (1), ¾″ × 17⅝″ × 32¼″
H Bottom back brace (1), ¾″ × 1¼″ × 31½″
J Top cross member (1), ¾″ × 1½″ × 32¼″
K Drawer braces (2), ¾″ × 1¾″ × 32¼″
L Bottom cross member (1), ¾″ × 2″ × 32¼″
M Upper back (1), ¼″ × 9¼″ × 32¼″
N Lower back (1), ¼″ × 27½″ × 32¼″

CUBBYHOLE SECTION
P Top/bottom (1 each), ¾″ × 8½″ × 30¾″
Q Sides (2), ¾″ × 8½″ × 6⅞″
R Center walls (2), ¾″ × 8½″ × 6⅛″
S Shelves (2), ¾″ × 8½″ × 7½″

CUBBYHOLE DRAWERS
T Fronts (2), ¾″ × 2¼″ × 6¹¹/₁₆″
U Sides (4), ¾″ × 2¼″ × 8⅛″
V Backs (2), ¾″ × 2¼″ × 5³/₁₆″
W Bottoms (2), ¼″ × 5¹¹/₁₆″ × 7¾″

DESK DRAWERS*
X Front (1), 1¼″ × 6¼″ × 32¼″
Y Sides (2), ¾″ × 5¼″ × 17⅜″
Z Back (1), ¾″ × 5¼″ × 29″
AA Front (1), 1¼″ × 7¼″ × 32¼″
BB Sides (2), ¾″ × 6¼″ × 17⅜″
CC Back (1), ¾″ × 6¼″ × 29″
DD Front (1), 1¼″ × 8¼″ × 32¼″
EE Sides (2), ¾″ × 7¼″ × 17⅜″
FF Back (1), ¾″ × 7¼″ × 29″
GG Bottoms (3), ½″ × 16⅝″ × 29½″

*Dimensions of drawer parts will change depending on the hardware used to mount the drawers.

HARDWARE
Drawer side rollers (3 pairs)
Desk lid hinges (1 pair)
Large brass knob
Small brass knobs (2)
Drawer pulls (6)
⅜″ screw plugs
No. 8 × 1¼″ flathead wood screws
No. 8 × 2″ flathead wood screws
4d finishing nails
1″ brads

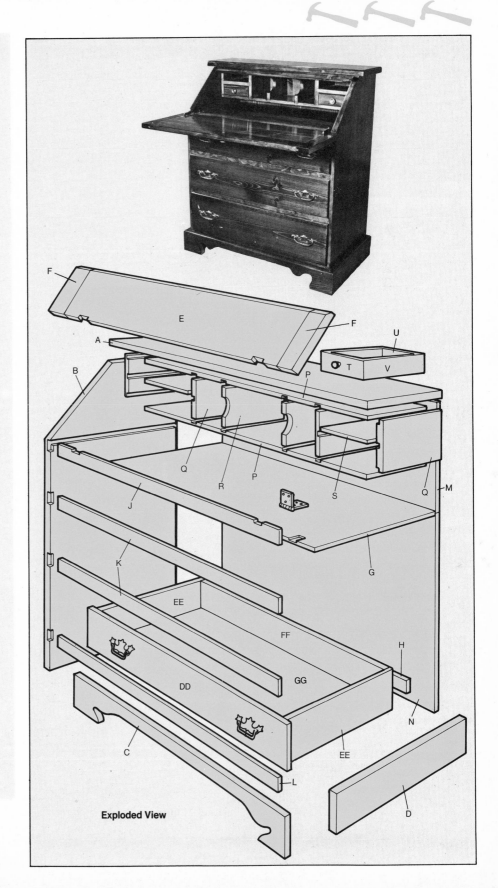

Exploded View

The secretary desk has a generous amount of storage in the three large drawers. In addition, the top section provides two small drawers and adjoining cubbyhole compartments.

This project is difficult. It takes great care to produce accurate angle cuts, machine the sides and drawers, and install the drop-lid desk surface.

As with several of the projects for larger pieces of furniture, the size and weight of the desk require handling by more than one person during the assembly stage.

STEP 1
MACHINING THE TOP AND SIDES
You may have to glue boards to width for the top and sides. See Gluing section, pages 11-12, for detailed instructions. After cutting the top, round the front and side edges with a 3/8-inch-radius quarter round router bit.

After cutting the sides to size, make the angle cut and cut the joinery, as shown in Detail A. The two sides are a mirror-image pair. Be especially careful when cutting the stopped dado for the top cross member, so that you do not break off part of the triangular area just above the dado at the end of the angle cut. See specification #5, page 17, for details on cutting the joinery.

STEP 2
MACHINING THE FEET
Since the foot arrangement wraps around the cabinet, cut 45° miters on both ends of the front piece and the joining edge of each side. If you want to make a 3/8-inch-radius standard rounded edging on the leading edge of these pieces, do it before cutting the miters.

STEP 3
MACHINING THE DESK TOP AND DROP LID
The desk top and drop lid are cut from 3/4-inch stock. To prevent cross-grain warpage, end pieces are splined onto the center section. See Detail B and specification #8, page 18, for details on machining the grooves for the splines.

Glue and clamp the sections

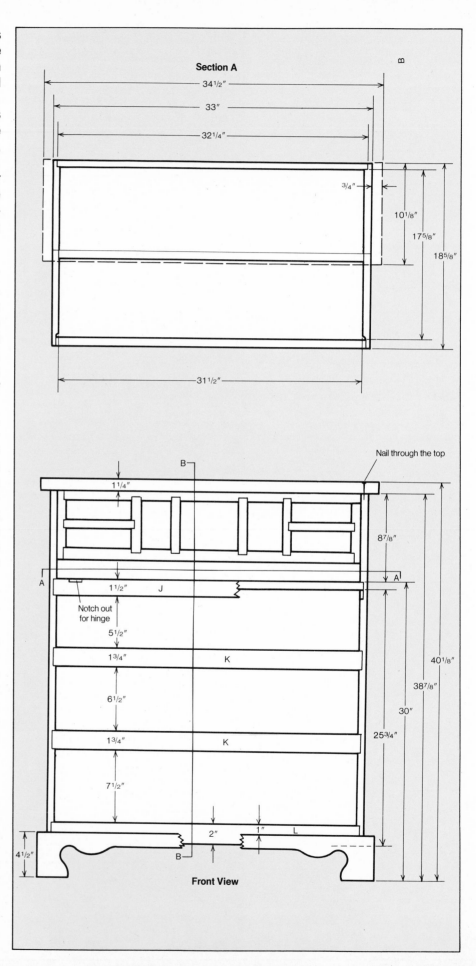

Section A

Front View

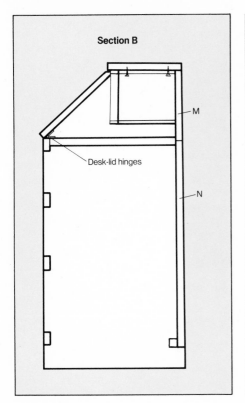

Section B

M

Desk-lid hinges

N

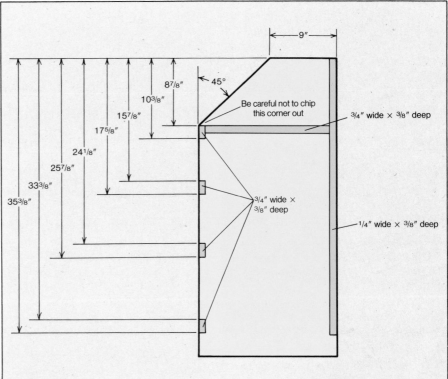

9″

8⁷⁄₈″

45°

10³⁄₈″

Be careful not to chip
this corner out

³⁄₄″ wide × ³⁄₈″ deep

15⁷⁄₈″

17⁵⁄₈″

24¹⁄₈″

25⁷⁄₈″

33³⁄₈″

35³⁄₈″

³⁄₄″ wide ×
³⁄₈″ deep

¼″ wide × ³⁄₈″ deep

**DETAIL A
SIDE LAYOUT**

together, placing glue in the grooves and then slipping the splines into the grooves. Check both for square and flatness.

When the glue has dried, rough-sand to make the splines even with the ends of the drop lid. Rout a ³⁄₈-inch 45° chamfer on the edge, as shown in Detail C.

STEP 4
MACHINING THE BACK PIECES
The back is made in two parts. The upper back is cut from ¼-inch plywood faced with the same wood you are using for the desk. The lower back will not be visible, and so it can be of any ¼-inch plywood sheathing.

STEP 5
MACHINING THE CUBBYHOLE PIECES
All cubbyhole-section parts are cut from ¾-inch stock. The top and bottom are dadoed alike, according to the specifications in Detail D; see specification #4, page 17, for details on cutting the standard shelf dadoes. The sides and center walls are also grooved with standard shelf

dadoes and rabbets, as indicated in Details E and F. Copy and transfer the center-wall pattern to two additional center walls, and cut them out with a band saw.

STEP 6
MACHINING THE DRAWER PARTS
The cubbyhole section has two hand-fitted flush-front drawers. For details on machining the parts for these drawers see specification #22, page 21.

For details on machining the parts for the desk's three larger drawers (with overlapping fronts, made for side rollers), see specification #17, page 21. Round the fronts of these three drawers with a ³⁄₈-inch-radius quarter round router bit.

STEP 7
SANDING THE PIECES
Rough-sand the underside of the top for the first 2 inches in from the edges. Rough- and finish-sand the front and side edges and the top surface of the desk top.

Rough- and finish-sand the inside

surface of the sides above the shelf groove, the diagonally cut edge, and the outside faces, as well as the top edge and face of the feet, the top face of the desk, and all edges and surfaces of the drop lid. The drop-lid pieces were glued and then rough-sanded during the machining step; now special attention must be given to finish-sanding the surfaces. The drawer braces and cross members need only be rough-sanded. Do not bother to sand the bottom back brace or the plywood pieces.

Rough- and finish-sand all components of the cubbyhole section except the upper surface of the top and the outside surfaces of the sides (these areas will not be seen).

STEP 8
ASSEMBLING THE DESK CABINET
Basic information on assembling a cabinet is given in the Assembly section on pages 25–27. The sequence for this project follows. Refer to the plans (Top, Front, and Side views) throughout the assembly sequence.

Assemble sides, cross members,

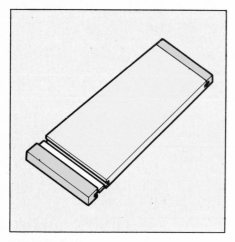

DETAIL B
DROP-LID JOINERY DETAIL

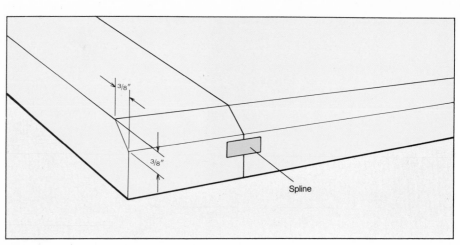

DETAIL C
DROP-LID EDGE DETAIL

Spline

drawer braces, bottom back brace, desk top, and lower back with glue and 4d finishing nails. Check for square and then clamp. Allow the glue to dry.

STEP 9
ASSEMBLING THE CUBBYHOLE SECTIONS

Glue and use 4d finishing nails to nail the top, bottom, and sides of the cubbyhole section. Check for square and clamp.

Apply glue in the dadoes and install the dividers. Clamp and allow to dry.

STEP 10
ASSEMBLING THE DRAWERS

Follow the instructions in the Assembly section, pages 29–31, to assemble each of the drawers.

STEP 11
ATTACHING THE FEET

Finish-sand all glue joints; then glue the front foot into position and clamp. Attach the side feet, carefully mating the 45° joints that have been applied with glue. Secure the corners with countersunk No. 8 × 1¼-inch wood screws and cover these with wood screw plugs.

STEP 12
ATTACHING TOP AND CUBBYHOLE SECTION

Secure the top with two 6d finishing nails driven into each side, or with

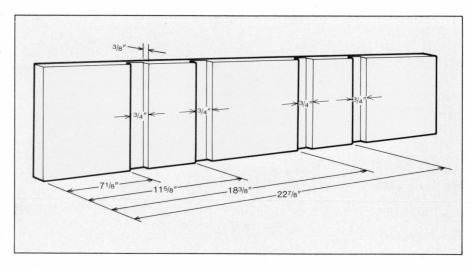

DETAIL D
CUBBYHOLE TOP/BOTTOM LAYOUT

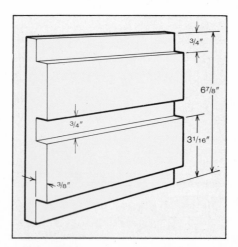

DETAIL E
CUBBYHOLE
SIDE LAYOUT

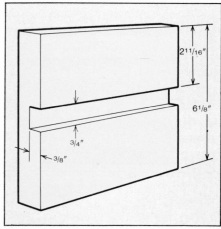

DETAIL F
CUBBYHOLE
CENTER WALL LAYOUT

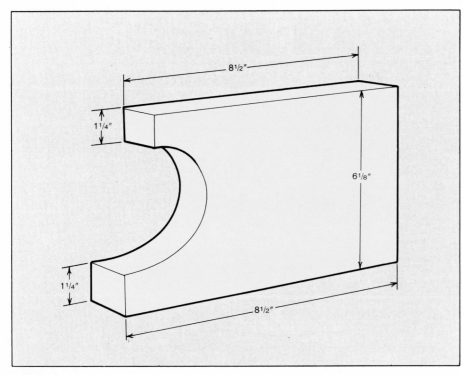

DETAIL G
CUBBYHOLE CENTER WALL PATTERN

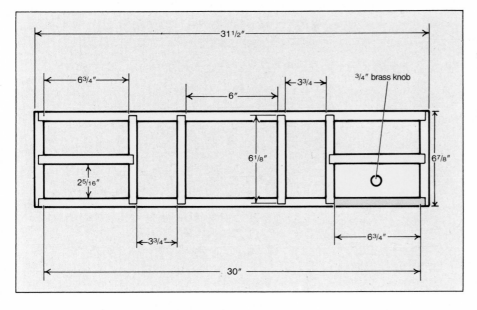

CUBBYHOLE FRONT VIEW

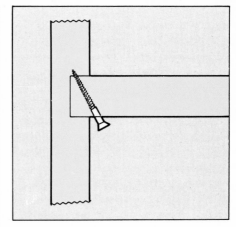

TOENAILING

No. 8 × 2-inch wood screws. Set nails and fill the holes.

Finish-sand all glue joints in the cubbyhole section. Install it into the desk by driving No. 8 × 1¼-inch wood screws into pre-drilled pilot holes through the top and sides of cubbyhole section and into the case top and sides.

STEP 13
COMPLETING ASSEMBLY PROCESS

When you have completed staining and finishing the desk, attach the upper back with 1-inch brads.

Check the fit of the small hand-fitted drawers and make any adjustments needed by sanding parts of the drawer.

After installing the pulls on the drawers, install the larger drawers, following the directions on pages 29–31 in the Assembly section.

Attach the drop lid, using the desk-lid hinges (see the plan, Side View). Mortise the desk top and drop lid for the hinges, as needed for notch required. Fit carefully so the lid moves smoothly.

SEVEN-DRAWER DESK

MATERIALS LIST

A Outer sides (2), 3/4" × 231/4" × 293/4"
B Inner sides (2), 3/4" × 23" × 293/4"
C Top (1), 11/4" × 24" × 57"
D Top middle cross member (1), 3/4" × 3/4" × 22"
E Bottom middle cross member (1), 3/4" × 11/4" × 22"
F Vertical cross members (2), 3/4" × 11/4" × 51/4"
G Top cross members (2), 3/4" × 3/4" × 16"
H Shelf braces (2), 3/4" × 11/4" × 16"
J Drawer braces (4), 3/4" × 11/2" × 16"
K Bottom cross members (2), 3/4" × 2" × 16"
L Connector braces (4), 3/4" × 11/4" × 51/4"
M Top back braces (2), 3/4" × 11/8" × 151/4"
N Top side braces (4), 3/4" × 11/8" × 201/4"
P Top center brace (1), 3/4" × 11/8" × 22"
Q Outer feet (2), 3/4" × 31/2" × 24"
R Inner feet (2), 3/4" × 31/2" × 233/4"
S Front feet (2), 3/4" × 31/2" × 181/4"
T Back (1), 1/4" × 293/4" × 543/4"
U Pullout shelves (2), 3/4" × 151/8" × 233/8"
V Shelf runners (2), 3/4" × 16" × 221/4"
W Shelf levelers (2), 3/4" × 3/4" × 211/8"

DESK DRAWERS*

X Fronts (4), 3/4" × 413/16" × 16"
Y Sides (8), 3/4" × 39/16" × 22"
Z Backs (4), 3/4" × 39/16" × 125/8"
AA Bottoms (4), 1/4" × 131/8" × 213/8"

KNEEHOLE DRAWER*

BB Front (1), 3/4" × 4" × 201/4"
CC Sides (2), 3/4" × 31/2" × 22"
DD Back (1), 3/4" × 31/2" × 177/8"
EE Bottom (1), 1/4" × 183/8" × 213/8"

FILE DRAWERS*

FF Fronts (2), 3/4" × 113/4" × 16"
GG Sides (4), 3/4" × 101/2" × 22"
HH Backs (2), 3/4" × 101/2" × 125/8"
JJ Bottoms (2), 1/4" × 131/8" × 213/8"
KK Drawer dividers (2), 1/4" × 10" × 131/8"

*Dimensions of drawer parts will change depending on the drawer hardware used.

HARDWARE

Side-mounted drawer rollers (6 pair)
Brass knobs (2)
Drawer pulls (7)
No. 8 × 11/4" flathead wood screws
4d finishing nails
1" brads
Felt

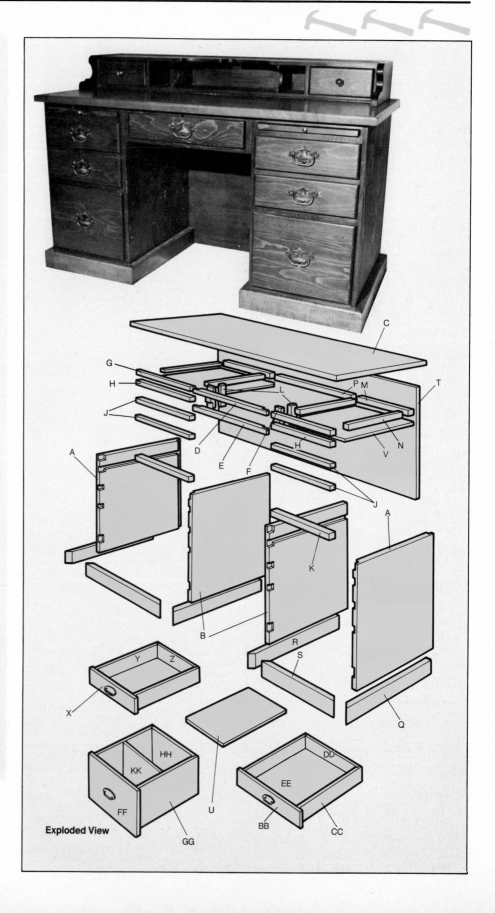

Exploded View

Because the machining for this project is very detailed and the assembly requires several subassemblies before final construction, this project can be quite a challenge.

This is also a desk of more than average weight. Before considering this project, analyze how much work and assembly space you have, and determine when you will need help in handling the assembly of the desk. Another consideration is getting the desk out of your workshop to its permanent location. You would be well advised to solve the logistical problems first.

STEP 1
MACHINING THE TOP
If you must glue boards to width for this project, see the Gluing section, pages 11-12, for directions. Use a ½-inch-radius quarter round bit around all four edges of the top to give it a rounded edge.

STEP 2
MACHINING THE SIDES
The two outer sides are mirror images. Rout or dado (with a table saw or, preferably, a radial arm saw) the top and bottom cross-member and drawer-brace dadoes, as shown in Detail A, as well as the standard shelf and flush-back joinery. See specifications #4 and #2, page 17, for detailed information on these grooves.

The two inner sides are also mirror images. Standard top and bottom cross-member, drawer-brace, and shelf dadoes are routed or dadoed into the inside faces of these pieces in the same manner as the grooves mentioned above, at the locations indicated in Detail B.

STEP 3
MACHINING THE FEET
The feet wrap around the entire cabinet, and all pieces are rounded with a ⅜-inch-radius quarter round router bit on the leading edge before mitering. The two front feet have 45° miters cut on each end to accommodate 45° miters on the side feet. Also miter the two outside feet exactly like the front feet.

The inside feet have only one 45° angle cut on each piece. These meet and fit the mitered front feet and butt into the back. The back foot has a 45° miter cut on each end.

The option of cutting a design into the feet is left to you. However, it is the opinion of the author that a flush foot without any design looks best for this piece.

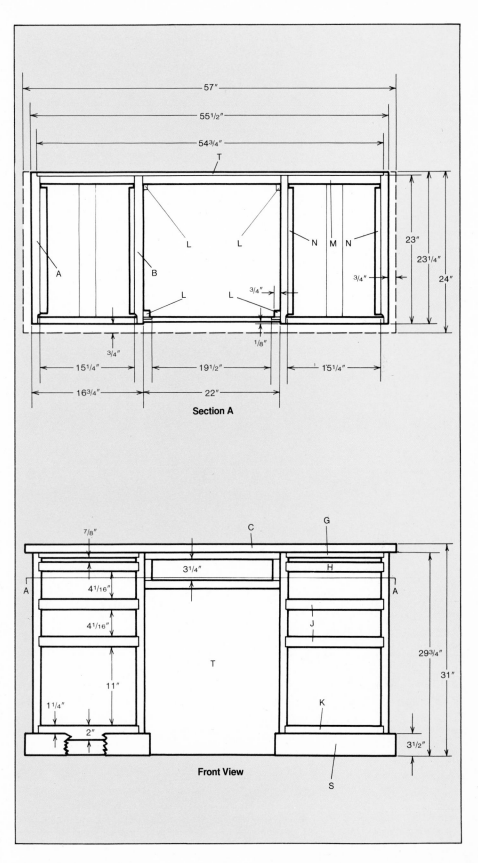

Section A

Front View

STEP 4
MACHINING THE CROSS MEMBERS, BRACES, AND LEVELERS

The top and bottom cross-member drawer enclosures are machined on the back sides, as shown in Detail C. The two vertical cross-member drawer enclosures are machined on the front surfaces, as shown in Detail D. This machining can be done with a straight router bit set for a 3⁄8-inch-deep cut or with a dado cutter head set up on the table or radial arm saw. The latter is preferable.

There are many braces for this project. Keep a list, and inventory these braces as they are completed. It is most efficient to identify them with small peel-off labels.

The 3⁄4-inch width on the shelf levelers is important and should be clearly marked so as to facilitate assembly.

STEP 5
MACHINING THE BACK AND SHELVES

The back and shelf bottoms can be cut from the same 4 × 8-foot sheet. See page 16 for details on how to cut a sheet of plywood for greatest economy. The face of the plywood should be of the same kind of wood as the solid stock used for the rest of the desk.

STEP 6
MACHINING THE DRAWER PARTS

The four desk drawers use side-mounted roller systems. Components for these should all be cut together for efficiency. See specifications #18 and #19, page 21, for details on constructing these drawers. The dimensions in the Materials List may change, depending on the hardware used to mount the drawers.

Round the edges of the drawer fronts with a 3⁄8-inch-radius quarter round router bit.

The front of the small drawer (the kneehole drawer) is rounded with a 3⁄8-inch-radius quarter round router all the way around.

The two larger file-size drawers are also built for use with side-mounted

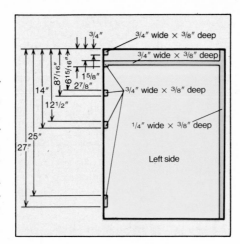

DETAIL A
OUTSIDE SIDE LAYOUT

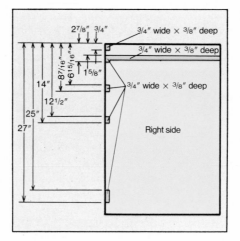

DETAIL B
INSIDE SIDE LAYOUT

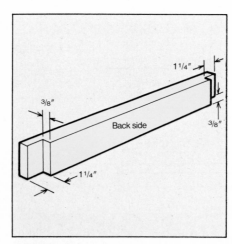

DETAIL C
TOP/BOTTOM
CROSS-MEMBER JOINERY

roller systems. They are machined the same as the desk drawer parts. See specifications #18 and #19, page 21, for details on constructing these drawers. Once again, the dimensions in the Materials List may change slightly, depending on the hardware used to mount the drawers.

Note the special 1⁄4-inch-deep grooves machined in the inside surface of the file-drawer sides to accommodate the drawer dividers (see Detail E). You may decide on other locations for these grooves; the file drawers can, of course, be partitioned in several locations. Make the drawer dividers as needed.

STEP 7
SANDING THE PIECES

Rough- and finish-sand the top and all sides, the feet, and the edges of the top and feet. The under and inside surfaces need not be touched.

The top and bottom cross members, vertical cross members, and all drawer braces only need be rough-sanded on the visible surfaces. Braces, such as the top connector and shelf braces, need not be sanded at all.

The shelf runners and levelers are never seen after the desk is assembled, and so they do not need sanding either. The plywood back and pullout shelves should not need any sanding, except, perhaps, light finish-sanding.

See the Sanding section, pages 13-15, for details on sanding the drawer parts.

STEP 8
CONSTRUCTING THE SUBASSEMBLIES

There are several subassemblies to be completed before the cabinet can be put together. Glue, assemble, and clamp the top, bottom, and two vertical cross members of the four components through which the kneehole drawer will pass and let stand until the glue sets up. Finish-sand this grille, or drawer enclosure. Attach the connector braces to the back sides of the vertical cross members in the drawer enclosure with No. 8 ×

1½-inch flathead screws as indicated in the plan (Section A).

Next, glue and use 4d finishing nails to nail the shelf runners into the grooves provided in the sides. These runners accommodate the pullout shelves. Glue and use 4d finishing nails to nail the top and bottom cross members, along with the drawer braces, into place on the sides. Clamp and square up the entire unit until the glue has set up. For details of this procedure, see the Assembly section, pages 26–27.

The drawer-enclosure assembly and the cabinet subassembly should remain clamped for about four or five hours to allow time for the glue to set.

Assemble the drawers next, following the instructions on pages 29–31 in the Assembly section.

After removing the clamps from the left and right drawer cabinets, countersink the nails, fill the holes with wood filler, and immediately sand off the excess. At this time, finish-sand the joints between the sides and the drawer braces and cross members.

STEP 9
JOINING THE SECTIONS
The center drawer-enclosure assembly may now be installed, using glue and No. 8 × 1¼-inch wood screws for each connector brace. Be careful not to spread glue on any area that will be stained later. Note that the drawer enclosure is positioned ⅛ inch back from the front edge of the sides.

Next, glue and nail the back into place, using 1-inch brads. Be careful to maintain the proper clearance inside the cabinets. Since the top braces inside each cabinet are cut to the clearance dimension, install them. Be sure to maintain these dimensions at the bottom of the cabinet too. Clamp the cabinet with bar or pipe clamps to make sure the joints between the sides and the ends of the back are securely glued.

While the clamped cabinet is setting up, fasten the rest of the top braces in place. See the Assembly section, pages 25–26, for details on installing the top braces.

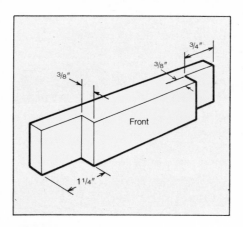

DETAIL D
VERTICAL CROSS-MEMBER JOINERY

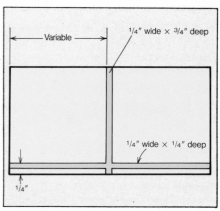

DETAIL E
FILE DRAWER SIDE LAYOUT

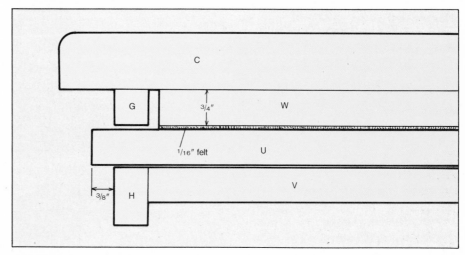

DETAIL F
PULL-OUT SHIELD INSTALLATION

STEP 10
ATTACHING THE FEET
Finish-sand the back and side glue joints as soon as they are set, taking care not to sand through the outer veneer of the plywood. The entire foot assembly may now be installed. See the Assembly section, page 27, for details.

STEP 11
INSTALLING THE TOP
Next, attach the top. Place the top upside down on a padded surface that is large enough and strong enough to support the whole unit. At this point you will need some help to invert the base onto the top. Since the installation of the top is the step used for squaring the cabinet—which is critical to a drawer cabinet such as this desk—it is imperative

that you closely follow the directions on pages 26–27. Use care in shifting this desk back to the floor.

STEP 12
COMPLETING THE ASSEMBLY
Attach felt to the bottom side of the shelf levelers so that the finish on the pullout shelves will not be scratched. Do not glue the levelers to the underside of the top. Simply screw them in place with No. 8 × 1¼-inch flathead wood screws.

Finally, install the monorail and side-mounted roller systems and their respective drawers (see Detail F). See the instructions on pages 29–31 of the Assembly section for installation details. Use the connector braces to mount the hardware for the kneehole drawer.

ORGANIZER FOR SEVEN-DRAWER DESK

MATERIALS LIST
A Back (1), 3/4″ × 6¹/8″ × 54″
B Sides (2), 1¹/8″ × 6¹/8″ × 13³/4″
C Top (1), 3/4″ × 7³/4″ × 53¹/4″
D Bottom (1), 3/4″ × 7³/4″ × 53¹/4″
E Envelope dividers (4), 3/4″ × 5¹/8″ × 7³/4″
F Side spacers (2), 3/4″ × 4³/8″ × 7³/4″
G Panel molding (1), 3/8″ × 3/8″ × 53¹/4″

DRAWERS
H Fronts (2), 3/4″ × 4⁵/16″ × 9¹⁵/16″
J Sides (4), 3/4″ × 4⁵/16″ × 7³/8″
K Backs (2), 3/4″ × 4⁵/16″ × 8⁷/16″
L Bottoms (2), ¹/4″ × 6³/4″ × 8¹⁵/16″

HARDWARE
Brass knobs (2)
1″ brads
4d finishing nails
Pressure-sensitive felt tape

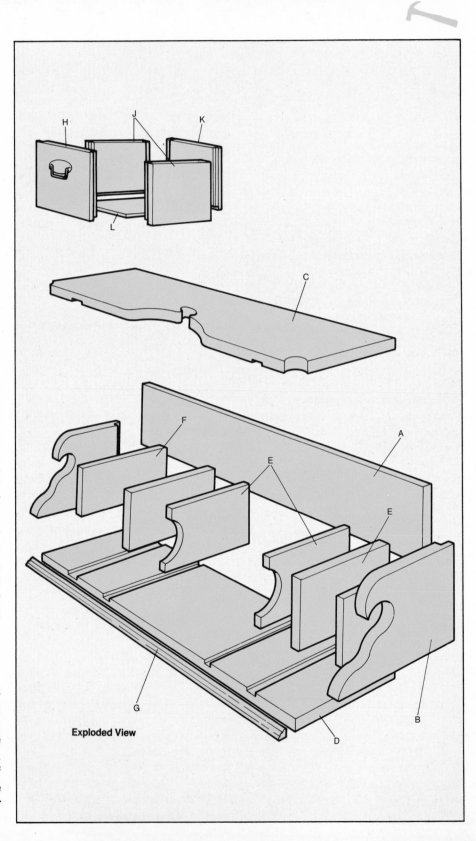

Exploded View

The organizer top for the seven-drawer desk, on page 124, is both attractive and very useful. It has two drawers and several envelope or cubbyhole compartments. In addition, the top surface provides a place for a desk lamp which, from this slightly elevated position, will provide better light.

After completing the desk, constructing the organizer top will seem very easy. The machining, sanding, and assembly steps will take about eight working hours plus the time required for the glue to dry during each of the assembly steps.

STEP 1
MACHINING THE SIDES
Cut the sides to the dimensions specified in the Materials List; then copy and transfer the pattern in Detail A. Cut this design into the sides with a band saw or a saber saw. Cut a rabbet into the inside faces of each side, as shown in the detail. See specifications #4 and #2, page 17, for details on these grooves.

STEP 2
MACHINING THE TOP AND BOTTOM

Cut the top to the dimensions given in the Materials List. Copy the pattern given in Detail B, transfer it to the top, and cut it out with a saber or band saw. The top is further machined with dadoes, as specified in the detail. See specifications on page 17 for details on these cuts.

The bottom has standard shelf dadoes for 3/4-inch stock, as shown in Detail C.

STEP 3
MACHINING THE DIVIDERS AND SPACERS

Cut two plain envelope dividers and two following the pattern given in Detail D.

STEP 4
MACHINING THE DRAWER PARTS

The desk organizer has two hand-fitted drawers with flush fronts. See specification #25, page 22, for details on cutting the parts for these drawers. Use the dimensions given in the Materials List for this project.

Round the leading edge on each front with a 3/8-inch-radius quarter round router bit. If you wish, machine the drawer fronts with the apothecary cut shown in specification #24, page 22.

STEP 5
SANDING THE PIECES

Rough- and finish-sand the back surface of the back, the cut pattern edges, and the top edges of the sides, as well as both faces of the sides. Rough- and finish-sand the top and front edges of the top and bottom pieces.

Rough- and finish-sand the two faces and front edge of each divider, as well as the front edges of the spacers.

Sand off and round slightly the two end edges of the panel molding to remove any saw-blade tear cuts. You probably will not have to sand the face of the molding. See the Sanding section, pages 13-15, for details on sanding the drawer parts.

STEP 6
ASSEMBLING THE TOP, BOTTOM AND DIVIDERS, AND SPACERS

Glue and clamp the envelope dividers in the dadoes in the top and bottom. Also, position the spacers, and nail them in place with 4d finishing nails. Check for square and clearance and, if square, allow to dry. Finish-sand the glue joints on the front surface of this subassembly before gluing it into the two sides and attaching the back.

STEP 7
ATTACHING THE SIDES

Glue and clamp the sides to the top/ bottom unit. Check for square and when square, allow to dry. Nail top and bottom into the sides for security, as shown on pages 29–30 in the Assembly section.

Once again, check the clearance dimensions, especially in the drawer area. The 3/8-inch panel molding can be spot-glued and nailed with brads. Be careful not to spread any glue onto areas that will be stained later.

STEP 8
ASSEMBLING THE DRAWERS

Assemble the drawers according to the directions on pages 29–30 of the Assembly section.

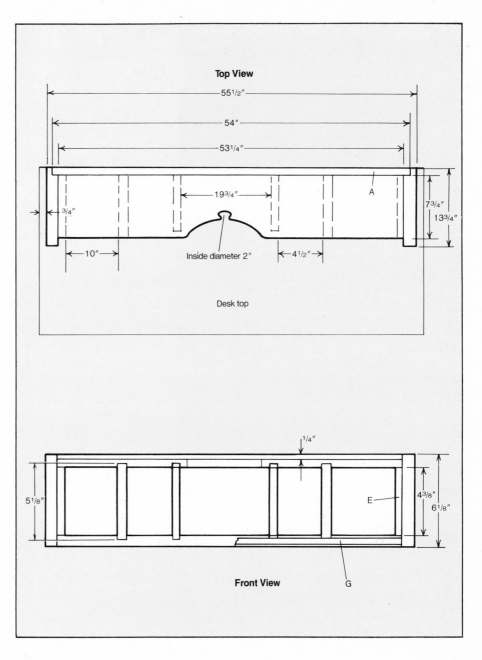

Top View

55 1/2"

54"

53 1/4"

19 3/4"

3/4"

7 3/4"

13 3/4"

A

10"

Inside diameter 2"

4 1/2"

Desk top

1/4"

5 1/8"

E

4 3/8"

6 1/8"

Front View

G

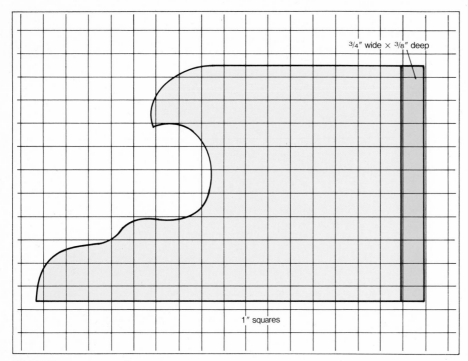

3/4" wide × 3/8" deep

1" squares

DETAIL A
SIDE PATTERN AND LAYOUT

STEP 9
ADDING THE BACK

Because of the small spaces of the cubbyholes, you should stain and finish the unit before adding the back. Use glue and 4d finishing nails to attach the back. Be sure to offset the nails so they do not bite into the same area of end grain in succession.

Apply 1½-inch-wide pressure-sensitive felt tape to the bottom. This will prevent the organizer top from scratching the surface of the desk top. The weight of the organizer should hold it firmly in position on the desk.

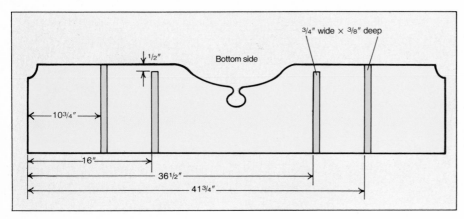

1/2"

Bottom side

3/4" wide × 3/8" deep

10¾"

16"

36½"

41¾"

DETAIL B
TOP PATTERN AND LAYOUT

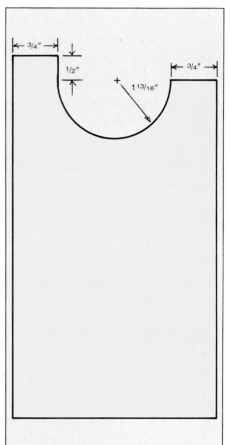

3/4"

1/2"

3/4"

1 13/16"

DETAIL D
DIVIDER PATTERN

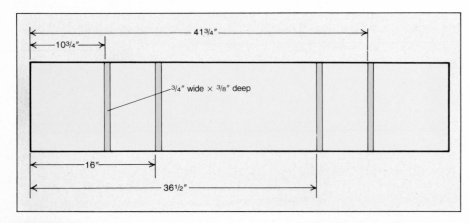

41¾"

10¾"

3/4" wide × 3/8" deep

16"

36½"

DETAIL C
BOTTOM LAYOUT

BABY-CHANGING TABLE

MATERIALS LIST

BASE
A Top (1), 3/4" × 173/4" × 331/2"
B Sides (2), 3/4" × 17" × 331/2"
C Half shelf (1), 3/4" × 131/2" × 311/4"
D Shelf (1), 3/4" × 163/4" × 311/4"
E Bottom (1), 3/4" × 16" × 311/4"
F Front foot (1), 3/4" × 31/2" × 32"
G Bottom cross member (1), 3/4" × 13/4" × 311/4"
H Top cross member (1), 3/4" × 11/4" × 311/4"
J Top braces (2), 3/4" × 3/4" × 141/2"
K Top back cross member (1), 3/4" × 3/4" × 301/2"
L Back (1), 1/4" × 303/4" × 311/4"

DOORS
M A stiles (4), 3/4" × 2" × 173/8"
N B rails (4), 3/4" × 2" × 1115/16"
P C panels (2), 1/4" × 1111/16" × 147/8"

HARDWARE
Brass knobs (2)
Decorating hinges (2 pair)
Magnetic catches (2)
No. 8 × 11/4" flathead wood screws
4d finishing nails
1" brads
Felt strips

This is a wonderful project to build for any household with a newborn. The baby-changing cabinet has room to hold all the items a parent will need to take care of the baby several times a day. The angled tray has plenty of room for the baby.

The cabinet is one of the easiest projects in this book—it involves no subassemblies beyond constructing the doors. The tray is somewhat more difficult. Although it has only five pieces to be joined, the angle cuts required must be made with precision. Use only nontoxic finishes on the cabinet and tray.

STEP 1
MACHINING THE TOP

If you need to glue up stock for the top, shelves, or bottom, see the Gluing section, pages 11-12, for detailed instructions.

Cut the top to size and round the upper edge on all four sides with a 3/8-inch quarter round router bit.

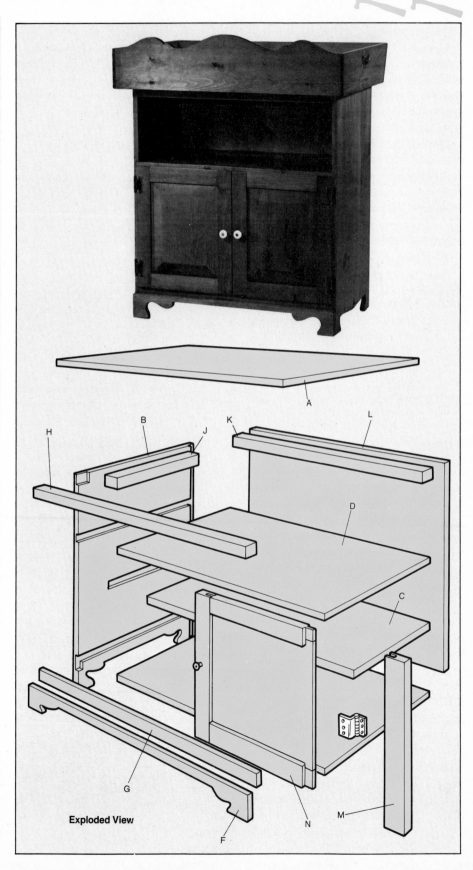

Exploded View

STEP 2
MACHINING THE SHELVES
Cut the shelves to size. Machine the half shelf with a standard flush cut ⅜ inch wide and ¾ inch deep. See specification #6, page 18, for details on this cut.

STEP 3
MACHINING THE SIDES
The two sides are machined with standard shelf dadoes, standard drawer-brace stopped dadoes, and standard back rabbets on the inside faces, as shown in Detail A, to produce a mirror-image pair. See specifications on pages 17 and 18 for details on these grooves. If you wish, cut a design in the lower ends of the sides; leave them plain for a modern look.

STEP 4
MACHINING THE FRONT FOOT
Cut the front foot to size. If you have cut a design in the lower end of the sides, cut the same design in the front foot; see page 24 for a selection of designs. Round the top leading edge of the front foot with a ⅜-inch-radius quarter round router bit.

STEP 5
CUTTING THE DOOR PARTS
The cabinet has two flush doors. See specifications #10, #11, #12, page 19, for details on cutting the door parts. Use the dimensions given in the Materials List for this project.

Because the door panels and the back of the cabinet are both of ¼-inch plywood, cut them from the same piece. The backs of the doors will show when they are open, so pick a plywood faced with the same kind of wood you use for the rest of the cabinet.

STEP 6
SANDING
Rough- and finish-sand the upper surface of the top and both surfaces of the sides. The half shelf, shelf, and bottom need only be rough-sanded. Rough- and finish-sand the routed edge of the front foot; the face need only be rough-sanded. The plywood sections will not need sanding.

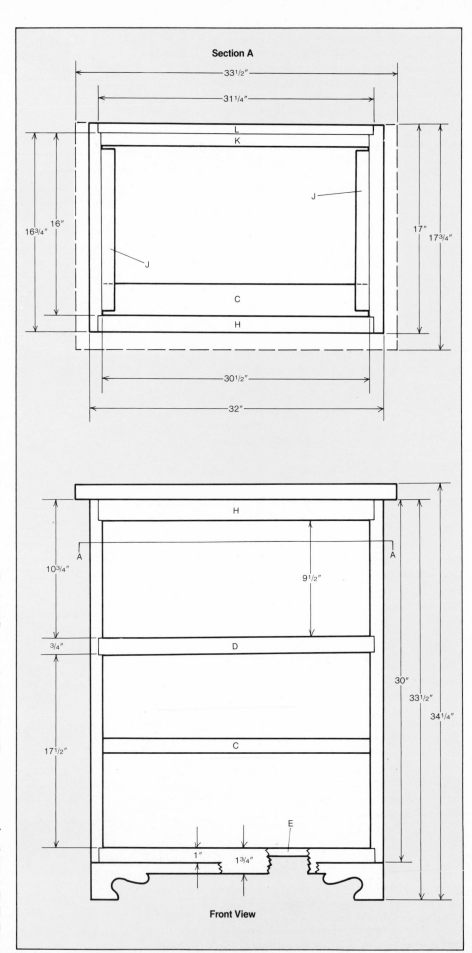

For information on sanding the door parts, see the Assembly section, page 28.

STEP 7
ASSEMBLING THE CABINET

Apply glue to the ends of the half shelf, shelf, and bottom, and also spread it into the grooves for these pieces in the sides. Fit the parts into the sides and then nail into the sides from underneath the shelves and bottom with 4d finishing nails. Clamp the assembly and check for square, adjusting if necessary. When square, allow the glue to dry.

STEP 8
ASSEMBLING THE DOORS

For instructions on assembling the doors, see the Assembly section, page 28.

STEP 9
COMPLETING THE CABINET

Attach the front foot to the cabinet with glue and No. 8 × 1¼-inch flat-head wood screws. Countersink the screws and cover with screw plugs.

Attach the top braces with No. 8 × 1¼-inch wood screws driven through the braces into the sides.

Place the top upside down on a padded surface and invert the cabinet assembly onto it so that the back edge is flush with the back edges of the sides, and so that the cabinet is centered on the top from side to side. Attach the cabinet to the top with countersunk No. 8 × 1¼-inch flat-head wood screws driven through the braces. If the cabinet is not completely square, pull it into square as you attach it to the top, driving nails through the braces just far enough to bite into the top and hold it square as you drive the screws; see the Assembly section, page 26, for details.

Install the doors according to the instructions in the Assembly section, page 29, and then remove them, marking the position of the hardware. After applying finish to the cabinet, reinstall the doors and attach the back with 1-inch brads.

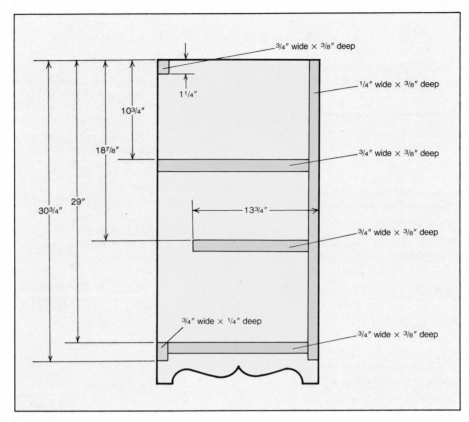

DETAIL A
SIDE LAYOUT

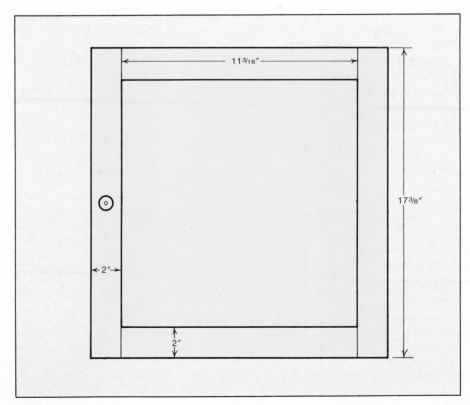

DETAIL B
DOOR LAYOUT

BABY-CHANGING TABLE TRAY

MATERIALS LIST

Q Back (1), 3/4″ × 5 11/16″ × 34 3/4″
R Sides (2), 3/4″ × 5 11/16″ × 20 3/8″
S Front (1), 3/4″ × 6 5/16″ × 35 1/2″
T Bottom (1), 3/8″ × 19 7/8″ × 34 5/8″

HARDWARE

4d finishing nails
Felt strips

STEP 1
MACHINING THE BACK

All the parts for the tray, with the exception of the bottom, are cut from 3/4-inch stock. Cut the back to size. Cut a groove 3/8 inch wide by 3/8 inch deep exactly 3/4 inch from the bottom edge, as shown in Detail A.

STEP 2
MACHINING THE SIDES

Cut the two sides to size. Cut a 3/4-inch-wide by 3/8-inch-deep rabbet along the back end of each side, as shown in Detail B. Cut a 1/4-inch-wide by 3/8-inch deep groove 3/4 inch from the bottom of each side on the same face as the first cut. Finally, cut the front end of each side (the end opposite the grooved end) at a 70° angle, as shown in Detail B.

STEP 3
MACHINING THE FRONT

Cut the front to size. Cut a rabbet 3/4 inch wide and 3/8 inch deep in both ends, as shown in Detail C. Next, make 20° cuts in the top and bottom edges of the front, as shown in Detail D. Finally, cut a groove 1/4 inch wide and 3/8 inch deep across the inside face of the front (the face with the rabbets at either end). This groove must be cut at 70°, as shown.

STEP 4
SANDING THE PARTS

Rough- and finish-sand the flat (outside) faces of the front, back, and

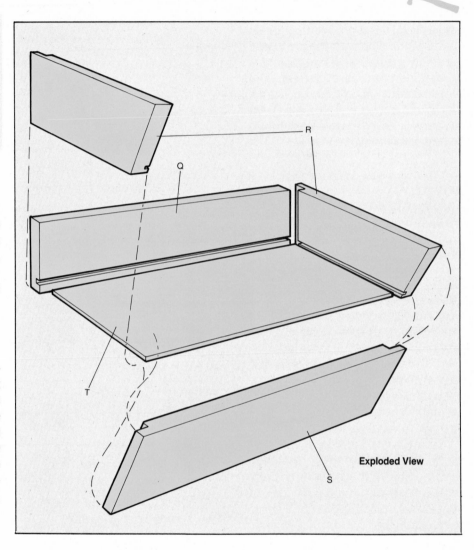

Exploded View

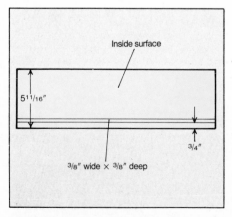

Inside surface

5 11/16″

3/8″ wide × 3/8″ deep

3/4″

DETAIL A
TRAY BACK LAYOUT

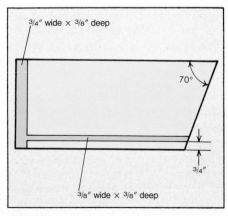

3/4″ wide × 3/8″ deep

70°

3/4″

3/8″ wide × 3/8″ deep

DETAIL B
TRAY SIDE LAYOUT

sides. The final sanding follows all assembly.

STEP 5
ASSEMBLING THE TRAY

Place the back on a flat work surface, inside face up. Put glue in the end rabbets and fit the sides to the back. Secure with 4d finishing nails. Set the nails and fill the holes with wood putty.

Slip the bottom into the grooves along the sides and slide it into the groove in the back. Do not glue the bottom in the grooves. Put glue in the rabbets on the ends of the front and set it into position on the ends of the sides. Secure the front with 4d finishing nails, set the nails, and fill the holes with wood putty.

Square up the tray and clamp with scrap wood under the clamps to protect the tray surfaces from dents. Let the glue dry.

STEP 6
FINAL SANDING

When the glue is dry, use a portable belt sander to smooth all the glue joints and the top edges of the tray. Finish the tray and, when the finishing process is complete, glue strips of felt to the bottom edges to protect the cabinet top from scratches.

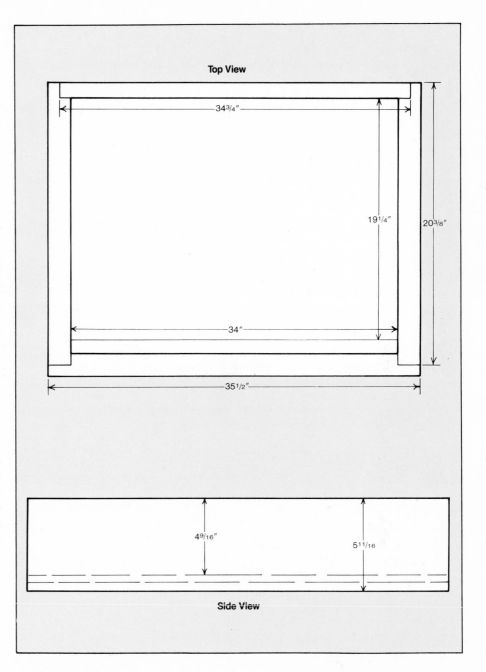

Top View

Side View

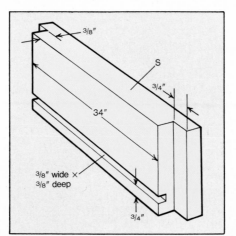

DETAIL C
TRAY FRONT LAYOUT

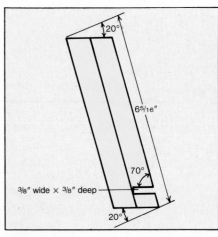

DETAIL D
SIDE VIEW OF TRAY FRONT

BABY CRADLE

MATERIALS LIST
A Head (1), 3/4″ × 15½″ × 17¼″
B Foot (1), 3/4″ × 15½″ × 17¼″
C Sides (2), 3/4″ × 11¼″ × 30⁹/₁₆″
D Bottom (1), 3/4″ × 14″ × 28⅝″
E Feet (2), 3/4″ × 4½″ × 24⅛″
F Braces (1), 3/4″ × 3″ × 23¼″

HARDWARE
No. 8 × 1¼″ flathead wood screws
No. 10 × 2″ flathead wood screws
6d finishing nails

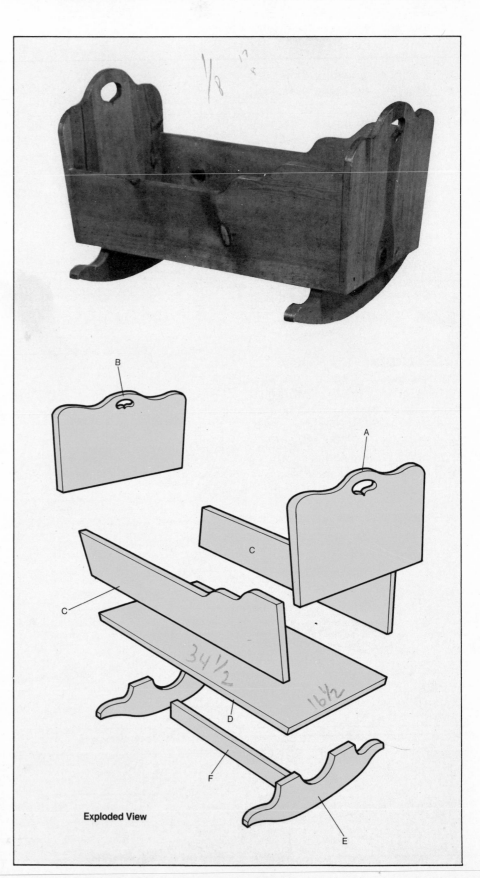

Exploded View

There are times in the lives of most woodworking hobbyists when a cradle is in order. This model will hold a baby quite comfortably.

The project requires a good hand with a band saw to cut both the decorative curves and the curve of the rockers. For the best possible fit, take care to get the angle cuts on the parts of the cradle body exact. When you sand the piece, take the time required to make it smooth enough for a baby. Use only nontoxic finishes on the cradle.

STEP 1
GLUING UP STOCK
Because several components are wider than the boards normally available in lumberyards, you will have to glue boards to width. See the Gluing section, pages 11-12, for details.

STEP 2
MACHINING THE HEAD AND FOOT
The head and foot are both 17¼ inches wide at the top and taper to a width of 15⅜ inches at the bottom. See Detail A for the necessary angle cuts. Use either a table or radial arm saw to make the cuts; then use a saber or band saw to cut the decorative curves on the top edge of each piece, as shown in the detail. Use the saber saw to cut the handle cutout after drilling a starter hole inside the handle for the saw blades.

STEP 3
MACHINING THE SIDES

The two side pieces are machined on either end with a 95° angle cut, as shown in Detail B. After cutting the sides to their gross dimensions, copy the pattern given in the detail onto the boards, and use a saber or band saw to cut the pattern.

STEP 4
MACHINING THE BOTTOM

The bottom is machined with a 95° angle all around the entire edge, as shown in Detail C. This machining may be done easily with a table saw or a radial arm saw.

STEP 5
MACHINING THE FEET AND BRACE

The cradle looks best if you use 1¼-inch stock for the two feet; however, 1-inch wood may be used if you prefer. Cut two pieces slightly larger than the dimensions given in the Materials List. Copy the pattern for the feet onto each piece and cut it out with a band or saber saw. When you have finished cutting the pattern, rout the entire perimeters of both feet with a ⅜-inch-radius quarter round router bit. Do not rout the top of the feet where they will attach to the cradle bottom.

Also, cut the brace according to the dimensions given. There is no special machining that need be done to the brace. But if you want, you can round the long edges. Do not round the ends.

STEP 6
SANDING THE PARTS

Rough- and finish-sand all the pieces except the underside of the bottom, which need not be sanded at all. Since the feet will be seen on all surfaces after installation, be sure to sand every edge and face.

STEP 7
ATTACHING THE SIDES TO THE BOTTOM

Pre-drill pilot holes in the sides for 6d finishing nails. Place these so that they will not bite into the same line of grain in the wood. Use glue and 6d

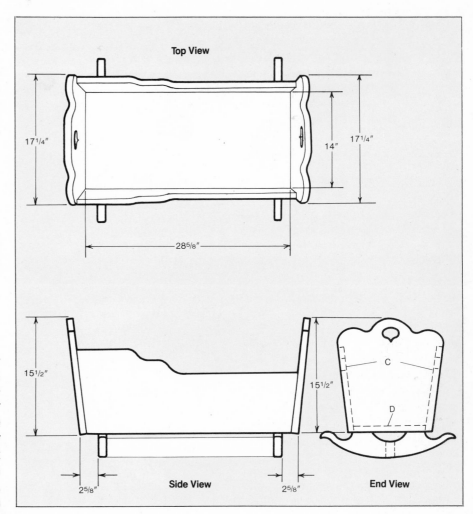

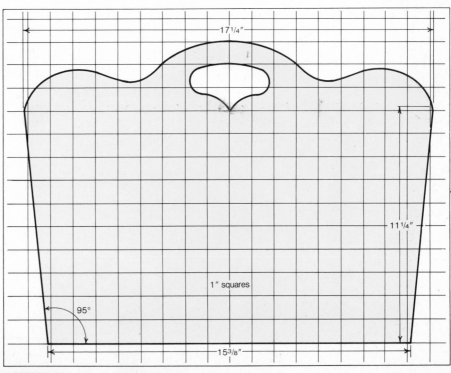

DETAIL A
HEAD/FOOT PATTERN

finishing nails to attach the two sides to the bottom. Use bar clamps to hold this assembly together temporarily while repeating the gluing and nailing process to attach the head and foot. At this point use bar clamps to hold all the components firmly in place while the glue sets up.

STEP 8
FINISH-SANDING THE ASSEMBLY

After the glue is set, use a portable belt sander to sand the edges of the head and foot flush with the sides. You will finish-sand the edges later in preparation for finishing.

STEP 9
ATTACHING THE FEET AND BRACE

Attach the feet to either end of the brace with No. 8 × 1¼-inch flathead wood screws and glue. Allow the glue to set, then locate the proper position for the two feet. Each is set in 2⅝ inches from the nearest end. (Note position in the illustration.) Attach the feet with No. 10 × 2-inch flathead wood screws driven through the bottom into the feet. Countersink and fill all screw holes. When the project is complete, lightly sand over all edges to eliminate any sharpness.

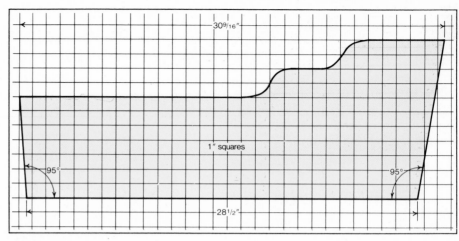

DETAIL B
SIDE PATTERN

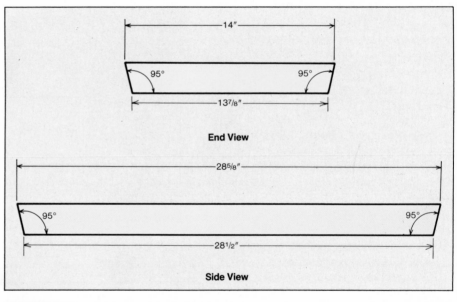

DETAIL C
BOTTOM CUTTING DIAGRAMS

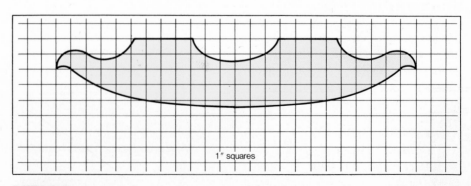

DETAIL D
FOOT PATTERN

CHILD'S CHAIR

MATERIALS LIST
A Sides (2), 3/4" × 12" × 32"
B Seat (1), 3/4" × 14 3/4" × 12"
C Back (1), 3/4" × 14 3/4" × 29"
D Front panel (1), 3/4" × 14" × 11 1/4"
E Scallop molding (1), 3/4" × 1 1/2" × 14"

HARDWARE
No. 8 × 1 1/4" flathead wood screws
4d finishing nails
1" brads
Screw plugs

This project is a simple piece of furniture which will delight any child. There are few pieces to machine, but the joinery required will allow you to use several tools and practice a variety of machining techniques.

STEP 1
MACHINING THE SIDES
You will probably have to glue up stock for the parts of this chair. See the Gluing section, pages 11-12, for details. Cut the sides to the size given in the Materials List, and then machine a flush-back rabbet and a shelf dado in each side, as shown in Detail A; see specifications #2 and #4, page 17, for details. Use a band, jig, or saber saw to cut the pattern design shown in the side view. Round the inside and outside edges of the pattern cut with a 3/8-inch-radius quarter round router bit.

STEP 2
MACHINING THE SEAT
Rout the leading edge of the seat and the first 3/4 inch back along each side edge with a 3/8-inch-radius quarter round bit as shown in Detail B. This rounds the exposed edge.

STEP 3
MACHINING THE BACK
Cut the back to the dimensions given in the Materials List and make the pattern cutout shown in the front view. A gothic arch pattern is shown here, but you can use whatever your imagination suggests. Rout a 3/8-inch

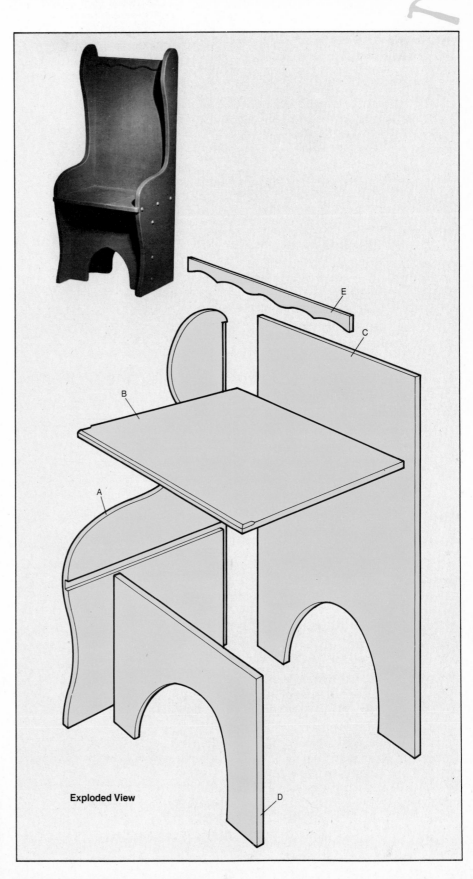

Exploded View

radius curve on the inside and outside edges, as shown in Detail C. The back is decorated with a strip of molding.

STEP 4
MACHINING THE FRONT PANEL

The front panel has the same pattern cutout as the back. If you made your own design, repeat it. Rout a ⅜-inch-radius curve on the inside and outside edges, as shown in Detail D.

STEP 5
SANDING

Rough- and finish-sand the inside and outside surfaces and front edge of the sides and the exposed edges of the seat. The two long edges that will be glued into the sides, and the bottom edge of the feet, need not be sanded at all. Also rough- and finish-sand all surfaces and exposed edges of the back and the front panel's front, back, and foot-cutout edges. Sand the scallop so that it will accept a stain evenly.

STEP 6
ATTACHING THE SIDES TO THE SEAT

Attach the seat to the side. Apply glue to the edges of the seat and the dadoes in the sides. Clamp and check for square. When the sides and seat are square, drive 4d finishing nails at an angle through the seat into the sides.

STEP 7
ADDING THE FRONT AND BACK

Install the front panel by nailing through the sides with 4d finishing nails. Do not glue. Countersink the nails. Secure the front panel with No. 8 × 1¼-inch flathead wood screws driven through the seat into the front panel. Also, secure the seat with screws, as shown in the Side View. Countersink all screws and fill the plugs. Glue the back in place and secure with 4d finishing nails.

Attach the scallop molding with a bit of glue and two 1-inch brads, or simply glue and clamp.

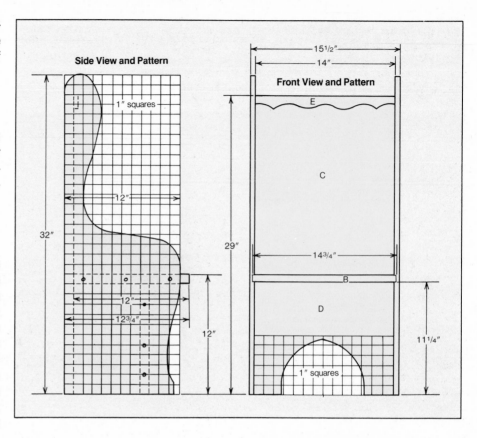

Side View and Pattern

Front View and Pattern

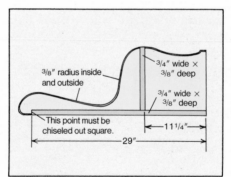

DETAIL A
SIDE LAYOUT

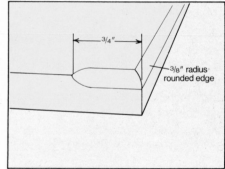

DETAIL B
SEAT EDGE DETAIL

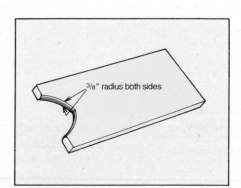

DETAIL C
BACK
ROUTING DIAGRAM

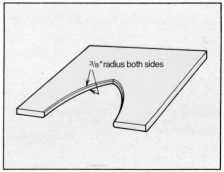

DETAIL D
FRONT PANEL
ROUTING DIAGRAM

CHILD'S BED AND DESK ATTACHMENT

MATERIALS LIST

BED FRAME

A Top (1), 3/4" × 387/8" × 747/8"
B Bottom (1), 3/4" × 377/8" × 741/4"
C Center divider (1), 3/4" × 11" × 371/2"
D Sides (2), 3/4" × 133/4" × 381/4"
E Back (1), 3/4" × 133/4" × 741/4"
F Drawer spacers (4), 3/4" × 2" × 36"
G Top side frame pieces (2), 3/4" × 2" × 761/2"
H Top end frame pieces (2), 3/4" × 2" × 39"
J Top cross member (1), 3/4" × 23/4" × 75"
K Bottom cross member (1), 3/4" × 23/4" × 75"
L Outside vertical cross members (2), 3/4" × 11/2" × 133/4"
M Center vertical cross member (1), 3/4" × 21/4" × 133/4"
N Feet (2), 3/4" × 21/4" × 371/2"

DRAWERS

P Fronts (2), 3/4" × 81/8" × 343/4"
Q Sides (4), 3/4" × 8" × 36"
R Backs (2), 3/4" × 8" × 303/4"
S Bottoms (2), 1/4" × 311/4" × 353/8"

HARDWARE

Drawer rollers (2 pair)
Plate casters (4)
Drawer pulls (4)
No. 8 × 11/4" flathead wood screws
4d finishing nails
Screw plugs

Here is a bed with storage drawers beneath the mattress support, both sturdy and very practical for a child's room, especially a small room. This project is relatively easy—a good one for the beginning woodworker, yet one which will be a pleasure for the more experienced craftsperson. The work does not require very precise machining, nor is the assembly very difficult.

The project on page 144 is a desk attachment for this bed.

STEP 1
MACHINING THE TOP, BOTTOM, AND CENTER DIVIDER

For economy, the top, bottom, and

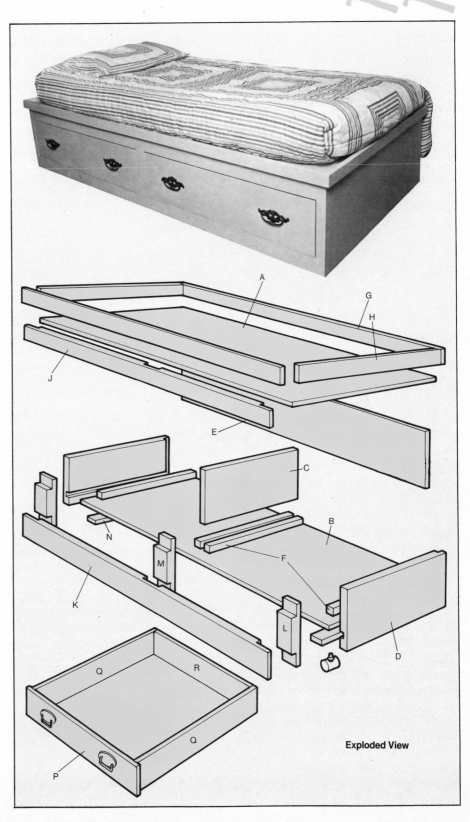

Exploded View

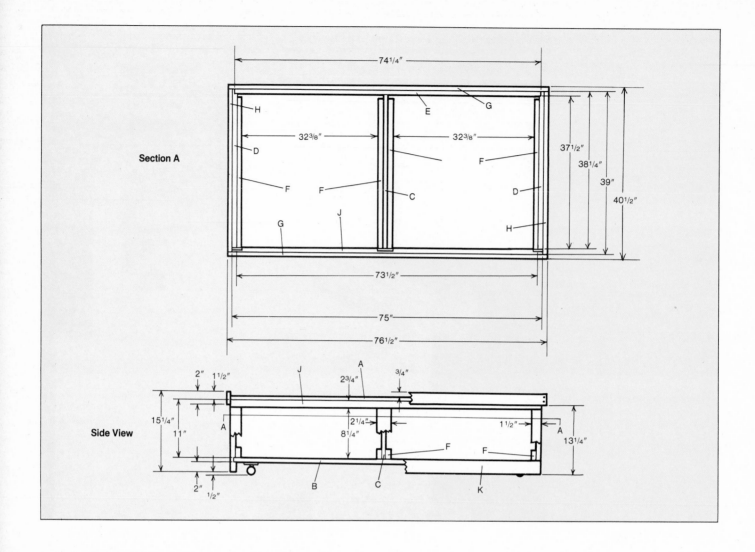

center-divider pieces may be ¾-inch flakeboard or plywood. You may want to drill 15-25 1-inch holes in the top. This will help ventilate the mattress. You can make the center divider by edge-gluing scraps left over from cutting the top and bottom.

STEP 2
MACHINING SIDES AND BACK
You may have to glue ¾-inch stock to create boards of sufficient width from which to cut the sides. These pieces are machined to create one left and one right side; see Detail A. Each side is machined with one flush-back rabbet and one shelf dado. See specifications #2 and #4, page 17, for details on this joinery.

STEP 3
MACHINING THE SPACERS AND CROSS MEMBERS
Four pieces of ¾-inch stock, each 2

× 36 inches, serve as drawer spacers to which the drawer roller system is attached. The top outside frame pieces simply hold the mattress in place. The top, bottom, and vertical cross members form a grille for holding the drawers in place.

Rout or dado the top and bottom cross members on the inside face, as shown in Detail B, to accommodate the vertical cross members.

Rout or dado the vertical outside and center cross members on the front face surface, as shown in Detail C, in order to mate them with the top and bottom cross members.

STEP 4
MACHINING THE DRAWER PIECES
The bed has two rather large drawers. These have flush fronts and are side-mounted, using rollers. Build them according to the plans

given in specifications #18 and #19, page 21. The dimensions in the Materials List may change, depending on the type of hardware used to mount the drawers. Round the front edges of the two fronts with a ¼-inch-radius quarter round router bit.

STEP 5
SANDING THE PIECES
None of the flakeboard or plywood pieces need be sanded. Make sure, however, that the top surface is not splintered, or it could tear your mattress cover.

Rough- and finish-sand the sides and back on the outside face only. The four drawer spacers and all the various cross members need not be sanded until after they have been glued together during the assembly process.

Rough- and finish-sand the top outside frame pieces on all edges and surfaces except the bottom edges.

Sanding instructions for all drawer parts are covered in detail in the Sanding section.

STEP 6
ASSEMBLING THE GRILLE

Use glue to assemble the grille (the front framework through which the drawers will pass—see Detail D). Check for square and then clamp. Recheck for square and adjust the clamps if necessary.

STEP 7
ASSEMBLING THE BOTTOM, SIDES, AND BACK

Install the bottom into the sides with glue and 4d finishing nails. Clamp and check for square. Invert the unit and install the back by nailing 4d finishing nails into the sides after gluing. Secure the lower edge of the back with No. 8 × 1¼-inch wood screws driven through the bottom into the lower edge of the back. Drill pilot holes, offsetting them slightly to avoid screwing into the same section of grain fibers. Turn the unit right side up.

STEP 8
ATTACHING THE GRILLE, SPACERS, AND DIVIDERS

Attach the grille to the sides, bottom, and top with glue and No. 8 x 1¼-inch flathead wood screws. Countersink all screws and fill the holes with wood putty or screw plugs.

Next, attach the top end frame pieces with No. 8 × 1¼-inch flathead wood screws, countersunk, driven through the sides into the frame. Clamp the frame to the side to hold it in place while driving in the screws.

In the same manner, attach the longer top frame pieces by screwing through the back and front grille top cross members. Clamp to hold in place while driving the screws.

Complete the top outside frame by driving 4d finishing nails through the face of the front and back top frame pieces into the ends of the shorter outside frame pieces, as shown in Detail D.

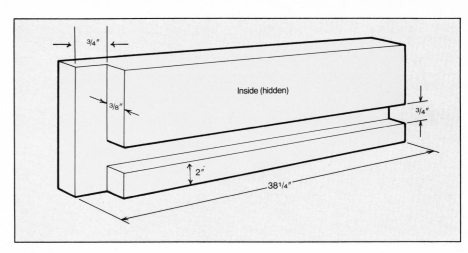

DETAIL A
SIDE LAYOUT

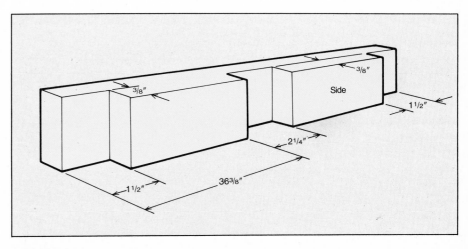

DETAIL B
TOP/BOTTOM CROSS-MEMBER LAYOUT

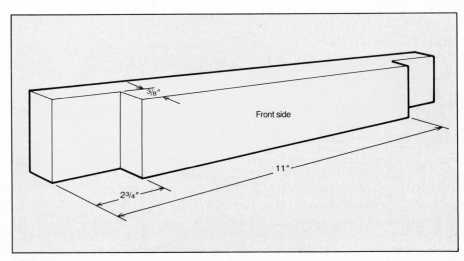

DETAIL C
VERTICAL CROSS-MEMBER LAYOUT

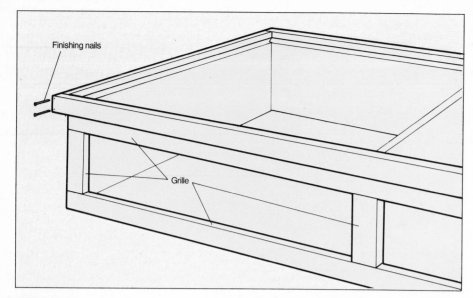

Finishing nails

Grille

DETAIL D
GRILLE AND TOP FRAME CONSTRUCTION DETAIL

STEP 9
COMPLETING THE BED

Invert the bed and install the feet and heavy casters near the corners on the bottom of the bed frame.

Place the bed on the floor. Drop the top into place on the bed. The top will support the mattress. The top itself rests on the top edges of the sides and on the center divider. Do not fasten it down. Finally, install the drawers.

DESK ATTACHMENT FOR CHILD'S BED

MATERIALS LIST
A Top (1), 3/4″ × 18″ × 42″
B Sides (2), 3/4″ × 5½″ × 17¼″
C Front (1), 3/4″ × 5½″ × 39¾″
D Top brace (1), 3/4″ × 1⅛″ × 36″
E Side top braces (2), 3/4″ × 1⅛″ × 13″
F Spacer (1), 3/4″ × 2½″ × 36″
G Leg (1), 3/4″ × 29¼″ × 39″
H Turned legs (2), 2¾″ diameter × 28″

DRAWER PARTS
J Front (1), 3/4″ × 4″ × 34¼″
K Sides (2), 3/4″ × 3″ × 15½″
L Back (1), 3/4″ × 3″ × 31⅞″
M Bottom (1), 1/4″ × 14⅞″ × 31¼″

HARDWARE
Monorail drawer slide
Drawer pulls (2)
Wood tape edging
No. 10 × 2″ flathead wood screws
No. 8 × 1¼″ flathead wood screws
4d finishing nails
1″ brads
Screw plugs

If you have room, you can attach this small but practical desk to the end of the project for a child's bed, on page 141. It provides a stable work area as well as a headboard for the bed. As with the bed, this is a project that any beginner can tackle with good results.

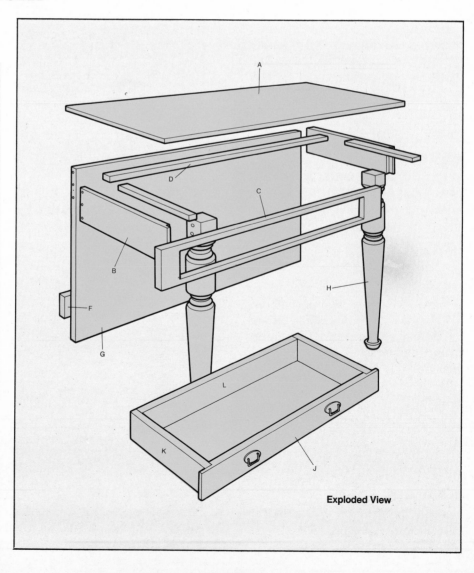

Exploded View

STEP 1
MACHINING THE TOP AND SIDES

Rout a ⅜-inch-radius curve around all edges of the top. Dado the sides, as shown in Detail A, so that you make left and right mirror-image pieces.

STEP 2
MACHINING THE FRONT PIECE AND BACK LEG

The front (drawer frame) has a 3¼- × 33½-inch cutout in the middle; see Detail B. Use a saber saw for this cutting operation after drilling ½-inch-diameter starter holes in each of the four corners of the cutout.

For strength and stability, the back leg is a piece of ¾-inch plywood essentially like a side. Use plywood faced with the same kind of wood you are using for the rest of the desk.

STEP 3
MACHINING THE DRAWER PARTS

Build one drawer with an overlap front for use with a monorail drawer roller system according to the plans given in specifications #17, #18, #19, #20, page 21. All the components are cut from ¾-inch stock, with the exception of the bottom.

STEP 4
PREPARING THE LEGS

You can order ready-made legs for this project or you can turn your own on a lathe. The specifications for the legs are given in the Materials List.

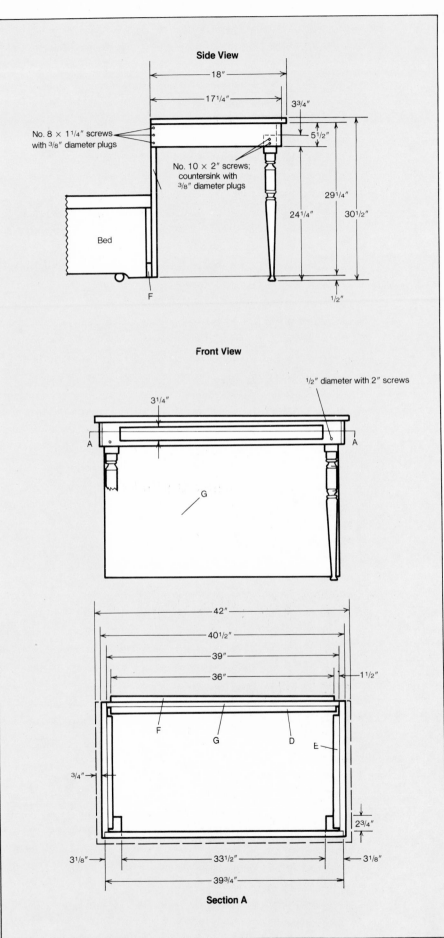

STEP 5
SANDING THE PIECES
Rough- and finish-sand the edges and upper surface of the top, along with the back edge and outside surfaces of the two sides and the outside face of the front. You do not need to sand the edges of the cutout area of the front.

Rough-sand the spacer on the two end edges, on one long edge, and on one face. The top braces, the plywood legs, and the turned legs do not need any sanding. Sanding instructions for all drawer parts are covered in detail in the Sanding section, pages 13–15.

STEP 6
PREPARING FOR ASSEMBLY
Read the instructions in the Assembly section for detailed information on the principles of assembling this item. The assembly steps for this project are given in order below.

STEP 7
ASSEMBLING THE DRAWERS
Place the drawer front face down on a padded surface and brace it securely. Glue and nail the sides to the front with 4d finishing nails. Set the nails. Slip the bottom into the drawer. Apply glue to the ends of the back. Place drawer on its sides and hammer 4d finishing nails through the sides into the back, and set nails.

Turn the drawer upside down and check that it is square. Drive 1-inch brads through the bottom into the sides—one on each side—to hold the drawer square while the glue dries.

STEP 8
ASSEMBLING THE DESK
Attach wood edging tape to the two side edges of the back plywood leg. Attach the top brace to the plywood leg with four No. 8 × 1¼-inch flathead wood screws. Pre-drill ⅜-inch-diameter plug holes into each side and the front, as shown in the plan (Front and Side views). Attach the two turned legs with No. 10 × 2-inch screws driven through the holes.

Install the two top braces onto the

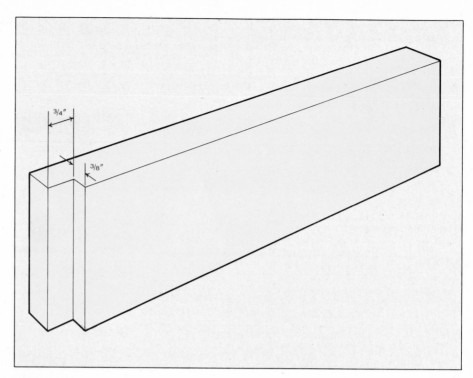

DETAIL A
SIDE LAYOUT

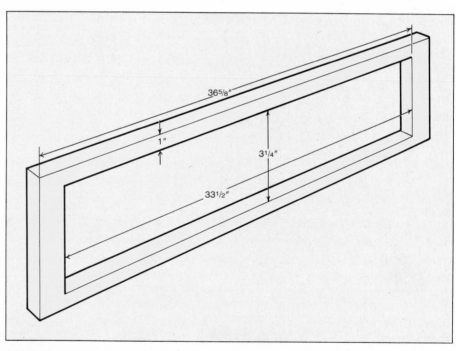

DETAIL B
FRONT LAYOUT

sides with No. 8 × 1¼-inch flathead wood screws. Attach the plywood leg using No. 8 × 1¼-inch flathead wood screws. Cover these wood screws by gluing in screw plugs. Invert desk and attach the top with No. 8 × 1¼-inch flathead wood screws through the top braces. Fit and install the drawer and attach the pulls. Lastly, when attaching the desk to the bed, screw the spacer onto the bed first, using No. 8 × 1¼-inch flathead wood screws; then screw the plywood leg to it.

ROUNDED-POST HEADBOARD

MATERIALS LIST

A Posts (2), 2¼″ × 2¼″ × 36½″
B Top cross member (1), ¾″ × (variable) × (variable)
C Bottom cross member (1), ¾″ × 5½″ × (variable)
D Dowels (8), ⅜″ × diameter × 3″

HARDWARE
No. 10 × 1½″ roundhead wood screws
³⁄₁₆″ washers

You can save money and earn satisfaction when you build this handsome headboard. You can create your own center pattern to suit your taste and harmonize with other pieces of furniture, or you may choose from the patterns offered here.

Little woodworking experience is required to build this simple project. The three primary operations are gluing, band (or saber) sawing, and sanding.

STEP 1
MACHINING THE POSTS

Cut the two headboard posts from 1¾-inch stock. At one end of each of the two posts, draw a 2¼-inch arc using a compass, as shown in Detail A. Note that the arc should not extend lower on the post than a maximum of ¾ inch.

STEP 2
CUTTING THE TOP CROSS MEMBER

The width of the top cross member depends upon the headboard pattern you select. The length, of course, depends on the width of the bed: the headboard for a twin bed is 39½ inches long; for a standard double bed, 54½ inches long; for a queen-size bed, 60½ inches long; and for a king-size bed, 66½ inches long. For any size, cut the headboard from ¾-inch stock.

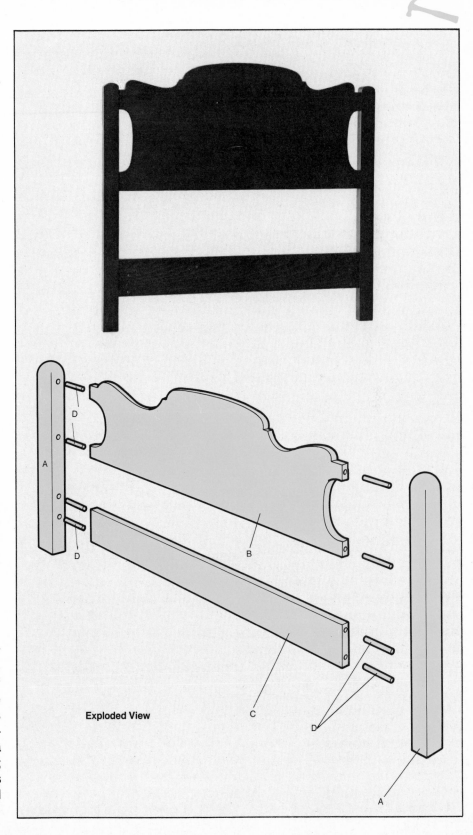

Exploded View

STEP 3
DRILLING THE DOWEL HOLES: BOTTOM CROSS MEMBER

Drill two ⅜-inch-diameter holes, 1¾ inches deep in each end of the bottom cross member, as shown in Detail B, to hold the glue dowels. These two holes must be centered on the thickness of the wood and drilled 1 inch and 4½ inches down from the top edge, respectively.

Note that the 1¾-inch deep dowel holes are deeper than necessary for the 3-inch-long glue dowels: this is because when glue is put in the hole, it occupies space. By drilling the hole a bit deeper than the length of the dowel, you avoid creating a hydraulic lock that could split the wood.

STEP 4
DRILLING THE DOWEL HOLES: TOP CROSS MEMBER

The top cross member is positioned 1 inch down from the top of each post. Refer to the Exploded View, and note that there are two ⅜-inch-diameter holes to be drilled 1¾ inches deep in each section of the flat edge that will touch the post. These holes, again, are for the glue dowels.

STEP 5
DRILLING THE DOWEL HOLES IN THE POSTS

Drill ⅜-inch holes 1¾-inch deep in the posts to accommodate the glue dowels. To locate the holes on the posts, use dowel centers inserted into the dowel holes in the ends of the top and bottom cross members. Set up the headboard assembly as shown in the plan, and press the top cross members and the bottom cross member onto the edges of the posts. The pins in the dowel centers will mark the centers of the dowel holes to be drilled in the posts. When the positions are accurately marked, drill the posts for the glue dowel.

STEP 6
SANDING THE PIECES

Rough- and finish-sand all four sides of the posts. The bottom cross member is only rough-sanded because it will never be seen. Rough- and finish-

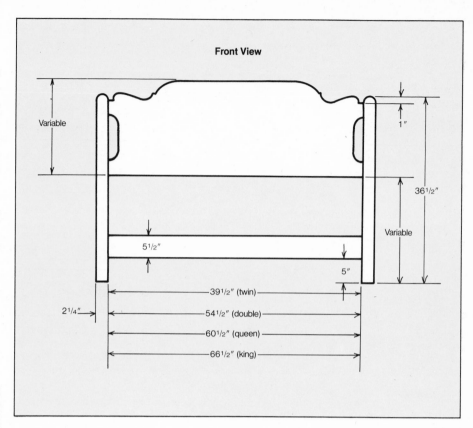

Front View

Variable

1″

36½″

Variable

5″

5½″

2¼″

39½″ (twin)
54½″ (double)
60½″ (queen)
66½″ (king)

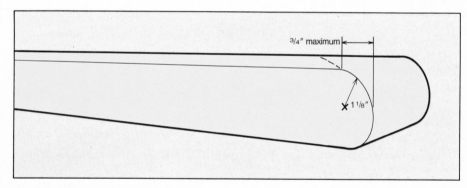

¾″ maximum

1⅛″

DETAIL A
POST END DETAIL

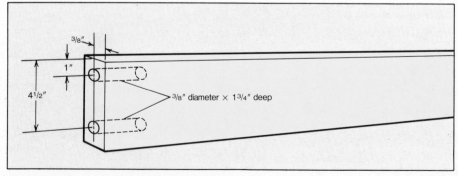

⅜″

1″

4½″

⅜″ diameter × 1¾″ deep

DETAIL B
BOTTOM CROSS-MEMBER END DETAIL

sand the top cross member. The decision whether or not to sand the back surface of the top cross member is up to you; if the bed will sit against a wall, don't bother, unless you want to be especially thorough.

STEP 7
ASSEMBLING THE HEADBOARD

Place the two posts and the top and bottom cross members on a surface large enough to lay out the pieces in position.

Inject glue into the holes in both the top and bottom cross members and in the posts. Insert the glue dowels and fit the parts together.

Use bar or pipe clamps across the posts to tighten the assembly. The clamps must be used on both sides (front and back) of the headboard so that when they are tightened, the headboard will not bow. Check for square with a framing square resting on the bottom edge of the top cross member and against either one of the posts.

Check to be sure no excess glue has squeezed out. If it has, wipe it off completely or it will prevent the stain and varnish from reaching the wood surface and the area will appear as a flaw in the finish.

Leave the headboard assembly in the clamps until the glue has a chance to set up.

When the headboard has been finished, use No. 10 × 1½-inch round-head wood screws and washers to attach your bed frame to the posts.

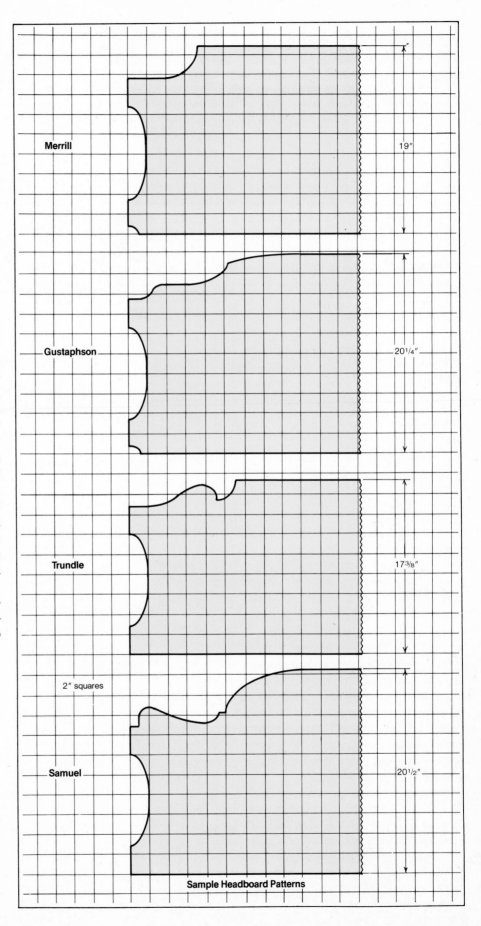

Merrill — 19"

Gustaphson — 20¼"

Trundle — 17⅜"

2" squares

Samuel — 20½"

Sample Headboard Patterns

SLIDING - DOOR HEADBOARD

MATERIALS LIST

A Sides (2), 3/4" × 103/4" × 401/2"
B Vertical dividers (2), 3/4" × 81/2" × 10"
C Shelves* (2), 3/4" × 10" × (variable)
D Upper back* (1), 3/4" × 21/2" × (variable)
E Under-shelf cross member* (1), 3/4" × 91/4" × (variable)
F Bottom front cross member* (1), 3/4" × 51/4" × (variable)
G Bottom back cross member* (1), 3/4" × 4" × (variable)
H Back* (1), 3/4" × 133/8" × (variable)
J Door rails* (4), 3/4" × 11/4" × (variable)
K Door stiles (4), 3/4" × 11/4" × 103/8"
L Spindles (8), 3/4" diameter × 93/8"

HARDWARE
4d finishing nails

*Depending on the size of your bed, the length of several parts will change. To determine the proper length for a given part, use this chart:

Part	Twin	Double	Queen	King
C	401/4"	551/4"	611/4"	671/4"
D	401/4"	551/4"	611/4"	671/4"
E, F, G	391/2"	541/2"	601/2"	661/2"
H	401/4"	551/4".	611/4"	671/4"
J	11"	13"	15"	17"

This attractive headboard provides generous storage space, making it ideal for a small bedroom. The version shown here suggests an Early American style, but you can give the piece a different look by choosing one of the alternate upper-back patterns shown on page 149.

The plans give dimensions for a headboard to fit a queen-size bed; to fit a standard or king-size bed, increase or decrease the length of the central section as necessary.

STEP 1
MACHINING THE SIDES
The two sides of the headboard are mirror images. If you wish, you can

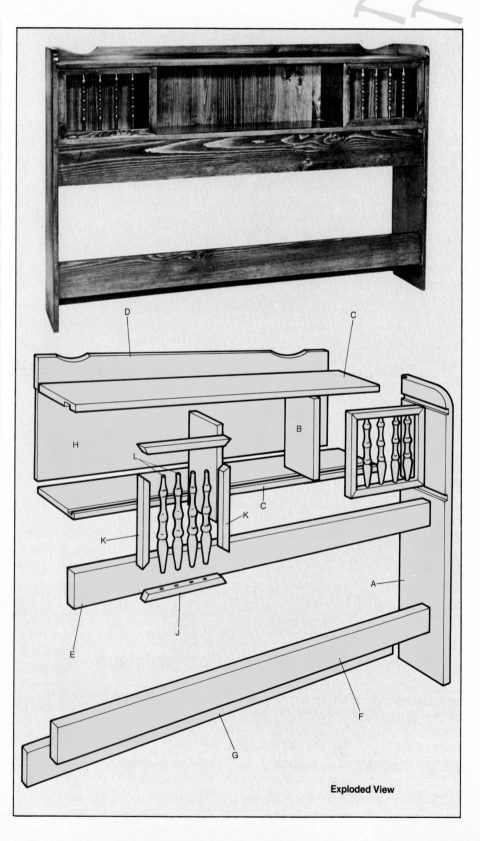

Exploded View

make a 1¼-inch-radius cut at the top corner on the leading edge of each side. Machine a 15⅞-inch-long rabbet and two shelf dadoes in both sides at the locations indicated in Detail A. See specifications #2 and #4 on page 17.

STEP 2
MACHINING THE SHELVES
The top and bottom shelves are grooved to allow the sliding doors to slip into them easily, slide properly, and be removed without difficulty when desired. The grooves are ¹³⁄₁₆ inch wide. The top shelf groove is ⁹⁄₁₆ inch deep, cut into the underside of the shelf. The bottom shelf groove, cut into the top surface, is ³⁄₁₆ inch deep. See Detail B for the location of the grooves.

STEP 3
MACHINING THE BACK PIECES
Cut the piece that forms the back of the storage section from ¾-inch plywood faced with the same wood that you choose for the solid wood pieces.

Cut the upper back from ¾-inch stock. Cut a design in either end; this design is up to you.

STEP 4
MACHINING THE DOORS
The two sliding doors on the headboard storage unit comprise four frame pieces of ¾-inch stock and four spindles. Each of the four frame pieces is mitered to 45° at both ends.

Before cutting the miters, drill ½-inch holes ¾ inch deep in the frame rails, as shown in Detail C, to accommodate the spindles. For two doors, you will need eight 9-inch-long turned spindles.

STEP 5
SANDING THE PIECES
Rough- and finish-sand the two face surfaces, as well as the front and top edges, of the sides; the front edge and two face surfaces of the vertical dividers; the top and bottom faces of the top shelf; and the top face of the bottom shelf. The front edges of the top and bottom shelves should be rough-sanded only.

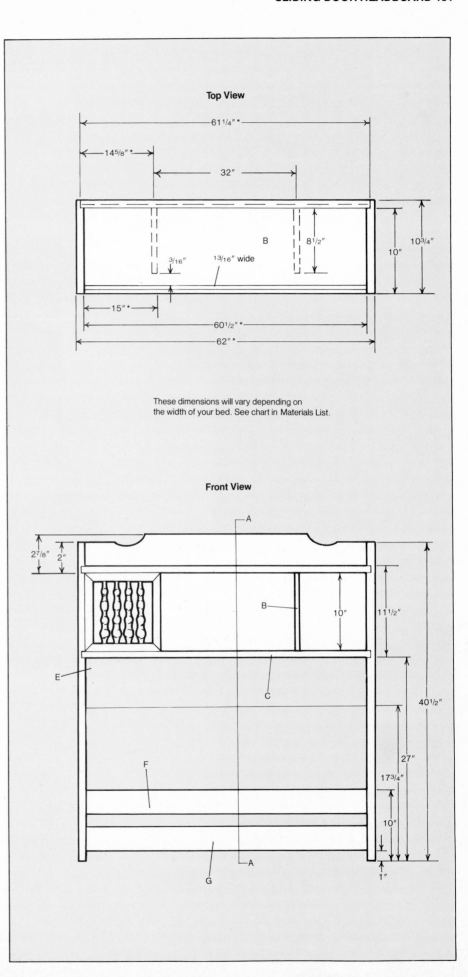

Top View

These dimensions will vary depending on the width of your bed. See chart in Materials List.

Front View

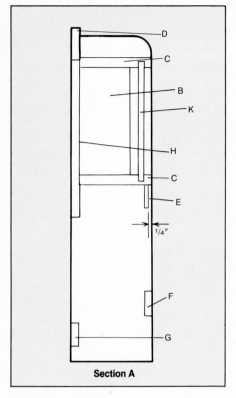

Section A

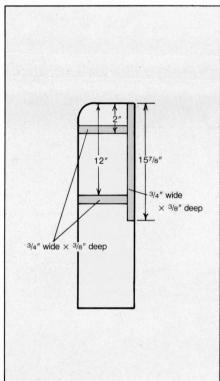

**DETAIL A
SIDE LAYOUT**

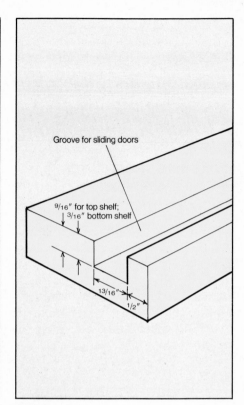

**DETAIL B
SHELF DETAIL**

Rough- and finish-sand the front face and the top edge of the upper back, and rough-sand the back face. Rough- and finish-sand the front surface of the under-shelf cross member; don't bother to sand the back side or any edges. Do not sand the bottom front or back cross member.

Rough- and finish-sand all sides and edges of the sliding-door frame pieces. Usually the plywood pieces and the turned spindles do not need sanding at all because they will have been finish-sanded during manufacturing or turning, but check for blemishes first.

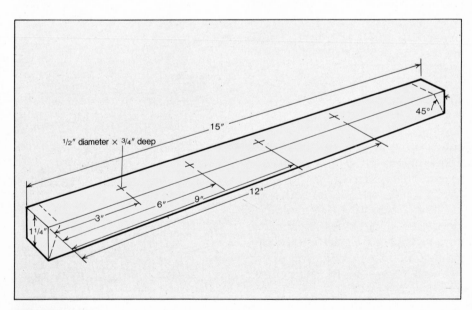

**DETAIL C
RAIL LAYOUT**

STEP 6
ASSEMBLING THE SLIDING DOORS

Before beginning the assembly steps, reread pages 28–30 in the Assembly section.

Apply glue to the mitered ends of the frame pieces. Insert the spindles into pre-drilled holes, assemble the four sides of each frame, and secure with picture-frame clamps to hold the frames square while the glue

dries. When the glue has dried, drill pilot holes and cross-nail all joints with 4d finishing nails.

STEP 7
ASSEMBLING THE SIDES AND SHELVES

Glue and nail the vertical dividers to

the shelves in the locations indicated in the plan (Top View), and then glue and nail the shelves into the sides. Clamp securely and adjust to be sure the sides, vertical dividers, and shelves are square. Let the glue dry completely before proceeding.

STEP 8
INSTALLING THE CROSS MEMBERS

Install the under-shelf cross member by inverting the headboard unit. Position the cross member under the shelf, then glue and clamp to shelf. When the glue is dry, secure the cross member with 4d finishing nails, countersunk, through the sides. Fill the countersunk nailheads with wood putty.

Glue and clamp the bottom front and back cross members to the sides in the locations shown in the plan (Front View and Section A). When the glue is dry, secure with nails, as described above.

STEP 9
INSTALLING THE UPPER BACK AND DOORS

Glue the upper back to the sides and top shelf. Clamp and let dry; then secure with nails, as you did the cross members.

STEP 10
COMPLETING THE PROJECT

Slip the doors into the groove in the upper shelf and let them drop down into the lower-shelf groove. A little paraffin wax in the shelf grooves will help the door slide smoothly.

When you are sure the doors move properly, remove them and apply the finish of your choice to the headboard. Apply finish to the exposed face of each back piece. When the finish has been completed, nail the back piece into place with 4d finishing nails hammered through the back into the sides and vertical dividers.

PORTABLE BAR

MATERIALS LIST

A Top (1), 3/4" × 18" × 39"
B Shelves (2), 3/4" × 10 3/4" × 27 1/2"
C Feet (2), 1 1/4" × 9 1/2" × 24"
D Front middle slats (5), 3/4" × 3 1/2" × 26"
E Front outside slats (2), 3/4" × 4 1/4" × 26"
F Side slats (6), 3/4" × 3 1/2" × 35 3/4"
G Top braces (2), 3/4" × 1 1/4" × 27 1/2"
H Top side braces (2), 3/4" × 1 1/4" × 9 3/8"
J Front slat braces (3), 3/4" × 1 1/8" × 27 1/2"
K Side slat braces (4), 3/4" × 1 1/8" × 10 3/4"
L Top cross member (1), 3/4" × 2 1/4" × 27 1/2"
M Footrest (1), 1 5/8". diameter × 29"

HARDWARE
No. 8 × 1 1/4" flathead wood screws
4d finishing nails
6d finishing nails

This portable bar is designed to be versatile. It goes well with both country and contemporary rooms and its compact size allows it to be stored close to a wall out of the way. The two shelves and top provide adequate space for storage and serving when entertaining.

This project is a simple one, even for the beginning craftsperson. Nearly all the pieces are rectangular and thus easy to machine. There are no intricate joints to be concerned about in the assembly process.

STEP 1
MACHINING THE SLATS
The six side slats and seven front slats can be made from 1x4 stock, (which is 3½ inches wide). Cut two side slats, as shown in Detail A, on a table or radial arm saw.

You might consider rounding the edges of the slats with a router to highlight the edges of both slats and shelves. This, of course, means a lot of work with the router.

STEP 2
MACHINING THE FEET AND TOP
Transfer the pattern given in Detail B to ¾-inch stock blanks. Cut out the

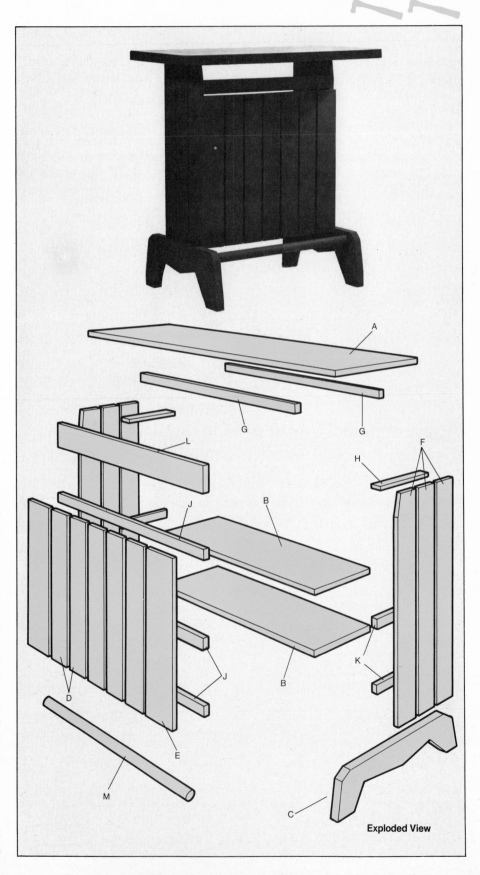

Exploded View

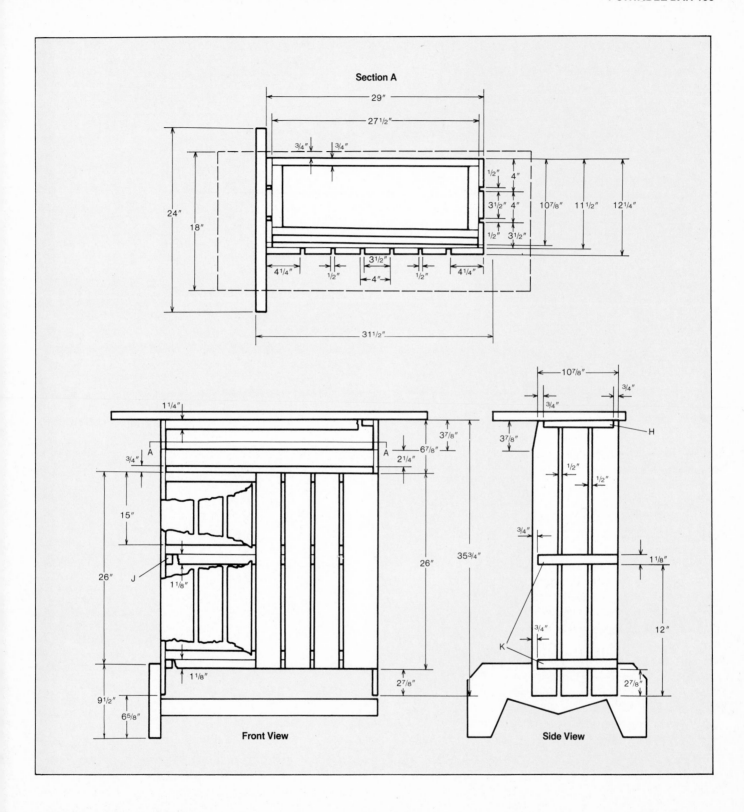

Section A

Front View

Side View

two pieces on a band saw and round the edges with a ¼-inch-radius quarter round router bit.

A stairway handrail, which is 1⅝ inches in diameter, can be used for the footrest. Of course, a brass rail may be substituted and the diameter may be altered.

The top specified in the Materials List is of ¾-inch solid stock, but it can also be made from ¾-inch plywood.

STEP 3
SANDING THE PARTS

Rough- and finish-sand the upper surface and edges of the top, all slats, slat braces, the top front and back braces, the top cross-member, the bottom, and the shelf on all surfaces and edges except their ends. The front slats are further sanded on their top ends, which will show. Finish-sand these as nicely as you can—the care will add much to the overall appearance of the piece. Rough- and finish-sand the foot except for the surfaces that sit on the floor. If you use a wooden rail for the footrest, it needs only finish sanding by hand.

STEP 4
ASSEMBLING THE SLATS
Position three side slats on a work table as shown in the plan (Side View) for both the left- and right-hand assemblies. Fasten the top braces with No. 8 × 1¼-inch flathead wood screws, as shown in the plan, taking care to keep the slats square; then attach the other two braces to each assembly.

Next put the side assemblies on the feet, centered and 4 inches deep on the feet as shown in the plan (Front View). Attach the feet with No. 8 × 1.¼-inch flathead wood screws driven through the slats into the feet. Check to make sure all parts are square as you work.

STEP 5
ASSEMBLING THE BAR
Assemble the front slats as you did the side slats, with braces in the same places as on the side slats. See Section A and the Front View of the plan. Use No. 8 × 1¼-inch flathead wood screws.

Attach the front slat assembly to the side slat assemblies with 4d finishing nails driven into the front edges of the side slat assemblies—fit the footrest between the feet as you install the sides. Nail the bottom and shelf in place on the braces as shown in the plan (Front View).

Put the top cross member in position and attach it between the side slats with glue and 4d finishing nails through the side slats into the cross member. Do the same with the top front and back braces.

After the glue has set up, place the top upside down on the work table and position the bar on it as shown in

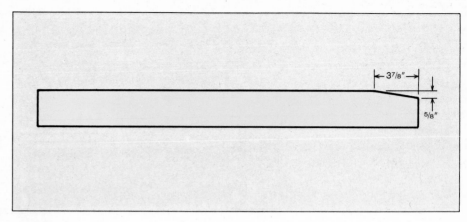

DETAIL A
SIDE SLAT LAYOUT

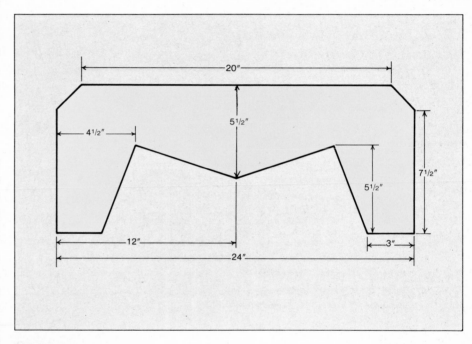

DETAIL B
FOOT PATTERN

the plan (Top View). Attach the bar to the top with No. 8 × 1¼-inch wood screws driven through the braces.

The footrest may now be firmly nailed into place. Do this by nailing 6d finishing nails diagonally upward from underneath the footrest, through the foot, and into the footrest. By performing this last task, you have completed the project.

GLOSSARY

Along-the-grain In the same direction as the grain; in plywood, the same direction as the grain of the face ply, usually the long dimension. Sometimes referred to as with-the-grain. Sometimes referred to as cross-grain.

Across-the-grain Perpendicular to the wood grain. Sometimes referred to as cross-grain.

Bevel To cut edges or ends at an angle.

Bow The distortion on a board that deviates from lengthwise but not across its faces.

Chamfer The flat surface created by slicing off the square edge or corner of a piece of wood or plywood.

Check A separation of the wood normally occurring lengthwise across the rings of annual growth; usually a result of seasoning.

Clamps Any of several types of device used to hold a joint secure and as desired until glue has dried and/or while nails or screws are driven into place.

Crook A distortion of a board in which there is a deviation edgewise from a straight line from end to end of the board.

Cross-grain *See* across-the-grain above.

Cross member A structural part of cabinetry, either horizontal or vertical, which adds stability.

Cross nail At a miter joint, nailing from each side through the joint for stability.

Cup A curve in a board across the grain or width of a piece.

Dado A joint made by cutting a rectangular notch across the grain of a board.

Dowel joint A joint created by fitting glue dowels into precisely-drilled holes that have been filled with glue.

Dressed lumber Lumber that has been faced with a planing machine.

Edge The narrow face of a rectangular piece of lumber.

End-grain *See* grain.

Face The wide surface of a piece of lumber; the side showing the better quality or appearance on which a piece is graded.

Finger joint A method of joining pieces of lumber by machining a series of dadoes in the ends. The joint is similar to interlocking the fingers of two hands.

Finished size The net dimensions after surfacing and machining.

Grain The direction of the fibers in wood. The direction may vary depending on the surface of the board referred to:

End-grain The grain at the end of a board, in which the fibers have been cut perpendicular to their length.

Long-grain The grain in the edge or face of a board, in which the fibers have been cut parallel to their length. Sometimes referred to as surface grain.

Grille A framework of horizontal and vertical cross members and braces which make up the front of a cabinet. The doors are attached to the grille and the drawers fit into it.

Groove A joint formed by cutting a rectangular notch along the grain of a board.

Hardwoods The botanical group of broad-leaved trees, such as oak or maple. The term has no reference to the actual hardness of the wood.

Heartwood The nonactive core of a tree, usually darker and more decay-resistant than sapwood because gums and resins have seeped into it.

Joint A point at which two pieces of wood are fitted together.

Jointer A power tool used to finish an edge or face of a board.

Kerf A slot made by a saw, the width of the saw cut.

Lap To position two pieces so that the surface of one extends over that of the other.

Level A tool which indicates whether a surface tilts, or the characteristic of not tilting in a cabinet.

Long grain *See* grain.

Loosened or raised grain A small section of the wood that has been loosened or raised, but not displaced.

Lumber-core Plywood construction in which the core is composed of lumber strips and the outer plies are veneer.

Miter joint A joint formed by fitting together two pieces of lumber or plywood that have been cut off at an angle.

Molding A strip of decorative material with a planed or curved narrow surface for ornamental use.

Panel faces   Outer veneers of a plywood panel.

Plywood   A panel made of three or more layers of veneer joined with glue and usually laid with the grain of adjoining plies at right angles. To secure balanced construction, an odd number of plies is almost always used.

Rabbet   A joint formed by cutting a rectangular notch in the edge of a board.

Radial arm saw   A stationary power saw designed to make cuts across a board accurately and easily.

Rail   The horizontal member of a frame.

Raised grain   A roughened condition of the surface of dressed lumber in which the hard summerwood is raised above the softer springwood, but not torn loose from it.

Resaw   To reduce the thickness or width of boards, planks, or other material by cutting into two or more thinner pieces on a resaw.

Sapwood   The living wood of pale color near the outside of the log, generally more susceptible to decay than heartwood.

Scarf joint   An end joint or splice formed by gluing together the ends of two pieces that have been tapered or beveled to form sloping plane surfaces, usually to a feather edge.

Select lumber   The higher grades of sound, relatively unblemished lumber.

Softwoods   The botanical group of trees that have needles or scalelike leaves. Except for cypress, larch, and tamarack, softwoods are evergreen. The term has no reference to the actual hardness of the wood.

Solid-core   Plywood composed of veneers over a lumber core.

Split   A lengthwise separation of the wood, due to the tearing apart of the wood cells.

Square   Either a tool which is used to check for a 90° angle or set of cabinet parts to 90°.

Stile   The vertical member of a frame.

Surfaced lumber   Lumber that has been planed or sanded on one or more surfaces.

Table saw   A stationary power saw with an adjustable guide or fence which can be used for crosscutting, ripping (cutting a board along the grain from end to end) or grooving.

Twist   A distortion caused by the turning or winding of the edges of a board so that the four corners of any face are no longer on the same plane.

Veneer   A thin layer or sheet of wood.

Warp   Any variation from a true or plane surface. The term covers crook, bow, cup, twist, and any combination of these.

PICTURE CREDITS

Arky, David: pp 8, center; 9, center; 41, 42, 43, 44, 45, 46, 47, 48

Price, Bernie: pp 8, right; 9, right and bottom; 10, 14, 15

Zernicke, Cal: pp 2, 5, 6, 7, 33, 34, 35, 36, 37, 38, 39, 40

Black & Decker: p 8, top right

INDEX

METRIC CHARTS

LUMBER

Sizes: Metric cross-sections are so close to their nearest Imperial sizes, as noted below, that for most purposes they may be considered equivalents.

Lengths: Metric lengths are based on a 300mm module which is slightly shorter in length than an Imperial foot. It will therefore be important to check your requirements accurately to the nearest inch and consult the table below to find the metric length required.

Areas: The metric area is a square metre. Use the following conversion factors when converting from Imperial data: 100 sq. feet = 9.290 sq. metres.

METRIC SIZES SHOWN BESIDE NEAREST IMPERIAL EQUIVALENT

mm	Inches	mm	Inches
16 × 75	5/8 × 3	44 × 150	1³/4 × 6
16 × 100	5/8 × 4	44 × 175	1³/4 × 7
16 × 125	5/8 × 5	44 × 200	1³/4 × 8
16 × 150	5/8 × 6	44 × 225	1³/4 × 9
19 × 75	3/4 × 3	44 × 250	1³/4 × 10
19 × 100	3/4 × 4	44 × 300	1³/4 × 12
19 × 125	3/4 × 5	50 × 75	2 × 3
19 × 150	3/4 × 6	50 × 100	2 × 4
22 × 75	7/8 × 3	50 × 125	2 × 5
22 × 100	7/8 × 4	50 × 150	2 × 6
22 × 125	7/8 × 5	50 × 175	2 × 7
22 × 150	7/8 × 6	50 × 200	2 × 8
25 × 75	1 × 3	50 × 225	2 × 9
25 × 100	1 × 4	50 × 250	2 × 10
25 × 125	1 × 5	50 × 300	2 × 12
25 × 150	1 × 6	63 × 100	2¹/2 × 4
25 × 175	1 × 7	63 × 125	2¹/2 × 5
25 × 200	1 × 8	63 × 150	2¹/2 × 6
25 × 225	1 × 9	63 × 175	2¹/2 × 7
25 × 250	1 × 10	63 × 200	2¹/2 × 8
25 × 300	1 × 12	63 × 225	2¹/2 × 9
32 × 75	1¹/4 × 3	75 × 100	3 × 4
32 × 100	1¹/4 × 4	75 × 125	3 × 5
32 × 125	1¹/4 × 5	75 × 150	3 × 6
32 × 150	1¹/4 × 6	75 × 175	3 × 7
32 × 175	1¹/4 × 7	75 × 200	3 × 8
32 × 200	1¹/4 × 8	75 × 225	3 × 9
32 × 225	1¹/4 × 9	75 × 250	3 × 10
32 × 250	1¹/4 × 10	75 × 300	3 × 12
32 × 300	1¹/4 × 12	100 × 100	4 × 4
38 × 75	1¹/2 × 3	100 × 150	4 × 6
38 × 100	1¹/2 × 4	100 × 200	4 × 8
38 × 125	1¹/2 × 5	100 × 250	4 × 10
38 × 150	1¹/2 × 6	100 × 300	4 × 12
38 × 175	1¹/2 × 7	150 × 150	6 × 6
38 × 200	1¹/2 × 8	150 × 200	6 × 8
38 × 225	1¹/2 × 9	150 × 300	6 × 12
44 × 75	1³/4 × 3	200 × 200	8 × 8
44 × 100	1³/4 × 4	250 × 250	10 × 10
44 × 125	1³/4 × 5	300 × 300	12 × 12

NOMINAL SIZE	ACTUAL SIZE
(This is what you order)	(This is what you get)
Inches	Inches
1 × 1	3/4 × 3/4
1 × 2	3/4 × 1¹/2
1 × 3	3/4 × 2¹/2
1 × 4	3/4 × 3¹/2
1 × 6	3/4 × 5¹/2
1 × 8	3/4 × 7¹/4
1 × 10	3/4 × 9¹/4
1 × 12	3/4 × 11¹/4
2 × 2	1³/4 × 1³/4
2 × 3	1¹/2 × 2¹/2
2 × 4	1¹/2 × 3¹/2
2 × 6	1¹/2 × 5¹/2
2 × 8	1¹/2 × 7¹/4
2 × 10	1¹/2 × 9¹/4
2 × 12	1¹/2 × 11¹/4

METRIC LENGTHS

Lengths Metres	Equiv. Ft. & Inches
1.8m	5' 10⁷/8"
2.1m	6' 10⁵/8"
2.4m	7' 10¹/2"
2.7m	8' 10¹/4"
3.0m	9' 10¹/8"
3.3m	10' 9⁷/8"
3.6m	11' 9³/4"
3.9m	12' 9¹/2"
4.2m	13' 9³/8"
4.5m	14' 9¹/3"
4.8m	15' 9"
5.1m	16' 8³/4"
5.4m	17' 8⁵/8"
5.7m	18' 8³/8"
6.0m	19' 8¹/4"
6.3m	20' 8"
6.6m	21' 7⁷/8"
6.9m	22' 7⁵/8"
7.2m	23' 7¹/2"
7.5m	24' 7¹/4"
7.8m	25' 7¹/8"

All the dimensions are based on 1 inch = 25 mm.